D0877960

Patricia Craig in Rannafast, 1959

asking for trouble

the story of an escapade with
disproportionate consequences

Patricia Craig

BLACKSTAFF
PRESS
BELFAST

First published in 2007 by
Blackstaff Press
4c Heron Wharf, Sydenham Business Park
Belfast BT3 9LE
with the assistance of
The Arts Council of Northern Ireland

Typeset by CJWT Solutions, St Helens, England

Printed in England by Athenaeum Press

A CIP catalogue record for this book is available
from the British Library

ISBN 978-0-85640-808-3

www.blackstaffpress.com

For my mother
Nora Teresa Craig (*née* Brady)
1913–2001

PREFACE

This is the story of an escapade with disproportionate consequences. When I was sixteen I was expelled from school. So
what, you may say: so were lots of people who never took it
into their heads to make a song and dance about it. True – but
I hope to show why this particular, infinitesimal injustice had
implications beyond the purely personal.

The contretemps took place in Belfast, still at the time an
unassuming small industrial city, keeping itself to itself, observing a certain order in its manner of living and turning a deaf
ear to any rumblings of unrest or aggravation issuing from its
interior. The school in question, St Dominic's, is filled with
nuns, cross and bitter nuns or those who are moderately kind, as
the case may be. They belong to an enclosed order, isolated from
worldly concerns, and to emphasise this fact they wear the
traditional medieval habit of cream serge topped by a black
headdress, and featuring conspicuous rosary beads. As well as
advertising their holiness, it gives them a look of being sinister
and intimidating. The teaching staff includes lay members too,
thank goodness, but these are subordinate to the *religieuses*. A
convent inflexibility has the place in its grip.

The year is 1959; hierarchical structures continue to function
– though not as strongly as they've done in the past; the Great
Northern Railway in Great Victoria Street, the Ulster Club and
Robb's Department Store are familiar landmarks; and an
innocence nearly unimaginable today prevails even among
inflammable adolescents.

The Catholic Church, our church, went on maintaining a
stern and strict policy with regard to sexual morality in particular,
and few among my contemporaries would have had the know-
how, or the will, to challenge it. I certainly didn't. Most of us

were secure and content enough in our small world, far from any centre of front-page events, and we thought that things would go on forever in much the same way: school with its pleasures and anxieties; marathon walks to the Hatchet Field up the Black Mountain via the Mountain Loney; minor flirtations in the Falls or the Ormeau Park; shopping in Brand's Arcade and browsing among the book stalls of Smithfield; cinema-going with friends possibly involving a spot of carry-on with schoolboys in the back row; Hallowe'en parties with turnip lanterns and fireworks ignited on the lawn to enchanting effect; bracing seaside holidays at Cushendall or Warrenpoint. If it wasn't exactly the life of Riley, back there in the late 1950s, it nevertheless held sufficient charm and vitality to render its transience regrettable.

Everything changes. That life, or my version of it, exists now only in my head, where – inevitably – it has acquired a powerful nostalgic overlay which goes on intensifying in tandem with the amount of time that separates it from the present. *Asking for Trouble*, then, the story of an insignificant upheaval, has a dual purpose. It's first of all a period piece, an attempt to retrieve a few of the aspirations along with the atmosphere of that distinctive time. But it's also a work of social criticism, undertaken partly to remind myself, and my contemporaries, of the obsolete embargoes we existed under, and the extent to which these were accepted or circumvented.

My concern is with 1950s attitudes, 1950s appearances, the mentality of the age – though of course I can't avoid the knowingness of hindsight, which causes one to contemplate with bemusement or dismay a lot of the things that once seemed perfectly reasonable. My main target, I suppose, is the type of sorry schooling I was subjected to; but then I'd have to admit that its churchly slant suited a good many of my fellow pupils better than it suited me. Of course, I experienced no sense of alienation and certainly didn't hanker after a secular education at the time, never having heard of such a thing. You didn't question the choices your parents made on your behalf, just as they didn't question the preordained course of their offsprings' lives. The handiest, denominationally appropriate school was the right one, as far as they were concerned; and in most cases it probably was.

It's just that, for some of us, the moral guidance we received seems equivalent to the practice of binding the left arm of a naturally left-handed child behind its back, in the interests of achieving a state of universal right-handedness. Conformity was the name of the game. Of course we needed to be instructed how to behave, but sometimes our instructors got it frightfully, spectacularly wrong. Fancy trying to impose sanctity and sub-missiveness on the devious, recalcitrant juveniles herded into their classrooms! The strong-arm tactics they engaged in to further this end didn't do a bit of good, either. The effect was to germinate a covert rebelliousness in a number of us.

However − as the following account will indicate − I didn't find my schooldays particularly onerous, pre-calamity. There was nothing crushing or joyless about the major elements of the life I was leading. Fun and games were not excluded from it. I didn't even find the school environment hostile. If I'd sailed through the whole six years of grammar school without coming to grief, it's possible that my recollections of the era would be couched in a different mode. But it seems worth taking a sharpish look at the reasons why I did come to grief. And even after all this time, I have an investment in getting it right, in presenting my version of events with as much accuracy and period-colouring as I can muster. I want to see what the whole episode looks like, from a distance, and to devise, if possible, a new conclusion to the old business of being brought to book.

PART ONE

Corrupting Influence

PC (front row, second from right) and class at Aquinas Hall, c. 1952

... Horses' dung is smoking on the cobbles.
Cobblestones?
I must have gone back further than I thought, to brewers'
    drays and milk-carts,
Brylcreem, *Phoenix* beer. Or candy apples – rich hard dark-
    brown glaze ...

CIARAN CARSON, 'Calvin Klein's *Obsession*'

It was like a scene from my least favourite type of school story, featuring a stern headmistress, a nameless delinquency and a trio of unhappy schoolgirls, the whole bound up with an evangelical intensity. There we stood in our royal blue gym tunics, heads bowed, lips trembling, undergoing a fearsome scolding on account of some major offence which had just that minute come to light. Lunch hour was drawing to an end; soon the first lesson of the afternoon would begin. We'd been accosted, though, on our way to the cloakroom, and summoned into an empty classroom by a nun white-faced with fury.

Exchanging dismayed glances behind her back, we wondered what we'd done wrong *now*. Our consciences weren't exactly clear. We were nine years old and addicted to adventure. But nothing came to mind at that moment to justify the stream of abuse coming down on our heads as the nun let rip with intemperate invective concerning our deficiency in the areas of obedience, trustworthiness and the grace of God.

3

We'd been rounded up by one of those nuns, quite common at the time, whose chief delight was wiping the floor with any pupil unlucky enough to be caught out in a misdemeanour. But what was this particular misdemeanour? A tentative request for information only results in extra upbraiding. We know perfectly well what we've done, we are told, and are actually making matters worse by pretending ignorance. How we have the gall to stand there denying our bad conduct passes all understanding ...

At this point two of us give way to tears. I feel pretty tearful myself, a captive audience while the details of my bad character are spat out at me; but I *won't* cry. Cry-babies are the butt of scorn in my schoolgirl adventure stories whose heroines persevere with dignity in the face of injustice and always win through. I have taken them as an example, and I will stick to an appearance of sangfroid if it kills me.

It doesn't kill me but it gets me further pounced on. The snivellers are at least exhibiting a modicum of remorse, our tormentor declares, whirling round to focus her attention on *me*, while I am so hardened in turpitude that rightful admonition just washes over me. A sentence is pronounced. The other two, being properly chastened, may join the rest of their class without further punishment, but I'm to go home and remain at home until I hear to the contrary. It's not an expulsion, exactly, but it might be the prelude to an expulsion. I am beset by all kinds of apprehensions as I retrieve my outdoor things from the cloak-room and leave the school premises without meeting anyone who might commiserate with me in my predicament. Then it's back to the Donegall Road in West Belfast, where I cause consternation in my mother and grandmother by landing in on them at the wrong time.

Part of the trouble is, I can't explain why this severe punishment has been visited on me. But I'm not as innocent of blame as all that. I have an inkling that it might have something to do with having been observed during the lunch hour up to no good in a forbidden portion of the school grounds. We are fascinated by the stable blocks, outbuildings, boiler rooms, kitchen gardens and other amenities round the back of the

4

school, partly because these areas have been placed out of bounds.

There are good reasons for the embargo on exploration. One furnace room, for example, has a door at ground level which opens on to a sheer drop of about twenty feet. It was clearly constructed by someone fiendishly eager to engineer an accident, and it seems miraculous that (as far as I know) no accident occurred. I suppose the door would have been kept locked, as a rule; but I can testify to the fact that it wasn't always locked. I had actually been down to the bottom of the iron ladder attached to the wall which descended straight from the outer door (though not on the occasion described above). Someone had dared me to lower myself over the threshhold and climb down, and I did it in the expectation that a secret passage would be revealed at the bottom, or a kidnapped heiress awaiting rescue, or at the very least a chest full of stolen treasure. But what confronted me, as I stood on the earthen floor still clasping the iron rungs, was out of a different kind of story – a horror story. The sight before my eyes, as I turned my head to take a look around the underground premises, had me scrambling upwards again at high speed. It had required the most tremendous effort of will not to cry out. A row of toads, an enormous quantity of them, it seemed, silently assembled against the far wall like the leitmotif of a macabre fairy story. (I'm assured that I have got this wrong, since Ireland is toad-free as well as snake-free – but the scene has remained fixed in my memory to this day in the way described. And whatever it was I saw over against the wall, it frightened the wits out of me.)

Frogs and toads, for some unfathomable reason, trigger a terrible reaction in me. I wish no harm to the species, but I need to keep the utmost distance between myself and them. I daren't reveal the presence of the toads to my friends at the top of the ladder, since we're all at an age when any contemporary's weakness is likely to be exploited, in the interests of fun. There's a short story by Alice Munro in which the phrase 'a condition of permanent vulnerability' appears. It's to do with the heroine's passion for lines of poetry and her awareness of the likely consequences, should such a passion get bruited about. I can't resist borrowing the phrase: a condition of permanent vulnerability wasn't just a risk for me, it was a certainty, if my friends had got wind of my aversion to amphibians … And with a supply of the creatures available for dispersal, it was more than likely that some irresponsible classmate would fetch one into the light of day, or – horrors! – into my desk in the second-form classroom. So I have to affect a composure I'm far from feeling, and announce that there's nothing whatever to see down there, it's totally boring and not worth the risk of being caught by a nun – or of breaking one's neck.

That's the end of that particular Toad Hall, as far as we're concerned; but the lure of forbidden territory remains. We keep pottering round the back pathways, strawberry beds and cabbage patches, even though there's nothing much to see or do there, dodging out of sight if a handyman or gardener should appear wheeling a wheelbarrow; and no doubt this is the reason for the trouble we're in, again. Someone must have reported us …

But a specific and more colourful transgression has stuck in my mind as a contributory factor, at least. I have a strong impression that we were held to blame for an accident featuring a small boy and a manure pit. Our school, Aquinas Hall, is a single-sex school; but once in a while, at the nuns' discretion, a very young boy is enrolled for a term or two. I remember the son of a Ghanaian lecturer at Queen's who briefly attended Aquinas Hall along with his sister (their exotic names were Grace and Raphael). And then came a small child called Patsy, around whom there hung an aura of unspecified deprivation – probably nothing more than the fact that he lived with his grandmother (lacking parents?), but we were instructed beforehand to be nice to him. It was Patsy who suffered the mishap with the manure pit, of which we weren't even witnesses, let alone activists. I don't know who got him out of it, but I can imagine the state he was in, and the annoyance of whatever teacher was charged with cleaning him up. And I'm not certain if he fell in or if he was pushed, but I know the incident had nothing to do with any of us. However, we may have been seen not far from the spot, and a wonky inference drawn from this circumstance. Nuns at the time were more interested in administering chastisement than in getting to the bottom of any supposed episode of rule-breaking.

I'm completely in the dark regarding poor Patsy's immersion in dung when I try to explain to my mother why I've been sent home in disgrace – indeed, I don't know where my subsequent information on the subject came from, or why it's connected so strongly in my head with that particular pickle … However, my mother doesn't waste a minute but straight away gets into her coat and hurries to Aquinas Hall to put things right, leaving me and my grandmother anxiously awaiting the verdict. It isn't long before she's home again with the business sorted out. Of course I'll be going to school as usual on the following morning! The incident is at an end, due to my intrepid mother and her persuasive tactics.

That's my first major bit of luck, having a mother who's as much a friend as a parent, who is efficient and resourceful, who is not only on my wavelength but unshakeably on my side, whatever infantile or reprehens-ible behaviour I am guilty of. (It's possible that her constant support gave me a false idea of the amount of leeway I could count on, but – if it did – my convent schooling would have gone some way towards redressing the balance.) My upbringing is left largely in her hands, though my cheerful father contributes his own brand of playfulness in the interval between returning home from his work at the Ulster Transport Authority in

PC, aged four, with her mother
at 551 Donegall Road

7

Duncrue Street and going out in the evening with his friend Jim Magee, who keeps a chemist's shop on the Glen Road. He needs an active social life to keep him in good spirits, while my mother is happiest at home reading a book. My long-widowed grandmother, too, who makes a fourth in our household, has a say in the way my life is organised, and a wholly benevolent attitude towards myself (though she's a bit bemused by my shyness, and keeps telling people not to mind me, that I'm very backward – which may have created an erroneous impression). All this I account as great good luck.

Of course, I'm painting too cosy a picture here. Tensions and resentments afflicted my immediate family, no less than any other – indeed, in some ways the scope for both was greater than normal, for reasons I'll return to. But as the only child of the household, and with my mother's ferocious partisanship to bolster me up, I was in a privileged position (the word 'spoilt', I am sure, was frequently on the lips of my more acerbic aunts, and others), and shielded as far as possible from inevitable adult discords. I was lucky, but in the normal course of things, just as patterns have a way of repeating themselves, luck has a way of running out.

'*Bíonn a mhí-ádh féin ag brath ar gach duine*' (their own ill luck is in store for everyone); '*Ní mar a shíltear a chríochnaítear*' (things do not fall out as we expect). These incontestable sayings are among the cache of six hundred Ulster Gaelic proverbs put together by an indefatigable nineteenth-century industrialist and scholar named Robert Shipboy MacAdam, who first saw the light of day in a room above his father's hardware shop in High Street, Belfast.

The year was 1808, and the town, being mainly Presbyterian, was more homogenous than it later became. Robert, a Presbyterian himself, soon joined a select number of pupils receiving an enlightened education at Inst (Belfast Academical Institution), a school founded on egalitarian principles. Inst, no doubt, was the scene of his first encounter with the Irish language.

A Reverend William Neilson taught Irish at the school, and it's easy enough to envisage MacAdam, in his antique schoolboy get-up, sitting in Dr Neilson's class demonstrating his flair for languages. It was enterprising of Inst to have Irish on the curriculum. The language, at the time, was either used in everyday transactions, which still held true for some parts of the North, or it was an anti-quarian pursuit. It wasn't until later in the century that it got itself tied up, once and for all, with the whole Catholic/nationalist package, to the chagrin of some of its Protestant upholders.

By the time he was twelve or so, young Robert MacAdam might have been aware, out of the corner of his eye, of changes happening in Belfast. For example, a lot of impoverished Catholics from country places were pouring into the Pound (named after an old cattle pound located about half a mile from the town centre), drawn in like flocks of migrating swallows by the presence of cotton and linen mills where they hoped to find work. The Pound, including streets such as Hamill Street and Barrack Street, was the oldest section of what later became the Divis area and the Lower Falls Road, and, from the 1820s on, it evolved into a counterpart of the even older, working-class Protestant Sandy Row, with its higgledy-piggledy housing, hardship and bravado. In these enclaves, and others like them, disruption and disaffection were rapidly taking root.

One of the factories offering work on a non-denominational basis was the Soho Iron Foundry in Townsend Street, estab-lished in 1834 by Robert MacAdam and his older brother James. The previous year – with both their parents dead – the MacAdam brothers had moved to a new address, 18 College Square East, a splendid four-storey town house in an imposing and atmospheric terrace facing the long, neo-classical façade of their old school, Inst.

College Square North, College Square East ... you have to close your eyes and think back, hard, to gain an inkling of this pungent fragment of bygone Belfast. It is nearly all gone, eradicated, bulldozed out of existence in the terrible rage for redevelopment which overtook so much of late-twentieth-century architectural thinking. In MacAdam's day, the town contained many graceful areas which stood as a testament to a local aesthetic – along with rough, insalubrious and dangerous quarters guaranteed to raise the hackles of social reformers.

'We had not the most remote idea that such a den of darkness and squalor could be the abode of human beings,' wrote the Revd W.M. O'Hanlon, with bated breath, following one of his investigative ventures into the slums in 1852. A certain hardihood was required to survive in a street like Rowland Street, off Sandy Row (say), or in the darker heart of the Pound – hardihood allied to a community spirit. And, of course, a sense of identity which could manifest itself in a number of ways. Some incomers into the Pound, through the middle part of the nineteenth century, had a resource in common with the factory-owner MacAdam: an enthusiasm for, and knowledge of, the Irish language.

MacAdam recruited certain Gaelic-speakers, such as Art Bennett, a stonemason from Forkhill, County Armagh, to transcribe manuscripts and collect songs and pieces of traditional lore from all parts of the North. Another of his scholarly employees was Peter Gallegan, or Galligan, a hedge-schoolmaster and farm labourer from County Cavan, whose son had a job at the Soho Foundry. But his greatest ally in these linguistic enterprises was Hugh McDonnell who lived at Millfield, just across the road from Hamill Street in the Pound. Breandán Ó Buachalla, in his study of 1968, *I mBéal Feirsde Cois Cuain* (In Belfast by the Harbour), gives due credit to this pair of conservationists and language supporters: 'It's enough for me to say that, 100-odd years ago in Belfast, you had Hugh McDonnell, a Catholic, and Robert MacAdam, a Protestant, working together to save the Irish language [from extinction].' And between them they established a tradition of admiration for Irish, and applause for those who spoke it, which has lasted right up to the present in the whole of West Belfast. The Ard Scoil (High School) in Divis Street and Cumann Cluain Ard (the Clonard Society) in Hawthorn Street, were centres of Gaelic expertise and sociability during the middle years of the twentieth century; and today you find a thriving cultural facility and meeting-place, Cultúrlann, occupying a one-time Presbyterian church near Broadway on the Falls Road.

From his handsome house in College Square East, Robert MacAdam was within easy walking distance of both the Pound (cow-keepers and mill workers) and Sandy Row (weavers and labourers) – and of Townsend Street and his place of work, when he wasn't travelling to Egypt on business, or taking down proverbs and stories from rugged old native speakers in the Glens of Antrim. Townsend: it wasn't too long before this thoroughfare ceased to live up to its name, as the instinct for urban accretion found a full-blown outlet in the Falls. (Falls, from *fál*: the Irish word for hedge, or pound, as in cattle-pound: nothing to do with waterfalls, despite a later street called Fallswater Street; or, as some wit suggested, with hordes of falling-down drunks emerging from pubs on a Saturday night. As far as hedge goes: it's tempting to associate the Falls with a repelling prickly hedge, growing higher and higher, as a nationalist exclusiveness, in later years, became its dominant tone.) First there were fields and orchards, then came the jerry-building programme that gave the area its doughty back-street ambience. The rows of red-brick houses, courts, entries, factory chimneys discharging billows of smoke, begrimed back-yards ... all these features of the Falls were in place by the mid-nineteenth century, though the workers' rows thinned out considerably as you progressed up the road.

Beechmount, for example, didn't come into being until the late 1890s, and even then it was still considered a rural area, mills and brickfields notwithstanding. When the Dominican Convent opened its doors in 1870, midway along the road, its situation was described as 'elevated and agreeable'. (I'll come back to that rebarbative institution and its role in my own little portion of *mí-ádh*, ill luck, in due course.) My own home territory, St James's – I was born at 551 Donegall Road, on the corner with St James's Avenue – was an even later development, a product of the 1920s: semi-detached, red-brick, bay-windowed houses with average-sized gardens, and plane trees at intervals along the pavement. It was nothing special, neither attractive looking in its own right, nor of historical interest. I was drawn to places that distilled a sense of the past, like the nearby tumbledown Milltown Row, adjacent to the Cemetery and the Bog Meadows, with its straggle of still-occupied minuscule dwellings and, behind it in the distance in a steep hollow, the half-ruined house probably once assigned to the manager of the eponymous mill.

I was also drawn to the Irish language, long before I got a chance to learn it: it wasn't on the curriculum of my posh primary school, the aforementioned Aquinas Hall (fee: four guineas a term) on the Malone Road – 'the *faubourg* Malone' – the preparatory department of the Dominican Convent after 1947 and the advent of the Eleven-Plus. Aquinas Hall, a large suburban villa, originally Benvue or Benview, was built in 1875 for a Belfast ship-owner. It stood on the corner of Windsor Park; and, from 1889, its next-door neighbour on the Malone Road was Dunarnon, the property of a Magherafelt tea merchant whose great-granddaughter happens to be the novelist Jennifer Johnston.

That late Victorian mansion has other literary associations: it was occupied during the 1930s by the father and stepmother of Louis MacNeice, and hence appears in the Belfast chapter ('A Personal Digression') of *Zoo* (1938), where it's described as 'a hideous house, but very comfortable … a front door with polished granite pillars and Corinthian capitals'. After the death of Bishop MacNeice in 1942, the house – 77 Malone Road – was divided into flats. A couple of years later, Dominican nuns acquired No. 75 and renamed it Aquinas Hall. It was, and remained, a hostel for Catholic women students, as well as functioning as a small private kindergarten school. By the late 1950s, the nuns had expanded their holdings to include Dunarnon, at which point, it seems, the whole caboodle became known as Aquinas Hall, with an address at 75–77 Malone Road.

This caused some confusion (in my mind anyway). Around 1970, Paul Muldoon – according to his poem 'History' – clambered, in pursuit of a Catholic woman student, through a ground-floor window of one or other of these Aquinas Halls, 'and into the room where MacNeice wrote "Snow", / Or the room where they say he wrote "Snow"'. For some reason, I'd got it into my head that these lines referred to the conservatory at the front of my old school, a room into which I was ushered in September 1949, along with a crowd of diminutive strangers. (With its glass roof and walls, it seemed to me an unusual and agreeable sort of classroom. However, I was soon transferred to a more advanced class in an ordinary schoolroom, and came to regard the conservatory as a mere infants' sanctum.) But it seems clear that this was not the room in which MacNeice wrote 'Snow'. Well, the clue is in the phrase 'the great bay-window' – though *my* Aquinas Hall boasted one or two of those as well, as far as I remember.

About ten years ago, coming down the Malone Road on a bus, I was horrified to observe that Aquinas Hall was flattened, and that building work had started in the once-abundant grounds where my friends and I held enthralled confabulations about the facts of life, or tried to think ourselves into an Enid Blyton adventure. However, when I remarked on this, several people assured me that I'd got it wrong, that Aquinas Hall wasn't knocked down, merely taken over by the Arts Council and renamed MacNeice House. Was I becoming subject to hallucinations? A second visit confirmed that my old school was indeed demolished (a whole new development now stands on the site): whatever the history of the house next door, and its association with the poet MacNeice, it definitely was *not* the place where I received the beginnings of an education.

That, with its royal blue uniform, its velours hat for winter and its summer panama, was considered a swanky school; French was taught to the top class there (ten- and eleven-year-olds) by a mad Dominican nun with a penchant for laying about her with a ruler. But, in my day at least, no Irish lessons were available. It is possible that Irish, with its bog-and-back-street associations, was considered insufficiently genteel by Aquinas Hall nuns, whom I remember as displaying a rather obsequious attitude towards the British royal family. The socially elevated location on the Malone Road may have gone to their heads. In the absence of formal teaching, I used to pester my mother to tell me any Irish words she knew, which weren't that many: *doras*, a door; *teach*, a house; *cat*, a cat. (She must have known more; she did study Irish at school in Lurgan in the 1920s and 30s, and even went to Rannafast once for a holiday.) Oh, and *sidhe*, a fairy, as in banshee.

Some children who used to visit relatives in our avenue were objects of wonder: they were being brought up as Irish-speakers, in the middle of Belfast (though of course in practice they were bilingual) – a *modus operandi* not at all common at the time. It's true that it wasn't without its hazards. Kudos might be heaped on your head on account of the dedication your Irish-speaking betokened; but, at the same time, you'd likely be judged a bit odd, a bit too fanatical or precious for your own good.

The poet Ciaran Carson, born in Raglan Street off the Falls Road, had the experience of growing up speaking Irish and English interchangeably – a circumstance some hold to blame for his subsequent stammer. However, he mastered both tongues easily, unlike certain victims of the policy of compulsory Irish in the South, who were said to have ended up 'illiterate in two languages'. Joking aside, the idea of undergoing instruction in every subject – geography, algebra, history, biology or what-have-you – through the medium of Irish, was daunting to the point of desperation.

I knew it would never come to that as far as I was concerned, and I looked forward to the time when I'd be able to study Irish as an ordinary school subject. To me, my supposedly native tongue was mysterious and glamorous, like a legendary forebear fallen on diminished days. The time seemed long in coming. I was eleven before I sat in an Irish class where we chanted in unison, *Tá mé*, I am; *Tá tu*, you are, and so on, which wasn't especially inspiring. The teacher was not inspiring either, being short and rotund and prone to point at herself while uttering the phrase *Beag agus maith*, small and good. We soon knew enough to go around pointing at one another while declaring robustly *Beag agus olc*, small and bad. It was a start. By this stage I was a Dominican pupil on the Falls Road, things, so far, having fallen out as expected. But, have patience, *Níor ith na madaí deireadh na bliana go fóill* (the dogs have not eaten up the end of the year yet).

By the time I was sixteen I knew enough Irish to pass exams and conduct an elementary conversation, but it wasn't until a year or so later that my career as an Hibernophile really reached its zenith. I might have been violently turned off the language, once it acquired certain doleful associations; but, in fact, I had sufficient wits not to hold the circumstances of my bit of *mi-ádh*, ill luck, responsible for the ill luck itself. However, it's possible that this was the point at which the summer school took root in my mind as a place of intrigue, elation and consternation, a theme worth pursuing.

That year, my seventeenth, I went with some friends and classmates to study Irish at St Brigid's College in Rannafast, County Donegal – a traditional rite of passage for Catholic-educated adolescents – and as a consequence ended up with no school at all to return to after the summer holidays. When school resumed in September 1959, and my class, now 6A, assembled at the start of term, I wasn't in it. I was skulking at home – at least, until a makeshift arrangement was hurriedly set up. I then became a pupil at a countrified convent, and spent the year obtaining a rough finish to an infelicitous education.

Since that time, I have not been well-disposed towards nuns, or piety, or denominational schooling. But, as I've said, my *afición* for Irish outlasted the upheaval. With a couple of like-minded friends, I began to frequent Cluan Ard in Hawthorn Street, a venue from which English was excluded. To participate in the desirable social activities of this club, you had to become fluent pretty quickly. Soon, among ourselves, we spoke nothing but Irish. We spoke it all over Belfast, in the Lombard Café over plates of apple pie and ice cream, at the Central Reference Library, on the top deck of buses going towards the Cave Hill. This practice was not without an element of showing off, indeed; but, at the same time, I believe, we genuinely wished to promote the Irish

15

language and culture, as well as presenting ourselves as fearfully dedicated and uncommon. (The last was confirmed by the curious glances we attracted from strangers.) For us, the language was an exciting emblem of identity, providing access to an inner core of Irishness. Though some of us were totally unmusical, we had the words of many eighteenth-century songs and poems by heart, and the lore of the Donegal Gaeltacht at our fingertips.

Joyce Cary begins his novel of 1941, *A House of Children*, by citing the effect on him of a swaying branch of fuchsia, glimpsed through the open window of a house in an inland town: suddenly, there's a tang of salt on the breeze, and some acute sensations of a childhood in Inishowen are returned to him in an all but tangible form. 'I was waiting for a sail, probably my first sail into the Atlantic. Somebody or something must have fixed that moment upon my dreaming senses, so that I still possess it.' Well, from Proust's madeleine on, literature is full of such mnemonic triggers, agents of all kinds of creative retrogression – and for most people too, in everyday life, the experience is fairly common. For example, it's virtually impossible, I would think, for any Irish person to get a whiff of turf smoke, in any circumstances whatever, without being instantly transported to an archetypal, agrarian-Irish domain. Sometimes, though, the movement backwards is precipitated by something more deliberate or mundane. We might be asked to recall an event from the past, or find ourselves in a backward-looking reverie, as a consequence of some chance reference or encounter. For myself, the act of 'thinking back' to the summer of 1959 and its aftermath, is a periodic occurrence, sparked off whenever I bump into one-time acquaintances (there seem to be a lot of them) who have the whole fiasco fixed in their heads.

In the autumn of 1992 I was at the BBC in Belfast to record a programme, in front of an invited audience, about the editing of anthologies. How do you go about editing an anthology? It wasn't a very exacting brief, but for someone who, like me, isn't a polished performer, *any* public appearance is apt to induce a state of the heebie-jeebies. Due to some unfathomable inadequacy, in these situations I lose control of my voice or my wits. A terrible tickle afflicts my throat, turning the whole thing into a coughing marathon. Fluster is not the word. Sometimes it's not so bad, when I've chivvied myself into a proper frame of mind beforehand, or when some contentious comment acts as a spur to loquaciousness.

On this particular occasion in Belfast I manage not to cover myself in ignominy, though signally failing to match the fluency of my fellow panellists, poets Tom Paulin and Frank Ormsby, and the chairman (the actor James Ellis). We sit at a table on a raised platform, microphones in front of us, facing the audience who don't give us too hard a time – well, they're there, presumably, either as friends of the speakers, or because of some professional or personal interest in how a compilation such as *A Rage for Order* or *The Faber Book of Vernacular Verse* is put together.

My role is to stick up for the prose anthology, my *Rattle of the North* having come out earlier in the year. A collection of excerpts from prominent Northern Irish works of fiction and non-fiction, this includes a passage from *Call My Brother Back* describing the removal of the MacNeill family from Rathlin Island to a street in Beechmount off the Falls Road. The new house, two-up two-down, is situated half-way along a run-down row; and beyond it are a brickyard and brickfields, with further 'fields straggling up to the foot of a mountain'. Michael McLaverty was a young schoolmaster when he wrote this partly autobiographical novel in the late 1930s, and he never again wrote anything that equalled its delicacy of expression and lucid proletarian innocence (though his second novel, *Lost Fields*, and a few of his stories come close).

'It's your fault I never learned to speak Irish.' This bewildering accusation, addressed to me after the anthologies broadcast, with everyone milling about the recording studio, comes (it turns out) from one of McLaverty's daughters, a Dominican past pupil of my vintage, who is fully au fait with the Rannafast crisis and its repercussions on the school. What does she mean? The explanation is pretty simple. Thirty-odd years earlier, our paltry delinquency had got itself blown up to such proportions that the Gaeltacht itself, the scene of our disgrace, was classed as forbidden territory for St Dominic's girls over the next couple of years. Encouraging senior pupils to spend a part of the summer in Donegal putting a gloss on their Irish was a thing of the past, at least for the time being. 'Rannafast' had become synonymous with 'fast' (well, there'd always been a tinge of that about the place, contributing to its fascination; but it was only now that it was out in the open, now the great scandal had broken and shame and infamy covered the school, the summer colleges, the insufficiently vigilant teaching staff and worst of all, us three expellees). Our unholy conduct was something no young pupil coming up behind us was going to get a chance to emulate. For some would-be Gaeilgeoirs, and others in search of extracurricular skylarking, this deprivation rankled – and we, idiotic enough to get caught out, were the authors of it.

Three old ladies attending the 1992 broadcast in Belfast are also keen to speak to me. While the programme was being recorded I'd dimly registered their presence as they sat sedately on their upright chairs and made no contribution to the debate. They'd seemed as much out of place as nuns at a fashion show, among the teachers and BBC personnel and council representatives and literary social workers who made up the bulk of the audience. And, indeed, they disclaim all knowledge of literary matters. They have come along out of loyalty to a dear friend, recently dead, who took a keen interest in books and writing, and, moreover, had been an admirer of mine: she had all my books, and used to cut out and place in a file every newspaper article by or about me that came her way. A Miss May Brannigan. I'm naturally gratified by this information, since it brings the number of fans I'm aware of up to two – the other being an elderly (male) eccentric and self-taught painter from Greenwich in south-east London. It isn't totally disinterested admiration, though. Local patriotism is at the bottom of it. It seems Miss Brannigan lived only a few doors away from us on the Donegall Road, just across from where her friends in the audience still live. Neverthless, I applaud her instinct to approve of someone's progress (however limited) rather than judging them incapable of anything simply because you knew them in their pram.

I am at a loss to recall any of these ladies, spinsters all, though I do remember others from the front of the road: Mrs Macnamara, who gave me Edwardian postcards to add to my collection; Mr and Mrs Clark, whose daughter married a Belgian soldier; the Armstrongs; Lily Beattie. While I stand there in the lecture hall at the BBC, with people commenting on various aspects of the programme, and friends trying to shepherd me across the road for a drink with the producer and contributors, part of my attention is focused on the Donegall Road in the 1950s – the far end of the road before the construction of the M1, with the Bog Meadows in one direction and the Black Mountain in the other: from my bedroom window, if you look to the right, you can see the mountain with its distinctive landmark, a field shaped like a hatchet, with a clump of trees and a barely distinguishable white house in the corner.

It was from this vantage point that Colm MacNeill, the young protagonist of *Call My Brother Back*, sat with his brothers looking down on dingy, pre-war Belfast: the patches of waste ground, the mill chimneys and dishevelled terraces. They can nearly make out their own street, down there among the homely architecture of Beechmount. Turn towards the Park, from the bottom of this street, and you soon reach the roads sloping up towards the mountain: the Giant's Foot, Rockville, Rockmount Streets and then the Whiterock Road with its comprehensive boys' school, where Michael McLaverty held the post of headmaster for a good many years. Beyond the top of the Whiterock Road comes the Mountain Loney, at that time a country lane with an old tin church half-way along it, and a well of pure spring water at the end to refresh you before you tackled the mountain proper. I think the whole area is now built over – while the streets which McLaverty evoked in the novel *Lost Fields* are now lost streets.

Michael McLaverty is very thick with the nuns of the Dominican Convent on the Falls Road, my old school. It is also the old school of my friend Patricia Mallon, whom – although we are almost exact contemporaries – I don't remember from those days of the late 1950s. It wasn't until 1985 that we met at an Irish Studies conference at Queen's University, at which I was reading a paper on the treatment of women in Northern Irish fiction (McLaverty's included), and struck up a friendship. She remembers me from our schooldays for the usual reason: the notoriety that was thrust upon me back in the past. (*Má's mór do chliú, ní maith*: if your fame is great, it is not good.) Her opening words – 'Does the name of Rannafast make you want to laugh or gnash your teeth?' – make me laugh, but ruefully. As I've said, whenever I go into any social gathering in Belfast, up comes an ex-Dominican pupil to remind me of the episode, which seems to have loomed very large in the lore of the school – though at the time, and for a long period afterwards, I was not aware of its impact. Indeed, I had thought my exit from the school went relatively unnoticed.

I can't imagine why I believed this: it was, after all, nearly a mass expulsion – three of us cast out at the same time – and clearly caused a scandal of sufficient intensity to mesmerise the school. How they must have lapped it up – I'd have done the same if it had happened to someone else – and how our mis-doings must have gained in exorbitance! What scope for the envisaging of lurid antics! I now know that we were held up as an awful warning for years to come. According to more than one teacher, signs of insufficient tractability were apparent in the three of us nearly from the minute we set foot in the school. We were blamed for holding far too good an opinion of ourselves, for being unamenable to discipline of any kind, whispering in class and eating ice-lollipops in the street, and forever carrying on insubordinately. Inter-house competition, games and other innocuous activities were supposed to have left us cold. (All this was conveyed to me, bit by bit, over many years.) We refused to pull our weight on netball field or hockey pitch, though perfectly robust in constitution, preferring to idle around making fun of those who exerted themselves in a proper spirit. The games mistress, in particular, claimed to have predicted our bad end. She was a Mrs Cumberledge, very bleak and bony, and infamous herself for being separated from her husband, for going to the Dogs (but only literally), and for turning up at the school every now and then wearing a fearfully moth-eaten old fur coat, which gave her the look of a shaggy snake. (I can still see that coat.) I detested her, with the kind of whole-hearted detestation that's rarely available to anyone over the age of seventeen.

Rumour had all three of us expecting babies, at the very least, after midnight orgies with Donegal turf-cutters, to account for the extremes of censure and innuendo surrounding our departure – and neither the games mistress, who certainly knew better, nor anyone else in authority went out of her way to contradict such misapprehensions. If the school, believing them, could be kept suitably cowed as a result, so much the better. (Some pupils, in shocked whispers, discussed the actual presence of *boys in our bedrooms*; while others, more admiring, wondered how we had pulled it off.) As for us – good riddance to the lot of us. At that juncture in my life, the future career that so engrossed Miss Brannigan from the Donegall Road very nearly remained as much a figment as the non-existent teenage pregnancies.

Every now and then there occurs a moment when events from the past assume a striking configuration – when accumulated connections and coincidences enrich the original occurrence, or begin to impose a pattern on top of it. You can suddenly see aspects of the thing that weren't apparent at the time, as well as marvelling at the way it all holds together. It ceases to be amorphous and acquires an outline – or at least, you're handed on a plate the means of achieving an outline. It makes a proper story, complete with plot and sub-plots. And more. 'We had the experience but missed the meaning,' T.S. Eliot wrote in 'Little Gidding'. 'And approach to the meaning restores the experience / In a different form … ' I'm all for having a pungent experience restored, though it's not so much meaning I'm after – futile to attempt so highfalutin an exercise – not so much meaning, as implications: the implications of what went on in Rannafast and Belfast at a particular period, and in distinctive circumstances, with myself and my friends at the centre of it.

It's that moment at the BBC in Ormeau Avenue in 1992, with the combination of Michael McLaverty, his one-time St Dominic's daughter and the late Miss Brannigan, that gets me thinking about the Falls Road and Rannafast, social history and convent benightedness, and the endless emphasis on chastity that marked our upbringing: all you've taken on board, as it were, merely by virtue of having lived through it. ('She was a middle-aged woman who had led a certain, not very varied but perceptive life, who had lived through enough time to write a narrative of it… ' – thus the heroine of A.S. Byatt's story, 'On the Day that E.M. Forster Died'.) It's true that that occasion at the BBC might have furnished a starting-point for other stories – if we're going to view the past as a succession of stories, carrying a particular import and with a beginning, a middle and an end; the Cobbles story, for example, or the Derby Street story, both capable of elaboration. However, it is Rannafast and its associations that suggest them-selves most insistently – that are going to nag at me, I know, until I get them off my chest.

There's already been a slight rehearsal for this undertaking. In 1982 I was asked by the *Observer* to contribute to a series of articles it was running on the subject of being expelled from school. The piece I wrote was very short and frivolous – short enough to reproduce here in full. It was printed under the title 'Corrupting Influence'.

> I was expelled from school for having once possessed a copy of *Peyton Place* and for having lent it to a classmate who thought it

was the *Kama Sutra*. In fact, it served her purpose just as well. After years of good conduct, this girl – stocky and bespectacled – suddenly developed an enthusiasm for the pleasures of the flesh (in a mild form).

What she learnt from Grace Metallious's helpful novel she put to good use in the course of a holiday we spent in Donegal, and ended by depriving the school of three of its most hopeful pupils (herself included). Our expulsion had a profound effect on us. Of the other two, one became a terrorist in later life and one married a policeman. I lost the taste for reading American bestsellers.

It happened the summer before we were due to go into the sixth form. Our school, a Belfast convent, was run on old-fashioned lines – no eating or going bare-headed in the street, no leaning out of classroom windows to wave at workmen building the new wing, light reading supposed to be confined to picturesque Catholic pamphlets with titles like 'The Devil at Dances'.

Seniors, however – those who could be trusted to uphold the standard of behaviour required by the school – were encouraged to attend an Irish language course which was held each summer in a Gaelic-speaking part of Donegal. Pupils from schools all over the province converged on this spot at the beginning of August, were allocated to various homes in the district and set about acquiring fluency in Gaelic. (Since this was the object, you were sent home if you were caught speaking English.)

The college authorities here, we discovered, were nearly as strict as the nuns we had left behind in Belfast. Ceilis – Irish dances – were organised for our benefit three times a week; but if you were observed dancing with the same partner more than twice, you were reprimanded. Pairing-off was frowned upon.

You had to be careful, too, how you dressed: one girl was taken to task for appearing in a blouse with the top two buttons undone. According to one rumour, priests and teachers attached to the college patrolled the roads at night shining torches behind turf-stacks and into ditches in search of concupiscent couples – making killjoys of themselves, it seemed to us, on the scale of Yeats's Father Rosicross.

Other rumours, however, had reached us before we left the city. We all looked forward to fulfilment, or at least entertainment, in the arms of some Donegal turfcutters; and we weren't disappointed. Groups of these local boys, home for the summer from part-time jobs in Scotland, used to roam the district between one and three in the morning, rapping the bedroom windows of girls who, they thought, might be game for a little hanky-panky behind a cow-byre. We quickly acquired the habit of scrambling out in the middle of the night (priests and teachers all safely in bed by this time – or so we hoped), wearing more clothes than we did in the daytime to discourage excesses of passion, and of scrambling in again at every intimation of danger. A dog barking or the glimmer of a torch in the distance was enough to send us scuttling for the windowsill.

So much hilarity was bound to be followed by sobriety: this nursery maxim proved well-founded in our case. Things began to go wrong. Our landlady at last realised what we were up to and nailed up the windows to stop us getting out. Worse, at a ceili on the last night of our holiday, we – pupils belonging to our school only – were summoned to the secretary's office and told that a letter, written by one of us and describing our activities in ribald detail, had reached our headmistress via the parents of the girl to whom it was addressed. As a consequence it was probable that we were all going to be expelled.

As soon as we were released, we headed for the girls' cloak-room where a state of extreme agitation soon prevailed. Who was to blame for this misfortune? We narrowed it down to two girls, both staying at a cottage at some distance from mine. I concluded, rightly at this stage, that I wasn't too seriously implicated in the business.

However, the fateful letter now in our Mother Superior's hands – all exclamation marks and knowing innuendoes, I believe – turned out to be the work of a girl whose supposed naivety had been a byword in the school. Clearly, some corrupting agent had been at work. What was it, the headmistress wanted to know.

It might have been a book she read. A book? What book? A terrible immoral novel called *Peyton Place*. And where had she got it? ... That was when my far-from-brilliant school career went bung.

There is nothing fearfully askew about this as far as accuracy of recollection goes (though I've presented some things as facts when they're only suppositions). But it is most unwarrantably simplified. It was wrong of me, for example, to apply the word 'terrorist' to my one-time best friend, who later went on to carve out a redoubtable career for herself in the South: her 'Irishness' took a different form from mine, or than mine would have taken if I'd stayed in Belfast, that was all. Living where she did (in West Belfast), at a particular time (the early 1970s), and as a crusader against social injustice, she didn't have the option of remaining neutral or disinterested as things fell to pieces around her, of observing excruciating occurrences from afar and forming judicious opinions on them. She was there in the thick of it, having her political consciousness raised along with her hackles: night raids, sectarian aggression, violence in the streets, vehement partisanship, an atmosphere of anarchy – anarchy tempered by a local republican camaraderie. What could she do but get involved – and once that had happened, a sequence of events including all the horrors associated with a clandestine affiliation was set in motion. This old friend, whom I shall call Olivia McAloon (more about her later), became famous, or infamous, for more than being expelled from school. Recently, yet another St Dominic's old girl, of a humorous disposition, bounced over to me in a public place to assure me that I was only the second most scandalous past pupil in the history of the school. In the notoriety stakes, our republican classmate had beaten me hands down.

As for the other delinquent (a most unlikely delinquent) specified in my *Observer* article, who was never a kindred spirit or even a close school friend – I don't know if it's appropriate to attribute to her as much of the blame for my downfall as I do, or even if it is true that she married a policeman (I seem to remember hearing something to this effect, but I can't be sure about this: I've chosen to assert it merely in the interests of symmetry). I've also conflated her character and that of a couple of lesser-known, more childish girls who were minimal participants in the dramas of that summer.

And yes, *Peyton Place* did come into the picture; but it was not the only, or even the main, reason why I was expelled. There's a lot more to the story than that, and several aspects of the business only became known to me after a considerable lapse of time. In the weeks after the verdict was delivered, I think I latched on to *Peyton Place* because I had owned a copy of this deplorable novel and it *had* gone the rounds of Form 5A; this provided an explanation of sorts when I was badly in need of one. I must have pieced it together from things said, or intimated, by some of the girls concerned; no one ever alluded directly to *Peyton Place* and its indecency, as far as I am aware.

But I was not in a state to make much sense of anything. The whole episode was devastating and bewildering. Like Sean O'Faolain after hearing that his novel *Bird Alone* had been banned by the Irish Censorship Board, I felt that 'Somebody had thrown me out of an accepted club without my knowing what I'd done.' First I was told that I might resume my place in the school at the start of the new term, then – after a reversal of opinion – that I was, instead, to be ejected (the second, I was given to understand, as evidence of my depravity came to light). These successive edicts were conveyed to my mother. It seemed I was too depraved to be actually summoned to the school on the second occasion, confronted with my supposed transgression and given a chance to defend myself. Nuns were very autocratic in those days. At the same time, they were under the thumb of priests. More than twenty years went by before I gained an inkling of the part played in the whole sorry affair by an extraneous character, a priest attached to Clonard Monastery in Belfast, a total stranger to me. ('*Is maith an scéalaí an aimsir*', time is a good historian.) I learnt of his existence, eventually, through the novelist Michael McLaverty.

It was after the publication of the *Observer* article. I've said that I wasn't acquainted with McLaverty's daughter, but the same was not true of her father, whom I did get to know, very slightly. In 1976, my parents had moved to a spot in County Down between Strangford and Ballyhornan, saying goodbye without regret to the Donegall Road and the sight of a burning bus forming part of a barricade every time they stepped out of the door. The owner of a weekend house just down the road, along the shores of the Lough, was known in the district as the author of several novels. One day my father was accosted while mowing the lawn by an elderly, gnomish gentleman wearing a black beret, and demanding to be told if a writer lived there. He was a writer himself, by the name of McLaverty. It was explained to him that the writer – me – was based in London, but came over to stay in County Down fairly frequently. (How had he heard of me? My 'writing' at the time consisted of a study of girls' fiction, written jointly with Mary Cadogan, and a handful of magazine articles.) It wasn't long before I met Mr McLaverty myself, some years before his astonishing loquacity and story-telling gifts were eroded by old age. (He ended his life being cared for in a nursing home.) We were all intrigued by him and his fund of anecdotes about Ballymurphy and the Strangford/ Portaferry districts of County Down. It's true that after a certain point we noticed a degree of repetitiveness and forgetfulness, or misremembering, beginning to afflict him. He sometimes mistook me for one of his past pupils (I think – or were they all boys?) and complimented me on having grown into a lovely big girl. (I was over thirty at the time.)

While he still had full command of his faculties, though, McLaverty read my *Observer* article and promptly paid a visit to his pal Mother Helena of the Dominican Order, the nun at whose hands my prospects for a university education came unstuck. To go by what he told me later, he found her in a penitent frame of mind. If she'd had the thing to do over again, she said, she'd have acted differently. At the time – well, drastic measures needed to be taken, to restore (as far as possible) normality and a high moral tone to the school. Mother Helena wasn't to know that the world was on the verge of change – that 1960s freedoms would soon extend even to the corridors and classrooms of St Dominic's High School on the Falls Road. The truth was, in the weeks following the discovery of our Gaeltacht goings-on, she came under tremendous pressure to make an example of me, me in particular, even though my relative innocence with regard to the Rannafast imbroglio had been more or less accepted. Father So-and-So of Clonard Monastery (if McLaverty ever mentioned this person's name to me, I quickly forgot it), in his full rage and indignation, was insisting on my removal from the school forthwith. Why, when he had no more personal knowledge of me than he had of Mata Hari – indeed had never set eyes on me in his life? An aunt now comes into the picture, the aunt of one of the other girls involved, my best friend, Olivia McAloon.

This aunt – Aunt Ita – was a gaunt woman, a cripple, who was often seen propelling herself about the town in an invalid carriage. Her great purpose in life was to carry out auxiliary work for the church, supplying flowers for the altar, organising collections on behalf of the Foreign Missions, that sort of thing. She was off to some non-essential church service every minute of the day. The Clonard priest was an acquaintance of hers, and it was to him that she went with the terrible story of her niece's expulsion. It was no skin off Aunt Ita's nose to cast me as the prime mover in the affair. She had never considered me a suitable chum for her niece. Something about me didn't commend itself to her. It may have been nothing more radical than my current hair style, which – by accident – produced an 'arty' impression. Up until the age of fifteen, I'd been subjected by my mother to a nightly ritual involving rags or curlers, the effect of which was to make me look a bit like a sheepish Young Christian or an exceptionally gauche barn dancer. (The look she was aiming at, sort of Margaret Lockwood-cum-Doris Day, was unfortunately not available to me: I didn't have the face or the personality to carry it off.) Then, the summer before Rannafast, I went to stay with the McAloons in a cottage in the Mourne Mountains, where my hair reverted to a natural state: straight. It was a revelation to me how much better it looked, and I resolved to hold fast to the inadvertent improvement.

But, in those days, to have straight shoulder-length hair, and a fringe to boot, proclaimed a deficiency of moral fibre, as far as women like Aunt Ita could judge. At the very least, it indicated a wish to attract attention; but it also suggested a dangerous leaning towards immoral archetypes seeping in from abroad. These might include X-rated films (Brigitte Bardot), or even Picasso's iconic images of Sylvette David of the socially defiant fringe and pony tail. I was certainly familiar with these and other romantic-delinquent images, and I can't deny their subversive appeal in constricted old Belfast. I remember a newsagent's shop in Donegall Street in the city centre which stocked a selection of foreign magazines, *Paris Match*, *Oggi* and so forth, and for a brief period when I was fifteen or sixteen I bought and scrutinised these intriguing periodicals in search of a kind of glamour which I felt was missing from the Donegall Road and St James's Avenue.

Though I hadn't contrived it with full consciousness, my new hair style was an approximation of those I'd noted in foreign or film magazines, and I suppose in a way it represented my first assertion of a social alignment that diverged from my mother's, being only available to the current generation of under-twenty-fives (those susceptible to libertarian promptings, that is). Protest and a heady non-conformity were in the air, even in the toned-down air of Belfast; and some of us were of a mind to latch on to those invigorating ideologies. We believed we'd got the hang of the unfolding era, the incipient sixties – or at least, that we were equipped to get it in due course.

Advancement-by-upheaval, though – in whatever area of life – is just a vague prospect for the future; in most respects we fit into the life around us and believe at some level that this life is changeless. Our everyday gestures of rebellion don't go much beyond listening to Radio Luxembourg, or sticking resolutely to our seats while the rest of a cinema audience rises to its feet for 'God Save the Queen' ... But now my innocent hair, my straight fair hair, has somehow got itself mixed up with that very tentative opposition to the status quo. At any rate, it acts on the older generation as a pointer to profligacy, inducing agitation in aunts, my own and others', as I suppose it was bound to do. Aunt Ita wasn't alone in her disapproval. But I read a unique vindictiveness into the officious poking of her nose into the matter of my Rannafast culpability, or otherwise. I imagine the tale she carried to the Clonard priest went something like this: I'd led the others astray, out of sheer badness, and then contrived to get off scot-free. God knows what evidence she produced to back up her story. Whatever it was, it sent him off in a jiffy on his mission of ill will. ('*Is fearr eolas an oilc ná an t-olc gan eolas*', better is knowledge of evil than evil without knowledge.)

When Michael McLaverty recounted to me his conversation with Mother Helena, in the early 1980s, he alluded to this priest as if I'd always known all about him and his impact on my life; but in fact I'd lived all those years in utter ignorance of his existence. (I have to try to be fair here: it is possible that Aunt Ita and the nuns and the priest were perfectly correct in their assessment of my character – that they all perceived, long before I did, my inability to subscribe to the system they revered; that they saw me, rightly, as a disruptive influence and an opponent of Catholicism – or, for that matter, any other dogmatic religion. But if this is so, it was on my future, not my present, behaviour that I was being judged.)

Father So-and-So: once his name came up, his role in the affair made perfect sense. This was one of the pieces that finally slotted into place, backed up by passing comments from my London friend and closest neighbour at the time, Rory McAloon (the brother of Olivia), with whom, for various reasons, I hardly discussed the matter at all. (I'm aware that the McAloons' version of the events described below will not coincide with mine.) In those days, I lived with my husband, Jeffrey Morgan, in the top half of a graceful Georgian house in south-east London, while Rory and his wife and daughters had the other half – and it was because of Rory, whom I bumped into in Blackheath in 1976, that this joint ownership came about. He and his family were installed in the basement of the house when it came on the market (it was in such a shocking state that it was under threat of compulsory purchase and demolition by Greenwich Council), and he went to considerable lengths to secure the property, finally bringing us in on the deal. As architectural enthusiasts, we were intrigued. Along with the house next door, ours had functioned as a hostel for the employees of a local drapery firm, Hinds (many of whom were Irish shopgirls, some from Donegal). In an earlier incarnation, under a Miss Mary Tatlock, the house had been a boarding school – and then a Miss Jane

Caroline Corbett and her heirs lived there between 1873 and 1940, after which began the long decline from London suburban respectability. Forty-odd years later, we moved in – after a full-scale renovation had been carried out.

It was a lovely and unusual place to live. (This is true also of our present home, a stone-built one-time manse in County Antrim.) And our occupation of it was due to a set of circumstances arising from a link with the past, my past – a link so tenuous it was down to a spiderweb thinness, though about to be solidly reinforced.

How it came about was this. For some reason, I was sitting on a bench at the end of Vicarage Walk in Blackheath, between a great friend in the area, a shrewd and incorrigible old lady from the north of England who concealed her formidable intelligence, but displayed her humour, by opting to look like an old-clothes woman, and an elderly black gentleman – idly sitting there, when Rory McAloon rode past on a bicycle, looked, stopped, looked again and rode back. It's an occurrence that calls to mind Anthony Powell's famous sequence of novels, *A Dance to the Music of Time*, in which the vagaries of social intercourse are likened to a dance whose complicated movements keep bringing you face-to-face with a particular person, and then out of their orbit for a time.

This fortuitous meeting, then, had consequences which none of us could possibly have foreseen. (To begin with, it's unlikely that I'd be sitting here, looking out at a pair of 200-year-old yew trees, in a house with a hidden garden and mysterious attics, if it hadn't taken place.) It nearly didn't happen. It was a wonder that Rory had recognised me, after a lapse of twenty-odd years, and given the fact that we'd only known one another slightly, between the ages of eleven or twelve and sixteen, while I knocked around with his sister. We arranged to meet, that day in Blackheath, and one thing led to another ... Our joint occupancy of No. 2 Cresswell Park proved to be quite a tempestuous business at times, Rory being volatile, maddening and moody, as well as amusing, generous and gregarious. As our friendship progressed, I became aware that his view of me was coloured ineradicably by the atmosphere in his home around the time of the Rannafast debacle. He envisaged me as a naughtier and more dashing schoolgirl than I ever was, cocking a snook at the Church and merrily getting up to all kinds of licentiousness.

He also had me down – rightly – as a poetry-lover, like himself, and would sometimes curb his wilder instincts if I was about. Once, when he didn't, I remember him charging at full steam after a crowd of juvenile intruders in the garden next door, yelling at the top of his voice; then coming back to where I was standing witnessing this performance, and declaring humorously, defiantly and apologetically all at once, 'It's the Falls Road coming out in me.'

Rory moved out of our Blackheath house a couple of years before his premature death in 1998 when he was fifty-three. An excess of drink on top of such perennial complaints as asthma, stomach trouble, migraine, insomnia, did for him in the end. We still find his absence upsetting and perplexing.

Long before I ran across Rory in Blackheath, my friendship with his sister had all but evaporated. It really didn't survive the Rannafast summer, though intermittent attempts were made to prolong it. By the mid-1970s, Olivia's life had taken a few dramatic turns. On top of being imprisoned for republican activities, she'd been shot in the head and stomach and was lucky to be alive. The expulsion from school, in Olivia's case, was only the prelude to a much larger expulsion – or exclusion: from the whole of Great Britain and Northern Ireland. Though her home was in Belfast she was exiled to Dublin, unable to cross the border without fear of arrest.

In the face of these nightmarish occurrences, Olivia's capacity for insouciance was somewhat diminished. When she read my *Observer* article in 1982 (it was reported back to me) she was affronted by the word 'terrorist' and consequently took a 'scunner' at me. Well, as I've said, it's understandable that she should resent the attempt of a one-time friend to blacken her deepest convictions, merely in the interests of obtaining an effect of smartness.

But it was a sorry end to an old school friendship. *Allies in the Fourth*, you might have dubbed us; and the Third, and the Fifth, while those early days threw up unimportant dramas, trivial school contretemps, around us. One of us might have to defend the other during a brief campaign by other girls of putting worms and spiders in her schoolbag, to see her lose her rag; or exercise her wits to concoct a plausible explanation for some bit of rule-breaking threatening to bring down ire on the other's head. The great topics of the day, to which we were devoted, included the question of who would get off with whose brother at a classmate's Hallowe'en party, whose end-of-term results were not up to standard, what teacher had it in for whom. (Some teachers were in a permanent condition of being fed up with the lot of us. I remember an occasion when a couple of us, caught frantically doing our geometry homework at the back of Sister Garcia's history class, were sent to report ourselves to the mathematics mistress, Miss Smith. Miss Smith – all five foot two, saturnine mordancy of her – when we'd tracked her down to the Dominican staff room, turned on us a look of infinite weariness and disdain. 'Go back and tell Sister Garcia,' she said, 'that I really couldn't care less if you sit in her class learning Hindustani.' And closed the door in our thunderstruck faces.) We were acting out in our own lives the substance of a thousand girls' stories, immersed as we were in classroom politics, the forming and reforming of alliances and cliques, the modish contingent versus the hard workers, the good sports and their opposite, the affected brats. Some among us (only a very few, alas) were admired for their beauty, their ostentatious cleverness, or their ability to make things hum. Where we departed from the standard school of fiction, Springdale, St Madern's or the picturesque Gulls' Haunt, was in the religious conditioning that permeated everything, down to the pain in your thumb. If you complained of a pain in the thumb, you were told to offer it up for the souls in Purgatory – who thereby got themselves associated with so many minor discomforts that they were eventually themselves thought of as a pain in the neck.

The scarcity of contiguous role models may have been a factor in the allure, for us, of more or less daring American teenage films including *Peyton Place* – shown, I think, at the old Imperial Cinema in Corn Market – whose delectable atmosphere was not reproduced in the book. When I read the book, I found it sickly and shoddy beyond anything I could have anticipated, and I couldn't wait to get it off my hands (with the consequences adumbrated above). No, throughout the 1950s, the figure most assiduously presented to us as a role model was that of Maria Goretti, an obscure Italian peasant girl who fought off a would-be rapist and literally died to stay chaste. (She'd achieved the status of 'Blessed' by the time we became aware of her – I think she was canonised later.) The fate worse than death, in this instance, really was, in her mind, worse than death. Not that we understood, for some years, what Maria Goretti's virtue consisted *in*, being insufficiently knowing to grasp the nature of the 'sin' she resisted so exorbitantly.

When we were only eleven or twelve, the nuns' version of the story – a 'man' had tried to persuade the devout young girl to commit 'a sin', but even the prospect of dying bloodily couldn't erode her aversion to wrongdoing – meant little to us. Was it a thieving enterprise he'd tried to coerce her into, or did he want her to tell lies on his behalf? Requests for enlightenment were met with evasion. Of course, before too long, we knew exactly what was entailed during the lethal confrontation in some backward part of Italy – by which point, I think, most of us were sufficiently pragmatic to reject the slant imposed by the Church over the pathetic occurrence. Better deflowered than defunct, in our opinion: or, what was the point in retaining an intact hymen if the rest of you was ripped to pieces? Nevertheless, the temporary popularity of Goretti as a Christian name among Irish Catholic parents testifies to the impact of the little Italian's senseless heroism.

Those girls (there were a few) among us who aspired to a similar invincibility were ripe for admission to a society called the Children of Mary (a Catholic coterie whose *raison d'être* is a blank to me, if I ever understood it); the rest of us were judged of insufficient piety to merit the broad blue ribbon, with holy medal attached, which denoted membership of this Mariolatrous, senior-school group. Entitlement to wear this ribbon on top of my wine-coloured gym-tunic was a status I never craved. I was more interested in acquiring a *fáinne*, or ring, to pin on my blazer: a silver *fáinne* to begin with and then a gold one, indicating degrees of proficiency in Irish.

My Irish was coming on, but it was still very much at the lesson-book stage; it wasn't yet a medium of communication with peers. I was fairly good at languages, though never outstanding – by languages I mean the two on offer, Irish and French. Among the fearsome grudges I've been harbouring against my old school, all these years, is its failure to provide for us, the A-stream, a grounding in Latin – an advantage you might have assumed to be inseparable from a Catholic education. But no: by some unfathomable quirk on the part of the curriculum-arranger, Latin was available to the B-stream in our year, but not to us – or not, at least, without an impossible jiggling of the timetable to fit it in. All the Latin I ever picked up was the word *veritas* – 'Our noble motto,' as the school song had it, 'blazoned on the shield we wear, / Truth in thought and word and deed, / The heritage we bear' and so on – the phrase *Per ardua ad astra*, our house motto, and as much of the Mass as stuck in my head.

This was supposed to be an efficient school, a school it did your reputation no harm to attend (unlike the supposedly inferior establishments for Eleven-Plus failures); but I remember it as a place where I was badly taught (with one or two exceptions) and badly treated (though I'd never want to play the 'poor me' card). I'm astounded whenever I read friendly references to nuns in general, and to those of my Dominican convent in particular – as, for example, in Mary Beckett's novel *Give Them Stones* (1987). In this novel, the heroine's sister wins a scholarship to the place – 'the school on the Falls Road' is all the identification it gets, but it's enough – and comes home enthusing about the quiet nuns in their long white habits and big rosary beads, 'the lessons and the kindness and the singing in the white chapel'.

She's writing about the 1940s, it's true, but I can't believe that things were so different then.

Kindness is not a quality I associate with nuns. *My* nuns didn't have it in them. They were nearly all ordinary, not very intelligent women driven to irascibility or worse by the artificiality of their situation. One or two, I am sure, were certifiably insane, like the physical-punishment addict of Aquinas Hall, or the uncontrollable hysteric I met at Ballynahinch. Nuns at the time were stuck with the veil for life – except in very extraordinary circumstances – and some of them must have regretted the virtual imprisonment they had set up for themselves. We were always hearing about this nun or that nun who'd suffered a nervous breakdown. Once professed, they didn't have the option of changing their minds – probably the last intake of convent fodder in that stymied position.

Soon, you'd get the cut-and-run syndrome which pulverised the whole idea of cloistered constancy. Starting as a drizzle, the I-leapt-over-the-wall brigade became a cloudburst, with nuns in droves ducking out of their vows as the life of holiness proved more than they could take. By the 1960s, even the Dominican Order was failing to hang on to its less-than-dedicated recruits. And when they resumed their laity, they went the whole hog. One contemporary recalls bumping into a young ex-nun at a railway station, and being slightly shocked by the extreme shortness of her skirt, the redness of her lipstick and breeziness of her manner.

The old perception of nuns as holy and good and the convent as a haven of stability was due for an overhaul, and, along with many ingredients of Irish myths and truisms, it was about to get it. Revisionism would soon come into its own. But, as yet, we had few intimations of upheavals in the political or the moral sphere. We thought we inhabited a world in which Catholic values were unchangeable, in which the Church hierarchy would continue to lay down the law, a law transgressable only by those already brimful of badness. All forces for change were regarded with suspicion by elders with mitres and elaborate headgear, and their stern views filtered right down to the lowest of their flock. At school debating contests, for example, those of us who upheld the mildest form of socialism were warned we were on a slippery slope: the merest push, we were told, would tip us over into a godless communism. (An alarmist attitude to a possible communist takeover was widespread at the time.) Communism, divorce and popular entertainment were the greatest evils of the modern world, and they were all tied up together. But Catholicism had its own, unassailable, resources, including the resource of domestic praying.

A few years earlier, our seven- , eight- , and nine-year-old heads had come under considerable liturgical pressure, as rosary dementia got the country into its grip. This craze, like a good deal of popular entertainment, was imported from America, and it smacked of a Catholic transatlantic smarminess which – even then – one or two of us found unpalatable. Well, I can only speak for myself, of course. At school (Aquinas Hall) we were urged to go around proselytising on behalf of the rosary, and in particular to persuade our parents to hold rosary sessions in their living-rooms in the evenings, if they weren't already doing so. Even at that age I had read enough, and was scornful enough of the 'ministering children' strain in Victorian fiction, to resent any attempt to cast me, me with my self-professed affinity with anarchic William Brown, and Jane Turpin of the tearaway in-genuity – to cast *me* as one of those goody-goody, obnoxious softeners of obdurate adult hearts. I'd no more have suggested praying to my parents than nude bathing in the Falls Park 'Cooler'. I couldn't imagine anything more preposterous than the four of us (grandmother included) down on our knees going 'Hail Mary / Holy Mary'.

There wasn't a chance of it: we were not that kind of family. But, to my consternation, it looked as though I was unique in this respect, as the whole school immersed itself in the devotional brouhaha. My family's cheerful impiety – well, relative impiety – seemed perfectly natural to me. But I hesitated to disclose our aversion to communal praying, since I could tell it ran counter to the stirred-up sanctity enkindling our classroom. I thought if I just kept quiet I could pass as a rosary devotee along with everybody else.

But then a nun, in a further access of zeal, came in one morning bearing a chart which she proceeded to pin up on the classroom wall. Across the top of this chart ran the names of every child in the class, with the days of the week down the left-hand side. The idea was that each of us should tick every day on which the family rosary was said in her home. As soon as this was explained to us, I was filled with anxiety and agitation. If I were to be honest, my column would remain a total blank, week after week, and there I'd be, exposed as the pitiable and freakish child of an insufficiently dedicated household. There was nothing for it but to grit my teeth and produce a row of deceitful ticks. It wasn't a complete row, as many people's were; but I simply had to pretend that we occasionally knelt down, beads in hand, to say the rosary in common with everyone else.

I hated doing it, it made me feel uneasy and grubby, and even though I kept my ticks to a minimum, each one jarred as I filled it in. I thought I was committing some kind of terrible sin, a sin peculiar to myself, and endangering my entrée into eternal bliss. I also worried that I'd be caught out. I wasn't, of course; no one ever questioned my claims to conformity in the matter of the family rosary. The only comment on the subject I remember was the observation that I should try to make it happen more often, to which I probably responded with a bashful smirk. I wasn't a natural liar, but common sense and expediency were turning me into one. *Is fusa tuitim ná eirigh*, it is easier to fall than to rise.

In 1920, the Archbishop of Armagh had decreed that the only acceptable form of Catholic education was the school in which Catholic children were 'educated as faithful Catholics in a Catholic atmosphere, and under the care and direction of their pastors, whose strict right and leading duty it is to watch over, direct and safeguard the religious education of the lambs of their flocks'. Blah, blah, blah. Such pronouncements boded ill for the prospect of integration. But integration as a concept carried very little weight at the time, or indeed later. Catholic bishops were still crowing over their exclusivity twenty-five years on, when they averred, 'We have had control of our Catholic schools for over one hundred years, and whatever the action we are driven to take we are determined to maintain it.' No surrender. They represented the Church as being in a state of siege, even when things in the North were relatively tranquil, harking back to the early days of the Northern Irish state, when 'the very existence of Catholicity [sic] in Down & Connor, and in Belfast in particular, was menaced, and [when His Grace the Most Revd] Dr MacRory, by an appeal to the Catholics of the world, was instrumental in procuring relief for his imperilled people'.

His imperilled people. The period in question, it's true, was a particularly fraught and traumatic era in Irish history, with a partial autonomy conferred on roughly four-fifths of the country, and the remainder sticking like glue to the UK connection. It was an awkward resolution of the Irish problem and bound to cause chaos and virulence; and chaos and virulence weren't long in coming. 'The outlook is desperate,' reported The Times newspaper in August 1920, while in the streets of Belfast newsboys bawled out the latest casualty figures: 'Twelve shot dead! Two hundred wounded!' The Northern government, once it came into being, didn't know what to do with the unruly minority it was saddled with, while those of the minority left high and dry by the terms of the Treaty seethed with disaffection and a sense of betrayal. Ambush, riots, machine-gun fire and pogroms were the order of the day. When District-Inspector Swanzy was shot dead in Lisburn, the ferocity of Orange reprisals caused a mass exodus out of nationalist quarters in the town, with whole families tramping by night across the Antrim Hills towards the (comparative) safety of Belfast.

There was misery for many, but the Catholic Church went out of its way to appropriate all the suffering and uprightness going. It was all 'his imperilled people', the highlighted image of 'bishop, priests and people [standing] together in unbroken and

… unbreakable solidarity', and Catholic integrity lording it over Protestant iniquity. You'd have thought that what was going on was a religious war, not the hoary old clash of ideologies, the struggle on the part of some political activists to obtain social justice and a chance of betterment for those who lacked these graces, the determination of others to preserve a way of life agreeable to themselves and to their followers. It was sometimes hard to tell where principle ended and pigheadedness began. Bigotry on one side was naturally answered by bigotry on the other, and when it came right down to fisticuffs and jeering at street level, the Catholic/nationalist contingent gave as good as it got. There were people in Catholic Belfast for whom it was a matter of principle not to buy a 'Protestant' loaf of bread (i.e. one manufactured by the Ormeau Bakery rather than Hughes's).

And there were other people, in other parts of the city, who knew absolutely nothing about the tradition of Protestant support for the Irish language, and couldn't have cared less if they had known. They knew where they stood on the language issue, that was all, and it wasn't the position occupied by Robert MacAdam, Sir Samuel Ferguson, Douglas Hyde, Francis Joseph Bigger and many, many others. 'If parents want their children to learn Irish or any other useless language, they should pay for it out of their own pockets,' snorted the opposition to state subsidies for voluntary schools, speaking in the infant Northern Irish parliament. Well, they weren't alone in this opinion. Daniel O'Connell, the great Liberator himself, in the nineteenth century was also convinced of the uselessness of Irish. It was, he believed, a hindrance to social progress and a millstone round the necks of those, mainly the rural poor, bogged down in its benightedness. The sooner it became extinct the better. If it had to survive, the best place for it was in the heads and hands of those with sufficient lesiure and money to cultivate it – i.e. the (mainly) Protestant middle and upper classes. It is by way of suchlike ironies, paradoxes and complexities that the fortunes of the Irish language may be traced.

As for native Irish-speakers themselves – socially they were the lowest of the low, despised as ignoramuses by those among their peers who'd mastered English and begun the upward scramble out of poverty and muck; or they were the last custodians of an ancient and endangered civilisation, and best approached as one might approach an unfathomable tribe discovered in the remotest corner of the earth. We may be certain that neither attitude was much to their liking.

If Catholic hyperbole is detectable in Cardinal MacRory and his 'imperilled people', it surfaces again in a comment made about MacRory's successor as Bishop of Down and Connor, the Very Revd Daniel Mageean. Dr Mageean was praised in 1941 as a pastor 'who has guided and defended the Catholics of Belfast through the fires of persecution', which makes him sound like a Gandhi or a Nelson Mandela. In truth, the fires of persecution added up to a moderately low-key affair in Belfast during the 1930s. Catholics on the whole remained unreconciled to the system they were living under, and the system itself certainly didn't have their interests at heart. Some cultivated subversion, and some went in for the kind of congregational freemasonry mentioned above. Most complained about the unionist regime from time to time. And the chronic debility of the body politic erupted occasionally in serious sectarian disturbances, like those of 1935.

But, for the most part, Catholics in the North got on with their lives like everyone else, aspiring to middle-class respectability if their origins were lower, consolidating whatever degree of comfort they'd attained. They bought summer outfits and other goods at enticing department stores like Robb's and Robinson and Cleaver's, and enjoyed the camaraderie of St Malachy's Old Boys' Club or the bustle of Campbell's Café filled with shoppers and dripping umbrellas on a wet morning in December.

My sense of the atmosphere in Belfast during those pre-war days comes partly from books, and partly from the recollections of people alive to its nuances, such as my mother. My mother, Nora Brady, was a student at Queen's University, where – among other things – she received a grounding in Scholastic Philosophy under the tutelage of Father Arthur Ryan (later Monsignor Ryan), a course of study unavailable to non-Catholics. As Marianne Elliott remarks in her magisterial history *The Catholics of Ulster*, this course came into being 'in response to a successful campaign to create separate Catholic teaching programmes in controversial subjects' – in other words, as part of the Church's endeavour to safeguard the faith of impressionable young Catholics exposed to the heady non-conformity of Queen's. It was no big deal, however, though probably it contributed to the undergraduate predeliction for religiously-differentiated alliances (a predeliction more pronounced at that time, I think, than it was a generation later – at least in my experience as a student at the Belfast College of Art). Overt sectarian prejudice didn't stand a chance in the (more-or-less) liberal ambience of Queen's, *c.* 1936, where my lively-minded mother had the time of her life. She never suffered personally on account of her (temperate) Catholicism, though she was well aware of the disabilities Catholics in general had to contend with, and deplored the subjugation of 'the nationalist people' – Cardinal MacRory's people – as much as anyone.

She was also in thrall to the nationalist version of history with its torments and triumphs (respectively inflicted by the English and achieved by the invincible Irish), though this didn't preclude an enthusiasm for everything to do with the First World War, and in particular its poetry – her father, whom she never knew, having died in that war. But, for the moment, tremendously exhilarated at having got to Queen's against the odds, she concentrated on enjoying as many undergraduate activities as she could handle. These included travelling on the train to Bangor with her friend Celia Lenaghan and heading for a prominent street corner where the two of them would stand flogging copies of the student magazine PTQ (*Pro Tanto Quid*, after the city motto of Belfast). This magazine was famous for the innocence of its dirty jokes – or the dirtiness of its innocent jokes, whichever way round you preferred – jokes along the lines of 'If I told you that I admired your bosom, would you hold it against me?' These ex-convent girls liked to be mildly shocked, as long as the shock didn't arise from anything seriously objectionable, such as blasphemy.

My mother at the time lived with *her* mother and sisters in a terrace house off the Stranmillis Road, from which she'd set out every morning, jaunty though myopic (and far too vain to wear her glasses), to walk the short distance down to Queen's and the day's lectures, past exclusive Friars' Bush Cemetery, once a magnet for grave-robbers, the new Ulster Museum and the delightful small gate lodge at the entrance to the Botanic Gardens, which always made her think of Hansel and Gretel.

English and History were her principal subjects, and she was and remained under the spell of these compelling pursuits for the rest of her life. She had her Palgrave's *Golden Treasury*, her Bradley's *Shakespearian Tragedy*, and copious notes taken down from Professor Savory to bolster her against inevitable ill hap. She was a scholarship girl, duty-bound to do well. Her anxiety to please, though, was tempered by a good-humoured, quizzical wilfulness which might have landed her in the soup with her tutors if the course she was taking hadn't proved to her liking. There were bits of it, indeed, such as maths, which represented an obstacle for her. But English and History, always a pleasure and never a grind, saw her through. These things really mattered to her: the Romantic Poets, the English Civil War, and the escape of Red Hugh O'Donnell from the English stronghold of Dublin Castle on a snowy night in 1591.

Selectively studious, she was nevertheless disposed to gaiety and enjoyed being voted the best-dressed girl at Queen's in 1937 (quite an achievement for someone with absolutely no money to spend on clothes). She relished the attentions of male fellow students, some of whom spent a large part of the summer break theatrically pining for her, and expressing their desolation in breezy, flirtatious letters, letters beginning 'Nora, my dove'. (It was around this time that Nora's paternal grandmother died and left her and her sisters five pounds each. She and her closest sister,

Kathleen, blued this windfall on a week's blissful holiday in Rannafast, where they inhaled the ethnically and ethically pure air of the Gaeltacht and grew familiar with its salient features.)

My mother's educational luck had begun when she was twelve or thirteen, and the nuns of her primary school in Lurgan had recommended her for a scholarship to a recently rehoused Sisters of Mercy convent, Our Lady's Secondary School, which quickly became known as Mount St Michael's, after its new setting. It was located within walking distance of hilly North Street, Lurgan, where Nora lived at the time: you went down the hill, up an incline, over a railway crossing, round a bend, and there in front of you was the convent perched on top of its own hill, a grand Victorian mansion known as Irishtown Hill House in earlier days, surrounded by trees, firs, pines and beech trees, and complete with gardens, tennis courts and hockey pitch, for all the world like something out of *Septima, Schoolgirl*. From its upper windows you could see Lough Neagh, with the occasional fisherman's boat or a tug guiding lighters to the Rivers Bann and Blackwater, and far away the mountains of Tyrone and Antrim contributing a suggestion of wildness – but only a distant wildness – to the scene. No mere school of fiction could hold a candle to Mount St Michael's, my mother thought; to be a pupil here was the summit of happiness, and a near-miracle in her case, in those days of deprivation and social stratifying. She was the youngest of five daughters of a strong-minded war widow who fully supported her brightest child's claims to be educated; but it wasn't easy, even with the scholarship.

There was no snobbery at St Michael's, yet Nora dreaded kneeling down for prayers and exposing the soles of her shoes to public scrutiny. This was because there was no money in the house to pay for mending: if a hole appeared, it just got bigger and bigger and you had to go on wearing the shoe regardless, until the sole fell off. To show herself in this condition was a torment for a sensitive girl with a horror of slovenliness. But the shame she felt was all in her head: no one ever taxed her with being ill-bred on account of her shocking footwear. (Money was very scarce, but she nevertheless managed to scrape up 4d a week to buy the *Magnet* and the *Gem*, essential items of juvenile reading, and had founded her own 'Famous Five' at school, in honour of Frank Richards's Greyfriars characters.)

In the novel *Call My Brother Back* by Michael McLaverty the hero's education at St Malachy's College is sponsored by a priest who has spotted the boy's intellectual gifts. This is fine – but then a moment arrives at the end of Colm MacNeill's first term when bills for the school fees are about to be handed out. The diffident fourteen-year-old is overcome by trepidation at the prospect of being conspicuously omitted from this ritual. When he receives an envelope along with everyone else, it's a relief at first, but then he is terrified that some awful mistake has been made, and an unpayable demand issued to his mother. In fact, inside the envelope is a slip of paper saying 'Father So-and-So's pupil'. Exactly the same thing happened to Nora at Mount St Michael's. She was only aware of one other girl at the school in a similar position to herself, and both of them, like the McLaverty protagonist, were included in the bill-distributing at the end of term to spare them embarrassment in front of their friends. The slip of paper inside the envelope addressed to Nora's mother bore the reassuring words 'No charge'.

It's hard for me to reconcile this solicitude for their pupils' peace-of-mind (I am taking the McLaverty account to be a true one) with the attitudes of those in religious orders known personally to me. *My* nuns would have been more likely to taunt a pupil for coming from a less than socially desirable area of the town, such as the Pound, Ballymurphy or Rodney Parade. During my first year at St Dominic's, one twelve-year-old, the oldest in a family of nine from the Lower Falls, was found crying in the cloakroom because a nun, in front of the class, had commented sneeringly on the less than pristine condition of her white Viyella blouse. (Such were the trivial barbs often directed at us.) This, mark you, was during the supposedly more democratic 1950s, when almost everyone was a scholarship pupil and the few exceptions, those whose fees were shouldered by their parents rather than the state, were looked down on, on account of their supposed intellectual incapacity. There was no winning with these nuns unless you had average brains, were exceptionally docile and could boast a rich, turf-accountant or solicitor father. (I am talking about the general run of things: exceptions here would be the odd girl taken under the wing of a particular nun and encouraged in whatever aspirations she might have. But this was rare.)

My mother rejoiced in her schooling and fitted in with her teachers' expectations in a way that I did not. She became a prized past pupil who'd conformed to an unspoken school code and ended by reflecting credit on the place, getting her graduation photo into the first issue of the school magazine, the *Michaelonian*, in 1938, and contributing to the same issue an appreciation of 'The School on the Hill' – an establishment which, she claimed, '… had grown into one of the finest Convent Secondary and Boarding Schools in a country famous all over the world for the excellence of the education and training imparted by its Religious Orders to the young'. Whew! Despite the punctiliousness of that assertion, however, I don't believe that my mother was inherently more tractable than I was, or any more committed to academic success. (Though she had, indeed, a lot of gratitude to express, and this was one way of expressing it.)

But between her schooldays and mine some vast changes seemed to have come about, social and psychological and in the reciprocal commerce of activity between church and community. At the same time, superficially, things went on in much the same way: Sunday church-going and other rituals were conscientiously observed, education continued in the hands of the clergy, sexual morality was still firmly in place. *We* were not aware of a general change in outlook, either present or impending; or if we were, it was only at a subliminal level. But something, other than my own incorrigibility (I think), brought about an extreme divergence in our respective school careers, my mother's and mine.

Of course it was a different world back there in County Armagh in the late 1920s, slower and steadier and a lot more sedate (or so we like to think). You were not exposed to un-settling furores via magazines, cinema and television, and altogether fewer channels existed to put ideas in your head. The concept of self-expression had not reached Lurgan. In Catholic circles at any rate, its opposite, self-suppression, was fostered in accordance with Church teaching. In practice, this could not work, or could work only partially, but it was kept to the fore as an idea, and incessantly enjoined on those in subordinate positions, such as schoolchildren.

You were supposed to put others before yourself, and to curb the instinct to go all out to achieve your own ends. If you hap-pened to be exceptionally talented in any area, the credit for this was due to God in the first place, not yourself; and your gift, what-ever it was, was meant to be employed in the service of the school, not the individual. This was not peculiar to the Catholic edu-cation, of course; as a ploy to quash self-conceit it was axiomatic, a defining feature (in its 'team spirit' version) of innumerable girls' and boys' school stories, though generally without overt reference to God. And it was all very well, most sensible children would have thought, though not especially to be applied to themselves. Still, the habit of obedience would have caused them to pay at-tention to this and other recipes for achieving a state of grace.

It was perfectly possible, even for an intelligent pupil like my mother, to regard nuns and their way of life uncritically – even to admire them for their piety and unworldliness. Convents, nuns, priests, the Mass, indeed everything to do with Catholicism, were part of the social fabric of that time and utterly taken for granted. They didn't stick out like a top hat at a football match. It wasn't until after the Second World War that convent life began to acquire an increasingly anomalous relation to ordinary life, and even then the winding-up of nunnish sequestration was a long-drawn-out process, and tied up with the secularisation of society as a whole.

Eventually, the idea of a religious vocation for Catholic women seemed so mad and outlandish that it has virtually ceased to exist (in the last decade or so).

But it wasn't like that in the past, not for my generation and certainly not for my mother's generation. And Nora in particular accepted the package of nuns and education without the smallest dissenting qualm. She was a Michaelonian, a hilltop girl; it wasn't in her to jeopardise that status. For her it was the school that distilled a magnetising glamour, not the wider world which contained such things as unemployment or lowly employment, scruffy corner shops, back-yard toilets, over-crowding, wet pavements and front doors opening straight on to the street.

The nearest my mother came to my Rannafast experience (without coming to grief) was a joyous occasion when she and four or five of her classmates (the brainiest girls in the school) were sent up to a convent at Ballycastle, on the north coast (*The School on the Cliff*), during the summer term, in order to sit some examination or other. They all failed the examination, but no one minded this very much; it wasn't important. This was a hiatus in ordinary school life: what was important was to make the most of the beach, the sea bathing, the country lanes, the girlish high jinks, the fizzy lemonade, the proximity of someone's male cousins who happened to live nearby. And they did make the most of all these delights. There are snapshots to prove it, showing my gamine mother looking pensive and self-possessed. Out of school hours, the girls loll about, picnicking under dry-stone walls and briar hedges, or stand on rocks accompanied by grinning schoolboys. They are out of sight of the Convent and free, for the moment, to gad about to their hearts' content, in their silky flapper tops loosely belted around the waist, and flowing skirts à la Jeanette McDonald. What larks!

Cardinal MacRory's successor, Dr Mageean, was Bishop of Down and Connor between 1929 and 1962. Dr Mageean

PC's mother Nora (fifth from left) with friends on the rocks at Ballycastle, c. 1929

presided over my schooldays as well as my mother's, setting the tone for Catholic life in the North during the long years of his reign. Catholics had to dance – if at all – to the tune of Dr Mageean, which boomed out as dreary and solemn as he could make it. He spent a lot of time ensuring that Catholic schools would not be contaminated by the smallest measure of 'Protestant' liberalism. No 'Inst' inclusiveness for him. There's an Ulster-Scots word 'jeuk' or 'juke', meaning to dodge or evade: to have any kind of a jolly time during those years you had to jeuk Dr Mageean's prescriptions for piety, such as shunning 'Protestant' entertainments and immersing yourself in the Rosary Crusade.

His doctrinaire assertions didn't stop with Church affairs. During the mid-1950s, as a young teenager, I held Dr Mageean personally responsible for the meagreness of my wardrobe and the cobbled-together nature of our summer holidays (a week here or there, usually with relatives in Coventry, Essex or Dublin). We had no money to spend on luxuries because of the ban imposed by Dr Mageean on married women teachers, who were ousted from their posts the minute they left the church and had picked the confetti out of their hair. Henceforth their skills, whatever they were, would be devoted to household management and the rearing of children. They were expected to stay put. 'Somehow a girl was meant for one spot,' says a character in one of Michael McLaverty's later, inferior, works of fiction. 'When she starts the roaming she's like a dog that goes after sheep – never contented.' Well! This striking pronouncement indicates the persistence of antiquated attitudes in the Catholic north of Ireland, while the rest of the world was moving on.

And indeed, there was no jeuking the Bishop's edict. So my mother, with one child – me – and her mother on the spot to act as willing baby-minder, was stuck restlessly at home until wartime marshalling of resources got her into the Censorship Office at Stormont. Post-war, it was back to the Donegall Road to sit looking out at the plane trees in St James's Avenue, or reading – and rereading – the works of Graham Greene. This state of affairs went on until 1956 or '7, when the pressures of modern life, not to mention the shortage of teachers as a vast new school-building programme got under way, caused the Bishop's ban to pass into history.

A few years later, it looked as though other malpractices, sectarian malpractices, might also pass into history, as voices of reason began to make themselves heard and egalitarian possibilities were bandied about. It was the mid-1960s, with its sense of new beginnings. Such a feeling of exhilaration hadn't flourished so strongly in the North since the last decade of the eighteenth century and the United Irish movement – about which Tom Paulin lamented, 'Hardly a classroom remembers / Their obstinate rebellion.' Alas, the twentieth-century revival of that democratic spirit wasn't destined, any more than that of the Lagan Jacobins, to come to fruition. Equally, it came up against intransigence, in the form of an awful atavistic figure popping up like an evangelical Jack-in-the-Box to rant about the Pope of

Rome and the threat to Ulster's Protestantism, and causing sectarianism to be reignited.

One shocking image from those years is the Burntollet marchers, those remaining on their feet after an ambush by loyalists in the Ulster countryside had left half their number unconscious, clutching their heads where batons had landed or streaming with blood, staggering on towards Derry in support of civil rights. Few at that moment could have failed to regard these people as heroes. They had looked at the society they inhabited, disliked what they saw, and tried to take some action to promote long-overdue reforms. The attack on them simply demonstrated to the world at large the justice of their position. But what was their position? As you find with almost everything to do with Ireland and its enormities, tangles and complications quickly enter in.

A book like Bob Purdie's sterling study of the Civil Rights movement, for example (*Politics in the Streets*, 1990), goes a considerable way towards indicating what the social reformer was up against. In the first place, the movement was never homogenous, but consisted of many small groups and sub-groups, all with slightly differing biases and objectives. They all, indeed, promised a better deal for those in the North enduring social disabilities; but some just wanted to knock humanity and a sense of justice into the existing state, while others were holding out for an entirely new system – Irish republicanism, socialism, Marxism or whatever. If some issues – principally, the issue of discrimination – caused sufficient outrage to bring them all, briefly, under the Civil Rights banner, there were still too many factions involved for anything approaching unity to be sustained. Looked at closely, the NICRA dissolves into the CSJ, CDU, NILP, CPNI, PD, NCCL, NDG, NDP, DCAC, RLP, RSSF … the abounding acronyms tell their own tale. It wasn't a pattern peculiar to the decade; ever since the establishment of the Northern Irish state in 1921, opposition to unionism had been marshalled under a whole spectrum of headings, from Catholic nationalism to communism.

It was, indeed, a place where it was easy to get into the grip of a grievance, and at moments it seemed as though everyone, everyone in the province was advocating some form of remedy for its discords. You had the nationalist remedy, the republican remedy, the reformist remedy, the conciliation remedy, the socialist remedy, the republican-labour remedy, the liberal-unionist remedy, the hard-line remedy, the Gaelic remedy, the priestly remedy, the cultural-nationalist remedy, the middle-of-the-road remedy, the atheist remedy, the anti-segregation remedy, the pro-segregation, or ghetto, remedy, the repatriation remedy, the Kilkenny cats remedy. In the face of all this, it's possible to feel some sympathy with a body like *Saor Uladh* (Free Ulster) which once opted out of the whole business by proclaiming a republic in the centre of a County Tyrone village.

However, it is probably true to say that the North, for all its unruliness, has never lacked a civilising spirit to interpose itself between competing prejudices. And this liberal spirit sometimes surfaces in unexpected places – I am thinking, for example, of the Irish-speaking club mentioned above, Cluan Ard, located in a street not far from St Dominic's High School, on which my social life was centred between the ages of seventeen (the year after I was expelled from school) and twenty. This club enriched the lives of a good many people, not all of them Catholic, and fostered wrong-headed aggression in no one. Even though English was never spoken on the premises, it held fast to the anti-sectarianism of the republican tradition. (This unfortunately could not be kept up. By the 1970s, with the 'Troubles' raging, very few Protestants, however liberal-minded, would have dared to set foot in West Belfast.) Whatever fluency in Irish I once had, it was acquired in this spot, or in the Gaeltacht, not at school; and here, as well, I gained a smattering of insight into the erotic, or bawdy, element in Gaelic literature, and began to understand that Ireland's literary heritage wasn't confined to the pious unrealities of a novel like *Mo Dhá Róisín* (My Two Roses) or Charles Kickham's *Knocknagow*. The eighteenth-century

County Louth poet Cathal Buidhe Mac Giolla Gunna, for example, has quite a bit about the delights of seduction, even if in the end it all boils down to a heart-rending renunciation: 'Acht anois, faraoir, tá mo shaolsa caite, / Is is miath liom stad agus léigean dóibh' ('Now, alas, my life is spent, / And I must stop and leave them to it.').

At the same time, at twenty or thereabouts, I was reading Brian Moore and relishing the cogency of his case against Belfast and against provincialism, including the provincialism of an Irish-speaking Ireland – not that I went along with it entirely, indeed, but it appealed to me at various levels. He made disgruntlement invigorating – the disgruntlement of someone whose birthplace is a backwater. Belfast, in the view of Brian Moore, does nothing for its citizens beyond stupefying and hamstringing them at every turn, lumbering them with deadly ideologies, dulling their perceptions and soaking them with its perpetual downpours. In the background to his writings of the 1950s and '60s, though it isn't singled out for special attention, is the unionist misrule which overshadowed all the other indigenous forms of oppression (church, economy or whatever). It's a place, he implies, from which anyone in his proper senses will remove himself as soon as possible. 'A dull, dead town', he calls Belfast, in *The Emperor of Ice-Cream*. And *Judith Hearne* positively bristles with the stifling effects of suburban Catholicism.

But it was the sexual failure – indeed the sexual shipwreck – of Diarmuid Devine in Moore's *The Feast of Lupercal* that most strongly alerted me to the horrors attendant on a puritanical education. Poor Devine, after an episode of excruciating ineptness, bitterly envisages the words of penitance he will offer the priest in confession: '… do not worry about that sin, Father. Tried it once and didn't like it.'

Tried it once and didn't like it. There's a powerful indictment of Catholic puritanism for you. Moore's point is that the school Devine went through, and to which he returned as a teacher, did for him in this important respect ('It was a matter of ignorance, pure and simple.'). He has neither a natural talent nor the skill acquired through practice to see him right – and when, at thirty-seven, he takes a fancy to a silly young girl from Dublin and tries, very tentatively, to involve her in a sexual relationship, an appalling evening ensues.

Moore has presented the schoolmaster Devine as a casualty of the Catholic education, a person in whom a natural modesty and primness interact with churchly inflexibility and the mood of the time (the book was published in 1958), to devastating effect. He is, indeed, an extreme case. Others, more pragmatic, would have sidestepped unacceptable embargoes, such as the embargo on 'company-keeping', or manoeuvred themselves into some kind of principled opposition to the religiose conditioning of the era. The years between fourteen and eighteen – say – are indeed a time when all kinds of passions are rampant, including the passion to purge society of its ills.

When I edited *The Oxford Book of Schooldays* some years ago (yes, there's a joke about my own educational experience) I called one section 'At Odds with the System' and into it I put the rebels, the dissenters, the social critics, the scoffers, the outsiders, the outraged – all those whose temperaments weren't in step with the schooling they received. My own temperament – it is now clear to me – clashed with Catholicism, though I certainly hadn't articulated any such unorthodoxy before the age of sixteen. I swallowed what I was told, and acted accordingly, going to Mass on Sundays, confession once a fortnight, and so on – though never in any spirit other than that of performing a chore. (Given the choice, I'd rather have tackled the back yard with scrubbing-brush and soap.) It was possibly a question of heredity: I didn't have a religious temperament, neither of my parents had a religious temperament, I don't think my grandmother had a religious temperament (though in her case it was harder to be sure, since the trappings of Catholicism, holy water, saints' statues and so forth, meant more to her). A secular, academic school would have suited me down to the ground. But there I was, pitched by circumstances into a convent, and – as yet – only moderately receptive to intimations of oncoming scepticism.

Of course I'd like to align myself with that intrepid group, those at odds with the system, but I fear I am not entitled to do so. I was one of the herd, never a leader or an innovator. I can't claim to have suffered for my principles; principles were not conspicuous as a motivating factor among my classmates of Form 5A. Such defiance of authority as we engaged in tended to be somewhat underhand (inventing excuses for not having done your homework; passing notes in class). It would have been a different matter if I had repudiated the nuns of St Dominic's and their restrictive ordinances, instead of sticking to their wretched code as far as I was able. I wish I had, but I lacked the gumption, or the insight, or the courage to be openly insubordinate. I was far from being an apostle for sexual liberation.

Still, the majority of us weren't as ignorant or inexperienced as Moore's Mr Devine, in our seventeenth year; for some of us, sexual intercourse existed as an intoxicating prospect. What would it be like? Wonderful, we thought, having gained an inkling – the merest inkling – of what might be in store for us, with the help of the more knowing boys of St Mary's or St Malachy's, at the back of the City Cemetery, in the Falls Park, up an alleyway, in a garden shed, on the slopes of the Cave Hill or up against our own back gates. It was always, at the very least, a compelling topic.

When I read a poem like Tony Harrison's enticing 'Allotments' – imbued with a frisson of the wayward and demotic – I find it strikes so many chords that it's hard to approach it in a proper spirit of detachment. 'And young, we cuddled by the abbatoir, / Faffing with fastenings, never getting far … ' Smoke, cobbles, brick, alluring darkness, industrial grime, frustrated lust … all that comes back with a full force of recollection.

In Leeds, though, they weren't inhibited into the bargain by a moral prohibition enforced so strongly that it nearly got absorbed into one's system. The poem's allusion to the River Aire,

> The cold canal that ran to Liverpool,
> Made hot trickles in the knickers cool
> As soon as flow …

prompts me to reflect that it wasn't a cold canal, but a cold doctrine of sin and damnation, that produced the same effect on us. It made us behave like prissy Sally Shannon, the bane of Gavin Burke in Moore's *The Emperor of Ice-Cream*. 'We can't,' she tells him, as he reaches for the waistband of her knickers. 'It's a mortal sin.'

The phrase 'It's a mortal sin' was uttered frequently, in those days. It's true that for many girls, some of my own friends among them (the hormonally challenged), the embargo on fornication wasn't especially irksome; for myself, at that age, it was manageable, as long as the sexual instinct had at least a partial outlet, and as long as I remained pretty confident that I wasn't going to end up like Elizabeth North's headmistress in the novel *Dames*, who only gained a vital bit of carnal knowledge in late middle age. 'So that is an erection, thought Miss Bedford.' Deferred fulfilment was all very well, but I didn't want it to be deferred as long as all that.

Ten years later, the authority of the Catholic church in Ireland was beginning to subside, even if Catholic attitudes didn't necessarily follow suit. An inexorable flexibility was in the offing, meaning in practice that you'd be able to call yourself Catholic, while picking and choosing among the tenets of Church teaching. It was an advance on utter authoritarianism, I suppose, but it came too late to be of any benefit to me, since my natural atheism had asserted itself once and for all as soon as I got to London and the Central School of Art at the age of twenty. I don't have any hankerings after a spiritual framework for my day-to-day activities. I'm also a bit bewildered by incomplete apostacy, believing, I suppose, that it makes more sense to be one thing or the other. But now the definitions have changed. You can be divorced and call yourself Catholic; you can be an unwed mother six times over and remain within the flock. Good heavens, you can be a Catholic bishop and go about fathering offspring if the fancy takes you. This is a newfangled Church. It is also a disintegrating Church, one that can't afford to alienate any of its adherents, whatever 'sins' they come laden down with. Well, all along, this Church showed an instinct for expediency.

I know the Catholic Church wasn't all bad. I know it performed many useful, indeed indispensable, functions. It acted as a curb on would-be violence and hooliganism. It knocked obstreperousness out of some of those harbouring anti-social inclinations. It provided a badge of identity, a stake in the community, for people who needed some guiding system they could fit into, to make sense of their lives. But some of its behaviour was very bad indeed. For example – during the 1950s and '60s, as I remember it, the onus on poor parishioners to subscribe to various Church Building Funds was completely over the top. The Church Building Fund and its needs were really dunned into us. One diabolical scheme to drum up money involved a solemnly touted bit of moonshine designated 'The Golden Book'. A donation of £5 or more entitled you to have your name inscribed in this metaphysical ledger; and once you were in, your place in heaven was assured. If your name was *not* in the Golden Book, due to parsimony or carelessness, you had to take your chance, but payment of the entrance fee would guarantee salvation. So we were told, and it may have given some of us an idea of heaven as a vaunted football match or celebrity concert for which tickets were at a premium.

On top of the cynical manipulation of the credulous suggested by this and other expedients for drumming up support, you have to consider into the bargain all this putative *church building* and what it entailed. What it entailed in many cases was the destruction of historic churches which distilled as much of a sense of the numinous as it was possible to attain; and what you got instead was a series of replacements in 1960s concrete-and-crassness. This may be read as a visible sign that the Church was relinquishing its role as custodian of anything at all in the way of spirituality.

'Puritan Ireland's dead and gone,' wrote John Montague; but it didn't go quickly enough to decontaminate our escapade. Indeed, it never died out completely; the puritan ethic is not a spent force even yet, though it's no longer backed up by social usage or an unassailable religious system. It survives as a caste of mind, not necessarily an unattractive caste of mind. A puritan note is sounded in Tom Paulin's 'dream of grace and reason', 'the sweet equal republic' that came to nothing. There are old Ulster churches, small, whitewashed, with polished pews, in which you can nearly see the point of puritanism, with its high regard for propriety, calm and order. And for plainness and sobriety, those Planter virtues which reached some kind of epitome in the poet John Hewitt, whom I used to visit in Belfast between the late 1970s and his death in 1987. *His* Ulster puritanism was carried with grace and vigour. There he sat, in his tweed armchair, looking upright and sturdy, with his pipe, his books and his strong liberal views, an old-fashioned latitudinarian secure in his humanism, while Belfast blew itself to pieces around him. Offered the Freedom of the City – or what was left of it – in eventual recognition of his importance as a poet, and as a conduit for civilising views, his comment was, 'I thought I already had it.'

Perhaps it's only when puritanism is tied up with sexual prudery that it turns disabling.

Unlike many people possessed by the urge to explore some aspect of their lives, or unfold a narrative to show themselves and their times in a particular light, I have very little to complain about. I didn't undergo an unsatisfactory upbringing. I was not deprived, abused, accident-prone, made little of, precipitated into awful circumstances or forced to grow up too quickly (some might say I've never managed to grow up at all). Of course, like everyone's, my childhood contained long stretches of boredom, doldrums interspersed with dolours. Sometimes a dreadful action was imposed on me, like having to appear as a flower in a silly school play. 'It'll all be the same in a hundred years,' my mother would say encouragingly, to put the thing in perspective.

I loved my wayward father and sometimes at night I couldn't fall asleep until the sound of his key in the front door announced his safe return from wherever he'd been out on the spree; and I loved my sharp-tongued grandmother whose hard life hadn't completely knocked out of her a capacity for fun. But the centre of my universe was my clever and affectionate mother, who ensured – among other things – that my infancy was enlivened by copious recitations of verses which she had by heart. Among these was one which I found particularly diverting. (I've never come across it in any other context.) It concerned a pair of namby-pamby mice: 'Now Horace and Willy were stupid and silly, / And couldn't say boo to a goose'; then there's a bit about 'tears', 'Which only made Daddy / Fly into a paddy / And give them a whacking, poor dears.' The two mice muffs are sent away to be educated at Rat College ('College' engagingly rhymed with 'knowledge'), where they do so badly that they are promptly returned to their doting parent with a letter of explanation. If he'd had them much longer, the headmaster tells her quite frankly, '… I'd have given them both to the CAT. / I remain, yours respectfully, Rat.'

I am two, three at most, and already able to distinguish between ruthless humour, which is bracing, and some ruthless threat creeping out of the night, which is disturbing. There's another story, in an old lesson book, about a wolf in sheep's clothing slinking in the dark towards a flock of unwary lambs, which I don't like at all. But my mother is always there to cushion me against upsets. It is also her role to adjust the dodgier bits of information I pick up at school. One day (I am five) I come home smugly repeating something I've just heard, about how it must be so awful to be a Protestant and banned from heaven, and how lucky we are that it doesn't apply to us. 'But your Grandma and Grandpa, your Aunt Charlotte, Auntie Ruby and all the rest of them are Protestants,' she says, matter-of-factly. This gives me something to ponder.

These relations, newly revealed as heathens according to my school theology, are my father's family and live in a gate lodge once attached to a grand house (now demolished) at the Malone Road end of Dunmurry Lane. It is very nearly right out in the country. My grandfather is a horse-trainer, riding instructor and head groom to a prominent local family. The defunct big house was called Lismoyne, and my grandparents' gate lodge has kept the name. It dates back to 1845 or thereabouts, later than the house, and is possibly the work of the architect Thomas Jackson. For me, though, visiting the place on Sunday afternoons, travelling from Belfast with my spruced-up parents on the Hillhall bus, it is just an intriguing small house, full of odd corners and enticing nooks, a house in which something is always going on. It is crammed with flighty young aunts and ebullient uncles and all kinds of distant cousins; there are dogs and horses and pecking hens about the place; I go on walks with my Auntie Ruby and drag my feet, for pleasure, through piles of autumn leaves down the road along the demesne wall, or, at a different season, up the lane behind the house to gather armfuls of bluebells. My grandfather persuades me to perch on a Shetland pony, and a photograph exists to proclaim my lack of horsemanship as I turn towards the camera, beaming all over my face but clearly ill at ease and not displaying a natural rider's posture.

Lismoyne is a part of my life. Orange lilies grow in my grandmother's garden (my Wexford grandmother, who never lost her southern accent), and a Union Jack is hung out on the Twelfth, but as yet I have no awareness of these emblems or what they signify. If I even register the fact that my mother's mother and my father's parents never meet – well, I'd have put it down to the fact that these are all old people for whom the journey between West and South Belfast would constitute an intolerable trek.

Protestant and Catholic. 'Not men and women in an Irish street,' William Allingham lamented, 'but Catholics and Protestants you meet.' And here I am, attached by upbringing and schooling to one of these sects, but with half my ancestry firmly located in the other. (More than half, actually, though I'm not yet aware of it.) As far as I know, no grand ideas of bridging the sectarian gap ever entered into my parents' heads. They married in spite of their differences, not because of them. Indeed, what drew them together in the first place was and remained a mystery to many. It was not a meeting of minds. She was bookish and he was convivial. She was pragmatic and he was feckless. She soon assumed her role as financial manager and stabilising influence, while my father went his own merry way.

How did they even meet? Looking back on their first encounter, in old age, my father endowed it with something of the force of an epiphany. (My mother was no longer alive at the time and couldn't confirm or deny his romantic recall, or attribute it to his recent, overwhelming bereavement.) The meeting between the two occurred early in the war, in 1940 or '41, at a dance in a Catholic church hall, St John's on the Falls Road. It seems that – for whatever reason – my father had already strayed into the Catholic world: the social, not the religious world (though he took on the religion as well, half-heartedly, to enable their subsequent marriage to take place within the church).

Arriving at the dance with a Catholic friend, a young barber's assistant by the name of Owney Muldoon, my father spotted one particular attractive face among the crowds of hopeful young women assembled at the far side of the hall, and knew in that instant (he says) that he was looking at his future wife. (What her view of the occasion was I don't know. Whenever anyone with typical Belfast impertinence asked her why she'd married him, she would say, jokingly, that he'd pestered her to the point where she had to give in for a bit of peace. He found this response hilarious.) They were married, then, at the same local church, and with the same Owney Muldoon as best man – not my father's elder or his younger brother, with both of whom he remained on excellent terms for the whole of their lives. In fact, as far as I know, not one of the Craig family was present at that Catholic wartime ceremony: the gulf was deep between the two sects and they tended not to set foot in one another's places of worship.

It's possible that, by going against the grain of Protestant Ulster, my father was indulging in a gesture of rebellion. It is also possible that this gesture was totally subconscious. He was not someone who was given to analysing his motives. But, whatever shocks he inflicted on his family – or they on him – a good supply of natural affection continued to bind him strongly to his siblings and to his parents, both of them, although by all accounts

PC's parents on their wedding day

my grandfather was a hard paterfamilias, especially as far as his sons were concerned. He may have applied a few of his horse-training tactics to their upbringing.

However much he upheld the cult of the firm hand and the steely temper, though, my grandfather William Henry Craig, born in County Leitrim in 1884, hadn't always acted in accordance with these principles himself. Among the things remembered about him was a strong streak of juvenile wildness. According to family lore, he ran away from home at the age of fourteen, in defiance of his parents' plans to get him a start in life as a railway clerk, and found employment for himself as a stable-boy at Finnebrogue near Downpatrick ... But then it seems the entire Craig family of six brothers and sisters ran away as soon as they were able. A couple of them went as far as Australia. The cause was a stepmother who appears to have acted in accordance with the Snow White stereotype. The children's real mother had died in 1891 at the age of thirty-six – and here the story takes an interesting turn. In every family tree there are people who stand out for one reason or another, and with me it's my great-grandmothers on both sides, Ellen Jordan on my mother's side (I'll take a closer look at her later), and Mathilda Clara Maria Heller on my father's.

Mathilda Clara Maria, born in Berlin in 1854, came to Ireland as a governess in the employ of the May family – one-time sovereigns of Belfast who gave their name to May Street, the street which contains the Presbyterian church specially built in 1829 for the Revd Henry Cooke ... The nineteenth-century governess, from Lucy Snowe in *Villette* to Dorothy Richardson's Miriam Henderson bravely taking on pupils at a finishing school in Hanover, is a common figure in literature, teaching being among the few resources of clever women with their way to make in the world. Thanks to these and other works of fiction, we know quite a lot about the courage it took to embark on a journey to a foreign country, at twenty or thereabouts, with no certainty of receiving kindness or considerate treatment at the end of it, just the prospect of grappling with a lot of potentially troublesome youngsters and trying to impose order and some linguistic know-how on them. And being in an anomalous position, embodying a status symbol for employers who required a Mademoiselle or a Fräulein about the place to underscore their affluence – not on their level, certainly, but not quite a servant either.

Well, every reader of *Jane Eyre* has the picture in their head: the physical discomforts, the slights and privations – and then at last the glorious reversal of fortune. Alas, in reality the governess was more likely to end up in the situation of my great-grandmother: pregnant by a fellow employee of the upper-crust family. In her case it was a handsome coachman of the Mays', another William Craig – and he seems to have hesitated to do the right thing by the young German woman he'd got into trouble, since no marriage took place until after the birth of their first child Bertha Elizabeth. (This pattern of a hasty – though not quite hasty enough – and more or less enforced marriage seems to have been quite common in nineteenth-century Ireland, in both Catholic and Protestant circles.)

What Mathilda Clara's family back in Berlin made of their daughter's disgrace, or even if they considered the illegitimate birth in the light of a disgrace, one will never know. The Hellers were Lutherans and one would assume they were reasonably strict as far as church dogma was concerned. My great-grandmother was the fifth child and second-youngest daughter of Friedrich Wilhelm Heller, a potter, and his wife Maria Dorothea Bertha Vogel, and the family would have had a certain standing and cultural aspirations beyond those available to a rough Irish coachman (I'm guessing here). Did Mathilda Clara find the Irish mists and rain and poverty-stricken countryside oppressive and hanker after the civilities of Berlin? In whatever spare moments she could snatch for herself, she wrote down lines of German poetry that came into her head (and maybe composed a poem or two herself). One poem she transcribed in her notebook, in a beautiful Gothic script, was written by Karl Simrock in 1838. It presents a luminous account of the Rhine with its legendary perils:

> To the Rhine, to the Rhine,
> Don't go to the Rhine,
> My son, this I advise:
> Life will seem wonderful there,
> And you will dare too much!
>
> You will see the maidens so free
> And the men so brave,
> As if they were nobility;
> You will join them eagerly,
> And it will seem good and right.
>
> And when on board,
> Castles will greet you,
> And the city with the ancient church!
> You will climb the heights of mountains
> And look down to the stream!
>
> And from the river below
> The water fairy will rise,
> And if you see her smile,
> And if the Lorelei should sing,
> My son, it will be your end.

You will be bewitched
By the sound and the vision,
You will be gripped by joy and fear.
And you will sing forever: To the Rhine, to the Rhine!
And never return home again.

'Und kehrst nicht wieder nach Haus': did she find that last line at all prophetic? As far as I know, she is buried somewhere in Ireland, probably in a Church of Ireland cemetery in County Leitrim … It is all irretrievably in the past, and family lore is a highly unreliable guide. I don't even know exactly where my great-grandparents made their home. But it's certain that poetry was a consolation to Mathilda Clara, enabling her to keep a hold on her sanity in alien surroundings far from the Tiergarten or Magdeburger Platz and with more and more children to raise. Her early death in 1891 one would naturally attribute to a calamity of childbirth.

I can't help seeing some parallels here with my parents' marriage: I mean the situation, not its outcome. My mother didn't have six children or die young. But here you have two clever women, readers, desperate for intellectual stimulus, married to men of a considerably less scholarly type. My mother, too, kept notebooks in which she transcribed the words of poems she was fond of, from early Yeats to Wilfred Owen. A modus vivendi more or less satisfactory to both of them, though, was hammered out between my parents (it wasn't exactly helped by the presence of my maternal grandmother who always took her daughter's part in any dispute) – and one would hope the same was true of Mathilda Clara and William Craig, in the few years of marriage allotted to them … One or two tantalising glimpses into their offsprings' lives exist in a couple of letters from Uncle John in Sydney to his niece Hazel (my aunt) in the 1950s. 'We all survived a lot and still a remarkable family,' he says. 'I am sure you heard your father tell the fireside stories many times.' Alas, the fireside stories are no more recoverable now than Mathilda Clara's state of mind on her wedding day, or the old Ard Scoil in Divis Street.

Uncle John, born in 1882, was the second child of Mathilda Clara and William Craig; next came my grandfather William Henry, then Charlotte Martha Jane (Aunt Charlotte), Frederick Arthur (Uncle Freddie) and Albert, who seems to have left no trace: possibly he died young. Aunt Charlotte, who married a man named Kennedy and lived on the wrong side of the Lisburn Road, in Great Northern Street near the railway line, has left a whiff of an odd impression of capability and vulnerability behind her. '… I am always worrying about poor Charlotte,' says Uncle John in a letter to Hazel. 'You keep a good eye on her as she has been a really great woman in her day. Big-hearted to everybody.' And: 'Have not heard from poor old Charlotte for a few months. I do trust she is well and her black cat.'

I do trust she is well and her black cat. Aunt Charlotte – unlike her stern brother William – possessed an engaging personality which endeared her to all. I can barely remember her, but I do remember a brisk, sedate and birdlike old lady, still with brown hair though she must have been seventy, bustling about and amiably involving herself in all manner of family goings-on. Old-fashioned. A dominant presence among the people of Lismoyne. She was my great-aunt, and – if I'd had the wit – I could have elicited from her the fireside stories, the German mother and the whole absconding family of Craigs …

As it was, the bulk of my elders only impinged on my consciousness as a kind of reassuring backdrop to my own prodigious, daily concerns – what mark I would get for my English composition, whether my friend Pauline Toal would accompany me to the Saturday afternoon matinee at the Broadway cinema. It could hardly have carried a charge of less significance, that world of school friends and adventure stories, admonishing nuns, the trees on the patch of waste ground behind St James's Park, the dog Kim, the sight of my mother alighting from the Donegall Road bus as we watched for her, my grandmother and I, from the sitting-room window – but at seven or eight I was immersed in it to the hilt.

And, so far as my allegiance was directed towards any ideology, it was Catholic Ireland, Irish Ireland, the romance of disaffection and potent nationalist identity that exerted the strongest pull. It was the way I was being brought up, the influences that surrounded me. Sunday mass, Easter lilies, the Falls Road ambience, 'All around my hat I wear the tri-coloured ribbon-o' … in such circumstances, the Protestantism of my father's family could only impress me as an anomaly.

My grandfather William Craig and his brothers and sisters would naturally have revered the mother lost to them so soon; and acknowledgement of the German element in their heritage came out with my grandparents in the naming of their children – Emily Charlotte Marie Heller (Marie), John Frederick (Ricky), Bertha Hazel – a practice not even curbed by the First World War (a war that adds further complications, for me, to a family tree already bearing unexpected twists and roots; it caused the death of my Catholic grandfather, not my Protestant grandfather of course, whose German blood would have kept him from enlisting).

The issue of nomenclature was among the things the Craig family might have held against my mother, but didn't (as far as I know). Not content with making an out-and-out Papist of my father (as it would seem), she'd even gone on to tamper with his good ancestral name, the name his parents had chosen with such devotion and care. William Albert Thomas. Albert, the name by which he was known, had an unpleasant, almost a ludicrous ring in her ears, and before they had been going out together for more than a month or so she had rechristened him Andy, a name that's stuck to him ever since, except with some recalcitrant relatives. It's true that it suits him better, but it's not what he was called, before Nora.

In spite of these and other dissonances, though, my mother became great friends with most of her in-laws, particularly those of her own generation – some of these friendships blossomed especially when my parents had moved out of what was un-deniably a Catholic quarter of Belfast, and into the religiously undifferentiated territory of County Down. But I'm getting into the future here. Back in the 1950s, my mother and I were welcomed at Lismoyne and made much of, ushered into the narrowest living-room I have ever encountered, with the table set for high tea at one end, the horsehair chaise longue before the black-leaded range, and the spaniel Sha – an abbreviation of Charlotte – in a frenzy of tail-wagging. Our regular visits continued even after the death of my grandfather when I was nine or ten; but gradually I asserted a preference for allocating Sunday afternoons to some teenage pursuit of my own. Lismoyne, though, the hospitable gate lodge, remains embedded in my recollection as a place of wellbeing and charm.

A Protestant, then, was never as alien to me as a Muslim; my experience to that extent didn't parallel Denis Donoghue's. Indeed, his remark to that effect made me jump when I read it. It occurs in his memoir, *Warrenpoint*: a mostly engaging, occasionally exasperating and wholly idiosyncratic account of an unrefractory boyhood in that County Down resort. What does he mean by it? As a boy growing up in an RUC barracks where his father was a sergeant, he must have been in daily contact with Protestants – but perhaps it's a Protestant particularity of outlook he has in mind. Whatever it is, it's an alarming admission. Clearly, for Ulster Catholics, there were degrees of circumscription.

'I could never understand,' Donoghue writes, 'how William Empson, a critic I revere, could hate Christians and especially Catholics, thinking their religion nothing but a sordid cult of blood and sacrifice.' I can't understand how Denis Donoghue, a critic I revere, could have submitted so readily to the Catholicism of his upbringing, using his tremendous intellectual powers to rationalise the tenets of the Church, rather than employing a more undermining strategy ...

For myself, I always preferred the spirited to the spiritual, protesters to accepters, intrigue to indifference. I relished the sense of things going on – though not, I think, to the point of upholding disruption. A tiny incident from the late 1960s illustrates *that* avowal. It was the time when civic disturbance was just beginning to get off the ground – or on to the ground – and I remember the affront I felt when an acquaintance described to me how she'd recently enjoyed a good night's rioting. A crowd of them, she went on, returned to the same trouble-spot on the following evening, and were terribly disappointed when a similar outbreak failed to occur. Of the first occasion, when a policeman hit her over the head with a baton, she remarked that she had never enjoyed anything so much in her life.

I think of Caroline Blackwood's jaded question in her 'Memories of Ulster'. Can there be, she wonders, 'a boredom so powerful that it finally acts like an explosive?' If there is, indeed, it's not a sound basis for political action – though it makes a vivid impression: all the wrongs and repressions and afflictions of Ulster simmering away for a couple of centuries and finally reaching bursting point. The Blackwood essay enumerates a few of Northern Ireland's ills – bigotry, inertia, 'an industrialised provinciality', a philistine mentality and so on. It harks back to MacNeice's 'Autumn Journal', with its

> the voodoo of the Orange bands,
> Drawing an iron net through darkest Ulster,
> Flailing the limbo lands –
> The linen mills, the long wet grass, the ragged hawthorn.
> And one read black where the other read white, his hope
> The other man's damnation:
> Up the Rebels, To Hell with the Pope ...

and forward to Derek Mahon's 'Pale light of that provincial town ... [punishing] nature in the name of God', while obliquely endorsing Brian Moore's critique.

These authors are all forceful commentators on a very flawed society, homing straight in on the causes of disaffection, and turning them, in their writings, to richness and stimulation. If it's tackled with sufficient energy, the whole bad business of Northern Ireland's awful heritage can gain an effect of piquancy rather than desolation. All these writers, though, approach the topic from a point of view of dislike, or at best ambivalence; they're not enamoured of the place.

I have to record that I never hated Belfast, never hated the North, never even hated the school that so readily washed its hands of me. On the contrary, I enjoyed the sense – however illusory – of living in a more interesting, more diverse, more complex society than anything available to an *English* contemporary, an inhabitant – say – of boring Slough or Crawley (I had no knowledge of these places, but they *sounded* pretty dull). The look of Belfast, even my part of Belfast, didn't have a lowering effect on me. I couldn't get enough of rain, back streets, waste ground, the back ends of laundries and cinemas, bleak playgrounds with bonneted toddlers going round and round on wooden carousels.

Most people looking back, I am sure, ascribe an immutable quality to their childhood surroundings – of course, you've only to look around you in the present to see how these have been overtaken by change, mostly destructive change; but at the time it seems they never will change. They've acquired a permanent form, you believe, by a process of accretion which will surely stop with the coming-to-consciousness of the egotistical infant (yourself), whose apprehension of the way things are arranged coincides with the arrival at an absolute culmination of that small local world round about. So, the city I grew up in was immeasurably more dense and physically integrated than the Belfast of today with its eclectic configuration, its dismal refurbishments and eroded singularity.

That old Belfast wrapped itself around you like the comforter specially procured for Baby Bunting in the nursery rhyme. It led you by the hand down its pungent entries and alleyways, along sedate three-storey red-brick terraces, up the sidestreets of Stranmillis and into la-di-dah Malone, through the fields at the back of the Falls Park where rough boys roamed with their dogs, past churches and flour mills and factories and primary schools, deeper and deeper into the throughother enchantments of Smithfield and the spirited byways of the Falls. It disclosed

70

unexpected embellishments for you to savour: a pair of stone lions guarding the entrance to an ordinary house at the corner of St James's Road; a small tin church halfway up the wild mountain loney; an intriguing effigy of an elephant presiding over a pub in Upper North Street. As an inhabitant of Belfast, you started out with a lot of affirmative possibilities which might lead you in one direction or another, as the city activated your conformist or dissenting tendencies. In certain circumstances, even its wrongs and infamy carried a romantic charge.

And as for the Dominican Convent – well, although most of the lessons I learnt there are now, in Philip Larkin's phrase, 'a forgotten boredom', the place afforded an outlet for the gregarious side of my nature. It was large and for ever astir and I had lots of friends; and something of interest was happening every day: a row in prospect over some misdemeanour, a glorious piece of gossip to recount, some unpredictable moment of elation. All the usual madcap enterprises. I rarely left the house with reluctance in the mornings, anticipating, rightly, some highlight of the day. 'Fourteen-year-old, why do you giggle and dote?' Stevie Smith wondered, before answering her own question: 'I'm fourteen years old, that's the reason.' At fourteen, a teacher's unbecoming hat was enough to set us off, and keep us entertained for days.

Now, when middle-aged women come up to me at literary parties, full of the half-remembered events of forty years ago, my strongest reaction is to amplify or correct what they have to say. It seems to matter, God knows why, that they should get the facts right – not mislay or muddle any detail of that shady business in the past. Yes, I suppose it makes the episode more colourful to lumber us all with illegitimate pregnancies when we came home from the Gaeltacht – that is one persistent chimera which I'm obliged to contradict. In that respect at least, I wasn't as headstrong as certain bygone members of my family, on both sides ... And when Rathmore is cited, as it frequently is, as the school I attended during my final year: this produces in me an agitated response, since it misses the significance of that part of the affair. No, I have to keep insisting, no, it wasn't Rathmore,

71

it was a different school entirely; and *that* ties up with my brief perception of myself – to borrow Karl Miller's motif in his engrossing memoir of his early days, *Rebecca's Vest* – as 'disastered me'. I wasn't, I believed, a natural magnet for disasters, but suddenly they seemed to be proliferating; and one could only meet them in a spirit of humorous lugubriousness, if such a thing were at all attainable.

As for Rannafast itself and what went on there: well, indeed, as I've said, that afforded enormous scope for speculation. And no, I find myself repeating obsessively, no, it wasn't like that at all, that didn't happen, this is what actually happened, this is the way it was.

PART TWO

Monkey Business

PC with friends in Rannafast

Even though it happened as long ago as the late fifties, I could
    still draw
you a picture of the place ...

PAUL MULDOON, 'One Last Draw of the Pipe'

The place, in my case, being Rannafast. The picture of
Rannafast that's stayed in my head is as decorative as a
Carrickmacross counterpane and as distinctive as an Aran *crios*.
It's composed in sombre tones, the bitter-chocolate browns of
turf bogs, greys of dry-stone walls and dark purplish blues of
distant hills. It is patchy and jagged, all scanty sloping fields and
rocky inlets and promontories jutting out as far as they can reach
into the daunting Atlantic ocean. It seems to have withdrawn, or
been cut off, from the rest of the world, and therefore has a
timeless or fairy-tale quality about it. It is wonderfully dissociated
from everyday banality. When I first set eyes on this radiant
locality, I was close enough to my childhood reading to be put
in mind of the storybook world of Patricia Lynch, with its bright
white cabins on rugged hillsides, its unrepining adversities and
heroic escapades. What follows is the story of some less-than-
heroic, indeed inescapably everyday escapades, and the dire
straits that resulted from them.

The custom of packing pupils off to the Gaeltacht for a month
in the summer has existed for many years, and has improved

the spoken Irish, temporarily at any rate, of more than one generation. Irish colleges, bleak box-like buildings, are located in four or five centres in Donegal, with accommodation for pupils, at a reasonable charge, provided by all the willing families in the neighbourhood. The Gaeltacht houses are nearly all one-storey, white-washed and stone-floored, with black-leaded ranges for heat and cooking, and turf fires kept perpetually alight. *Tithe na Rosann* – the houses of the Rosses – were originally built in clumps of ten or twelve, but by the middle of the nineteenth century they had become more scattered. Thatched roofs were once, not so long ago, a feature of these districts, but most dwellings now are roofed with ordinary slate. They are sturdy houses, built to withstand fierce winds from the Atlantic.

Every year, the influx of rampant teenagers from all over the province causes problems of discipline for those, priests and Christian Brothers and lay teachers, whose task it is to nip incipient sexual encounters in the bud. The billeting of pupils on the local families is organised on a gender basis. At times during the day when segregation isn't possible, a sharp look-out is kept for signs of sexual attraction, excessive conversing, hand-holding and the like, between any two pupils: if detected, such signs will procure a scolding for those concerned.

At the evening ceilidhes, which take place between eight and half-past ten, priests and teachers keep an eye open for couples dancing together more than twice. Those caught doing so are instructed, after the third dance, to find different partners. Since this regulation is not specified, newcomers often break it un-knowingly, and are surprised to be reprimanded. In the eyes of priests, dancers singling one another out in this way are heading straight for an occasion of sin. Very zealous priests are known to walk the country roads after nightfall, armed with blackthorn sticks to rout out concupiscent couples from ditches or the back of turf-stacks, or wherever they've positioned themselves. It is not known if the priests are often successful in this manoeuvre. The boys and girls studying Irish in the Gaeltacht – according to rumour – always find ways of getting round such embargoes, to a greater or lesser degree.

It is our first experience of the Gaeltacht. Of the Dominican pupils who've signed up for the course – ten or twelve in all – only two are my particular friends, Olivia and Colette (and especially Olivia). There are several others, though, belonging to our class, or our year, with whom we're on friendly, if not intimate, terms. The convent's senior Irish teacher, a Miss Boyle, has us all in her charge. We assemble at ten past eight in the morning at the Great Northern Railway terminus in Great Victoria Street, an excited group clutching oblong suitcases with padded handles, loaded up with shoulder bags and raincoats, ready to board the 8.25 train for Derry.

The train is not full. Olivia and I bag an empty carriage, and keep it to ourselves for most of the journey. There are movable armrests between the green upholstered seats, which we keep pulling up and down as we try out different postures for maximum comfort, and framed sepia photographs of Dunluce Castle and the Giant's Causeway above our heads. We tear the wrappers from bars of Fry's Chocolate Cream and discuss our prospects for getting off with boys. Olivia is an animated redhead, an inch or two shorter than I am, with a droll manner and a keen sense of mischief. We are wearing our school blazers, maroon-coloured with a black-and-white emblem on the top left-hand pocket, over wide-skirted summer dresses made of gingham, or of some other kind of patterned cotton material. We are geared to the fullest extent to have an enjoyable time.

A bus has been specially hired to take us on from Derry, along with others of our age-group bound for the Gaeltacht, and their teachers. A meal of sorts is consumed before we board the bus, chips in paper bags from a down-market café (the nuns of St Dominic's would consider this to be letting down the side by acting in a common manner, but they aren't there to object), and bottles of orange squash. A bee-line is afterwards made for the lavatories. Eventually we are all rounded up and shepherded on to the bus. Olivia and I get a seat at the back and sit there casting an eye over the strange girls and boys arranging themselves and their belongings for the three-hour journey with a lot of noise and hilarity. Only one person, as far as I can judge, looks at all right to fit the part of an object of infatuation: a young male teacher, harrassed by his responsibility for a crowd of unruly boys from a County Antrim school. I say as much to Olivia, who agrees that he's not bad-looking. We lean back in our seats, gazing out at the passing fields and forests and villages.

After an hour or so, the landscape begins to change. Less vegetation; hedges giving way to uncemented stone walls. Little steep fields strewn with boulders and yellow gorse. Occasional trickles of water running down to join the roadside ditches. The few trees are low, and bent in one direction. Then there are no trees at all; purple mountains suddenly spring into view; fields turn dark brown with turf. It's like no countryside that I have ever seen. I can't avoid the impression that we've entered a foreign country.

As the bus gets closer to the coast some trick of atmospherics makes the landscape seem at once shimmery and distinct – all clear-cut edges, and changing colours as a mass of clouds behind a blue hill splits and shifts. Grass devoid of lushness, yellow, straw-coloured or olive green. White cottages standing out dramatically against dark fields and hills. The bus moves forward slowly along an uneven road. Behind stretches an interminable bog, conducive to agoraphobia. Black water, tufts of marsh grass, a trail of small white flowers ... Bog cotton: *ceannavan*. Along a side-track a lorry is parked; turf-cutters lay down their spades to watch the bus go by. To the left, in the distance, rises a conical gothic peak, veins of quartz running downwards from its crystallised summit.

One of the teachers on the bus claps his hands for silence. 'Right, everybody. That's it. *Sin é – labhróimid i nGaeilge as seo amach.*' He's telling us we have to speak in Irish from now on. Some of us look at one another in consternation. Of course we knew that English was forbidden among the holiday visitors to the Gaeltacht, but now that it has come to the bit ... The babble on the bus resumes, in a garbled form. Fortunately, as long as the bulk of the sentence is in Irish, or what passes for Irish, we're allowed to insert an English word in a pinch. A lot of very peculiar, half-baked, macaronic exchanges can be heard all over the Donegal coast during the holiday season.

The college authorities are right, of course: if you're forced to make the effort to start with, it soon becomes more or less natural. And since the acquisition of Irish is the official purpose of our visit, persistent English-speaking isn't tolerated. Once or twice you may get away with, but after that you run the risk of expulsion, of being sent home in ignominy. Only dunderheads can't at least pass themselves in a language they've been studying at school for years, and dunderheads aren't supposed to be there in the first place. We are all senior pupils, fifth- and sixth-formers, and some of us even have the right to wear, on our lapels, a gold or silver *fáinne*, or ring – the emblem of an Irish-speaker of at least moderate proficiency.

We're nearly there. Just ahead, indicated by a lightening of the air, and a faint saltiness mixed with the smell of turf, lies the sea. We've reached the extreme edge of Ireland. Everywhere you look, you see grey rock jutting above the surface of the land. Stony and barren, Denis Donoghue called the place when he came with some fellow Newry schoolboys in the 1940s, all six foot six of him, to attend Coláiste Bhrighde, St Brigid's College, outside which we're deposited in our turn: a bit bedraggled from the journey, but in high spirits nevertheless. We have to sign a register and wait to be allocated to our lodgings. The first slight contretemps occurs when Olivia and I are put in different houses. It's hard to explain in our untried Irish that we'd asked to be together, but we persist until the point is grasped. The *rúnaí* – secretary – a man called George McAdam, with a fraught look on his face and a pencil behind his ear, says he'll see what he can do, but could we please go along with the arrangements as they are at present, until everyone gets settled. People are being sent off in groups of five or six, in various directions, and with local children to act as guides and carry the girls' cases.

Every house in the district is known by the name of its most prominent inhabitant. *Teach* Pheadair Bhig – Little Peter's house – is the address given to Olivia and Colette, who turn left beyond St Brigid's College, while I turn right, in a group that includes my classmate Angela Magill, a tall blonde girl not quite spirited enough for my taste but otherwise unexceptionable, and

Maire Maguire from Form 5B – another redhead – about whom I know very little beyond the fact that she lives near St Peter's Pro-Cathedral on the Falls Road in Belfast and has something of a reputation for bumptiousness. *Teach* Eddy Doyle is the house we're heading for. The turf smoke which pervades the whole countryside is the most striking thing about the place so far – that and the rugged landscape, which already I find entrancing.

The house is set back from the road, and halfway up a hillock. We trudge, in single file, up a mud track to the front door, where the *bean a' tí* – woman of the house – is waiting to greet us. A lot of the welcoming expressions she uses pass right over our heads, but we grin and nod to indicate our satisfaction at being there. All the time I am wondering how quickly I can get transferred to the same lodgings as my best friend, Olivia McAloon – if she doesn't join me first at *Teach* Eddy Doyle. Surely someone will be willing to swop!

In the meantime, I deposit my belongings in the large back bedroom of the cottage where I'm to share a bed, provisionally, with Angela Magill. The room contains three double beds of brass and iron, with horsehair mattresses and rather unimpressive, 1930s or '40s, crude patchwork quilts. (To find the indigenous red-and-white Irish chain or double Irish chain quilts in everyday use you'd have had to go back to the 1920s or beyond – and at sixteen I certainly didn't have the knowledge, or the prescience, to look out for these and all the other country artefacts, the spongeware bowls and so forth, which came to activate my collector's instinct so extremely from about the age of twenty-five on. In those early Rannafast days it was boys, first and foremost, that dominated all our thoughts – with schoolwork and exams some way behind.)

As soon we are ready, we set off in a group of five or six to explore the countryside surrounding *Teach* Eddy Doyle. I am getting on rather friendlier terms with Angela Magill, and also discovering something of a rapport with Maire Maguire, whose irreverence and vivacity strike a chord with me. I think we may turn out to be kindred spirits. It strikes me how odd it is that I always get on with redheads. Turning towards the shore, the three of us cross-question a couple of new acquaintances about their school in County Tyrone or Fermanagh – I forget which – one of those country places which I regard as the back of beyond: cattle in the streets, old-fashioned front parlours, that sort of thing. Such places, to my mind, lack the wildness and glamour of Donegal, which – so far – is living up to my expectations. I am revelling in the invigorating atmosphere. One of these countrified girls, Kathleen Shannon, is large and amiable and a bit slovenly in appearance. I like her. The other, Maureen Gearran or Garrity or something, is merely a mouse: mouse hair, a mousy cardigan, a self-effacing demeanour. Glasses to boot. At this stage in our lives, I and my friends are very intolerant of insignificance. We judge people on their looks (though fearfully insecure with regard to our own) but if these don't come up to scratch, a decided talent or characteristic, a bright, engaging or amusing manner, makes an acceptable substitute. All of us take the utmost interest in one another's doings and appearances.

We haven't gone far along the road before we spot Olivia and Colette coming excitedly towards us, waving their arms and breaking into a run. Olivia grabs me by the shoulders and twirls me round and round in the roadway. There are three lovely boys in their house, she announces jubilantly; wild horses won't get her out of it. Sons of the family, all tall and handsome, though the house is Peadar *Beag*'s; Little Peadar has three big sons. I respond suitably to this information.

A path leading down to the beach is just in front of us, and at the last moment we remove our sandals and launch ourselves, barefoot, on to the loose, warm sand. At the moment of impact I am conscious of a sharp pain in my right foot. I have hit a spot where a rock is concealed below the surface of the beach. For a moment or two I think I am only bruised and decide not to mention the mishap. But a trail of blood on the sand soon alerts the others. 'What have you *done*!' they shriek. 'Oh dear,' I say, looking down, 'I seem to have cut my foot.'

This seems to me the right line to take: I think we'd all have gone to any lengths to avoid losing face by making a fuss about a tiny accident. It is perfectly permissible to make a fuss on someone else's behalf, however. The others gather round and force me to sit down on the beach while someone dabs at the injury with a pocket handkerchief to get the sand out of it. The handkerchief is then wrapped around my toe and tied in a knot. Angela Magill, who's taken charge of these operations, dispatches Olivia and Colette for the resident nurse. I feel this is going too far; I am really not that badly hurt. It's the blood that makes it look worse than it is. After sitting there for a bit I insist on hobbling up to the road, leaning on Angela's arm.

And there approaching us are Olivia and Colette, accompanied by a trio of sturdy looking boys. Having failed to find the nurse, they'd spotted Little Peadar's sons and blurted out, in garbled Irish, an account of the accident to my toe. These boys are Maghnas, Frank and Dermot Bell. They are very nearly as presentable as Olivia has claimed, and one in particular I am instantly drawn to. He's the middle one (I think), the one called Maghnas, auburn-haired, assured, not in the least a bumpkin. Clearly all three are accustomed to making a good impression on the summer visitors, as indeed are many more of these local boys whom we get to know over the next few weeks. The whole place is seething with adolescent ardour, in a framework of denial and restriction which only adds a savour.

On this first occasion I am helped by many hands across the fields to *Teach* Pheadair Bhig, where the woman of the house, standing in for the nurse, applies disinfectant and elastoplast to my damaged toe. The worry uppermost in my mind at this moment is the question of whether I might be incapacitated for the dance, the ceilidhe, due to take place on the following – Wednesday – evening. I keep comparing myself to an *amadán* (a fool); at the same time, I am exhilarated because I think, I *think* it is just possible that Maghnas Bell has reacted to me in the same way as I have reacted to him. I am sure – almost sure – that a *frisson* of sexual attraction has passed between us. Either that or I'm deluding myself – of course I don't rule out the possibility. We've hardly exchanged a word, but there is *something* … I am sure there is.

I find I can get about quite well as long as I remember to put my right foot to the ground quite gingerly. (In fact the cut heals quickly and doesn't inconvenience me at all, though it leaves a scar that has never gone away; that and a mark on the palm of my hand from an encounter with barbed wire on a later visit to Rannafast are two of my legacies from the Gaeltacht. The journalist and author Cal McCrystal ended up similarly afflicted, when he showed off before his classmates by once going swimming during an Easter visit to the place, and had his stomach cut by a shard of glass for his pains. Not profiting sufficiently by this experience, he showed off again by eating an oyster dug from the shore and made himself fearfully sick – thereby demonstrating how 'Providence punishes those who step out of line and allow their attention to wander from the righteousness of fireside storytelling.')

That August evening, more than forty years ago, I spend some time hanging about the secretary's office at Coláiste Bhrighde, trying to effect a transfer to *Teach* Pheadair Bhig. For some

Five girls in the Gaeltacht (PC third from left)

reason, I don't know why, nothing comes of it. I am billeted on Eddy Doyle and his family and there I stay, with some disgruntlement at first but later in a spirit of enthusiasm. I like the house, and the people in it, and make some friends there, and generally have a whale of a time.

There must have been problems, however. For example: what on earth did I eat? I wasn't a tea-drinker then, any more than now; bread and jam held no appeal for me, and as for meat of any sort … even the sight of it brought on a feeling of revulsion. These peculiarities were accommodated at home, but they certainly didn't add up to a dietary principle that many people would have understood. Vegetarianism was not in vogue. I hardly knew the term, and would not have thought of applying it to myself. I didn't eat meat, that was all. It was a matter of taste, not an ideology. (It wasn't until much later, after I'd lived in London for a bit, that I formalised the practice I'd more or less abided by for most of my life, and became an out-and-out vegetarian.) It was also an inherited trait. At some point in her remote infancy, my mother took a scunner at onions and then somehow the whole range of vegetables, apart from potatoes, peas and beans, got tainted with the same unpalatability. As the youngest child, spoilt, her sisters said, she got away with being pernickety. Then she passed the same pernicketiness on to me, only it was meat and fish that made me go 'Ugh'. Jack Spratt would eat no fat. But despite her odd aversion to vegetables, my mother was never an avid carnivore. This was someone who had to give up Domestic Science at school for fear of opening an exam paper and finding herself required to stuff a chicken.

In the Gaeltacht, on my first holiday with friends rather than relatives, I suppose I lived on boiled potatoes and carrots, bread and butter, biscuits and so forth, eked out with numerous bars of chocolate and packets of crisps from the local shop. It doesn't sound like a healthy diet, but it seems to have kept me going. If anyone wondered at my constant refusal of this and that at the dinner table, they didn't comment on it. There were more enticing topics to engage our attention.

Not that these would have come up for discussion at mealtimes, with the presence of the Doyle family – to start with at any rate – imposing an inhibition. '*Cuir chugam an salann, le do thoil*' ('Pass the salt, please') and '*Lá breá atá ann*' ('It's a fine day') would have been about all the conversation we could manage, at least until we settled in and became more daring. Of the people of the house, I don't remember Eddy Doyle at all, probably because he left for Scotland after about a week; his wife, the *bean a' tí*, has left a slightly clearer impression on my mind but not much: stout and friendly and never seen without that ubiquitous Gaeltacht garment, the navy overall patterned with tiny white flowers. I remember two of the younger Doyles, a boy a year or two older than us and a girl of thirteen or fourteen; but these, though perfectly agreeable, don't loom very large in the network of friendships, intrigues and infatuations which soon developed. A younger brother of the *bean a'toigh*'s, called Cathal I think, appeared at some time during the month of August and *did* take part in the – what to call it? *Sexual* isn't right, since it implies rather more than the truth: perhaps *amorous* is a better word. The amorous free-for-all which dominated the district for a month in the summer, in opposition to the decorum required by the authorities. Cathal, from our house, proved as prone to flirtation and horseplay as anyone, even though he must have been thirty at least.

It wasn't all fun and games, of course. We're obliged to attend classes at Coláiste Bhrighde for a couple of hours in the morning and the afternoon (apart from weekends and Wednesday afternoons, which are free). It's our first experience of the direct method: instruction doled out to us, not in English, but in the language we're striving to acquire. This, at least to begin with, has the charm of novelty. We listen hard and absorb as much as we can. At the same time, among ourselves, we vigorously disclaim any wish to *work*. We are playing the part of giddy girls – aided and abetted by the holiday spirit. It's de rigueur to flaunt the amount of indolence you can get away with. We loll at the back of the classroom, pretending to doze, and putting it down to luck if we manage to answer correctly when addressed. The teacher, who after all is on holiday too, isn't very strict with us. He, to my delight, is the personable young man who amiably laid down the law on the bus from Derry. Martin Henderson, his name is. God knows why he's been assigned to a class of girls; but there it is. All the other classes in the building are mixed, while ours, for some reason, consists of girls only. Thirty or forty of us, all shapes and sizes, all varieties of temperament and intellectual capacity.

The teacher exerts himself to deal with the more alarming forms of girlishness, and manages very well. He doesn't mind if we call him by his Christian name, but makes it plain that his patience and good humour aren't inexhaustible. Somehow he keeps us in order, while tolerating our pretence of idleness, and actually duns into our heads – some of our heads – a fair amount of information. One or two of us benefit from his teaching to the extent of achieving an interest in Donegal idioms. *Cora Cainnte as Tir Chonaill*, I remember, was the title of a book he used. As for me – I am so taken with Martin Henderson's appearance and manner that I never can decide finally between him and Maghnas Bell as the ultimate man about the place to hanker after.

The stations of the west, Seamus Heaney wrote. 'But still I would recall the Stations of the West, white sand, hard rock, light ascending like its definition over Rannafast and Errigal, Annaghry and Kincasslagh …'

Light ascending like its definition. I think by this Heaney means that everything is reduced to its essence, its most elemental form, in this wild place. 'I had come west to inhale the absolute weather.' He had also come with his school, St Columb's in Derry; but he seems to have been younger at the time than we were and less emphatically primed for merriment. It's the more serious aspects of the Gaeltacht that have lingered with him, if we're to go by the prose poem in *Stations*: history, famine, injustice, insurrection, 'Croppies' graves'. The stations of the west modulate into the stations of the cross, and thence point forwards and backwards to Station Island, St Patrick's Purgatory, Lough Derg in another part of Donegal, all the emblems of a persecuted, an austere and glamorous, Catholicism.

Lough Derg never held the slightest attraction for me, or for anyone I knew well; but there were girls at school who had made the pilgrimage, gone there to fast and pray all night and trudge over sharp stones reciting the Rosary in their bare feet. I'd no more have considered inflicting these privations on myself than going in for flagellation. Lough Derg and everything it stood for seemed to me to be the opposite of Rannafast. It was like some kind of medieval torture chamber, and I hated the thought of it. However, at sixteen I was no enlightened renegade either. If I'd been aware of it I'd certainly have repudiated William Carleton's repudiation of the whole sorry, penitential business. Carleton's 'The Lough Derg Pilgrim', written in 1828, is the first of his *Traits and Stories* and announces his incipient apostasy, as repugnance for Catholic chicanery grows on him in the course of his sojourn at Station Island. I suppose, if I'd thought about it at all, I was still, at some level, equating Catholicism with integrity, and apostasy with some depravity of character. This had something to do with the actual religious force but more, I think, with a sense of national identity – the immense allure of ill-treated Ireland, martyrs, misgovernment, indomitability and all.

Carleton, who took as strong a line as anyone concerning the abuses of his day, turns up among Heaney's formidable revenants in the poem 'Station Island'. 'Your Lough Derg Pilgrim,' says the narrator,

> haunts me every time I cross this mountain –
> as if I am being followed, or following.
> I'm on my road there now to do the station.

– which draws an exasperated retort from the forthright old turncoat, 'O holy Jesus Christ, does nothing change?'

Things *were* changing, but slowly. By the 1940s and '50s, goings-on at St Patrick's Purgatory were likely less gaudy and disorderly than those recalled by Carleton; but the features of Catholicism provoking the fullest outrage in non-believers were much the same: superstition, priestly greed, hypocrisy, the whole repressive repertoire. Carleton's singling out of 'that jealous spirit of mistaken devotion, which keeps the soul in perpetual sickness, and invests the *innocent* enjoyments of life with a character of sin and severity' certainly strikes a chord with me, when I consider my schooling in Belfast, and the way it ended – even though I know it isn't sex but boisterousness, play and conviviality the nineteenth-century novelist has in mind.

As far as sex is concerned – there is nothing in the whole of Carleton's output to suggest the smallest deviation from the conventions of the day. You get the feeling, from his books, that any failure to uphold a po-faced purity would be tantamount to traducing the national character. It's only the odd inferior gentleman, like Hycy Burke in *The Emigrants of Ahadarra*, who has trouble damping down his erotic impulses. In this world of make-believe, of course, women *have* no erotic impulses. What they have instead is an unshakeable morality. 'In no country on the earth,' William Carleton assures his readers, in the preface to *Fardorougha the Miser*, 'or among no class of females, could the eye of an observer discover greater truth, sincerer religion, or firmer principle, than among the wives and daughters of the Irish peasantry.' Whew! It's a far cry from Brian Merriman's

> twenty-year-old with her parts untamed.
> She was no ignorant girl from school
> To whine for her mother and play the fool
> But a competent bedmate smooth and warm
> Who cushioned him like a sheaf of corn.
> Line by line she bade him linger
> With gummy lips and groping finger ...

In the Irish poetry book we used at school, *Filidheacht na nGaedheal* (Poetry of the Irish), the innocent opening section of Merriman's *Cuirt a' Mheadhain Oichdhe* (*The Midnight Court, c.* 1780) was included under the heading 'Nature Poetry', but not the rest: the rest was definitely out of bounds as far as school children were concerned.

And not only schoolchildren. When Frank O'Connor's spirited translation of Merriman's masterpiece came out in 1945, it promptly fell foul of the Irish Censorship Board, which left the poem doubly banned in Ireland. '... I believe the best authorities hold that it is almost entirely my own work,' O'Connor wrote in 1959 (our Rannafast year), 'the one compliment Ireland has ever paid me.'

Na Rossa go Bráthach (The Rosses For Ever) is the title of another of our school readers. Rannafast is a townland in the Rosses, north-west of Lough Derg – a poor district, abundant in memories of hardship and exploitation, and also in local lore. Many stories are current about the heroes of the Rosses and their epic deeds, whether these have to do with fighting, piety or scholarship. Some of these stories are recounted in Séamus Ó Grianna's *Nuair a Bhí Mé Óg* (*When I Was Young*), a charming exercise in autobiography published in 1942. Séamus Ó Grianna (James Greene) belonged to the famous Mac Grianna family of Rannafast – authors, storytellers, broadcasters, folklorists and singers – some of whose members were still around at the time of our first visit to the district, though unfortunately not of a generation to attract our interest.

'Ignorant girls from school' that we were, we were happy to assign any kind of scholarly pursuit to some date in the duller future. Well, we had a lot on our minds – whether we'd be shamed as wallflowers at the very next ceilidhe, or caught infringing some rule and sent home in disgrace. ('Disgrace': the word conjures up a whole different ethos, the world of those enticing English stories of the 1920s and '30s with titles like *A Disgrace to the Fourth*, *The Worst Fifth on Record*, *Expelled from St Madern's*, or *Averil's Wild Oats* – titles not without a bearing on our impending predicament. These, it's true, and others like them, would have meant not a thing to me at the time, having been consigned by me, some years earlier, to the literary scrapheap of the staid and old-fashioned. At nine or ten, I'd judged them vastly inferior to the sparkling adventure stories of Enid Blyton and Malcolm Saville, the Bunter books or the girls' and boys' papers of the Amalgamated Press and *their* brand of school fiction. It took me a long time to get around to the older school stories. It was only when I decided to form a representative collection of children's books from about 1900 to 1955 that I came to revel in their appearance and associations – though less perhaps in their actual content. But, as evocative items of juvenile reading, they are now at the core of a collecting enthusiasm which surpasses even the quilts and spongeware mentioned above.)

The School – or summer school – of Ups and Downs (to borrow another title) does very well to describe the events of that August, and our fluctuating moods. We were all up and down, for one reason or another – though not down and out completely before the end of the month. Occasionally – very occasionally – a fit of holiness would come over one or two of us and we'd attend early morning Mass without being obliged to. On the other hand, we were soon regaling one another with bilingual jokes like the one about the two nuns, one of whom is called Charlotte. The Irish for 'Sister' is '*Siúr*', and, in the vocative case, the 'S' is aspirated to give an 'h' sound. 'Ch' also becomes 'h', so, when the two nuns meet in a corridor and exchange greetings, you get something that sounds like: 'Well, a *hoor*'; 'Well, a *harlot*.' This tickles our sense of irreverence.

I'd like to think that the atmosphere in Rannafast that summer was closer to Merriman – the well-named Merriman – than to the 'ologroaning and ologoaning' of Station Island, but of course it wasn't as simple as that. The two things existed side-by-side, inculcated piety and would-be licentiousness – and existed in a heightened form for reasons not to be wondered at: among them the supercharged locality and the closed community. Merriman again (via O'Connor):

> The girls at home and the boys in college.
> You cannot persuade me it's a crime
> If they make love while they still have time,
> But you who for learning have no rival,
> Tell us the teachings of the Bible;
> Where are we taught to pervert our senses
> And make our natural needs offences?

This bygone Gaelic outcry had a lot of relevance, but very little currency, in the Ireland of the mid-twentieth century.

I have in front of me a picture postcard showing the road in front of Coláiste Bhrighde, *c*. 1955, complete with groups of sedate looking girls wearing knee-length cotton dresses, neat school blazers and ankle socks; aside from a certain period charm which attaches to the image, willy-nilly, these fifth- and sixth-formers look infinitely biddable and sensible, with never a hint of caprice or unruliness to ginger up the scene. So might we Dominican pupils have looked, I suppose, a few years later, to any chance photographer who happened along that stony road; strolling in

Postcard featuring schoolgirls in Rannafast, 1950s

twos and threes towards the Post Office or Sharkey's shop, affecting the utmost indifference to any boys who passed us but inwardly seething at the prospect of coming face to face with some particular object of attraction.

Wednesday evening. After class at the college, and tea at the Doyles', we set to work on our faces with Woolworth's powder and lipstick, and sort out what we hope are our most becoming dresses, in preparation for the opening ceilidhe of the season, which, as ever, is due to take place in the central classroom at Coláiste Bhrighde: a spot on which, around eight o'clock, the entire population of Rannafast, both permanent and temporary, seems to be converging. There's a tendency, at this stage, for boys and girls from the various houses to go about in separate clumps. Clearly, a lot of adolescent awkwardness is going to have to be overcome before a proper mingling is achieved; and in the meantime, being embosomed in a group bolsters up one's confidence. Some of us, it's true − myself and Olivia, for example − have already decided to disparage the whole flannel-trousered ungainly crew of schoolboys attending the college (boys whom we'd have been happy enough to be associated with at home). It's only the *muintir na háite*, the people of the place, as far as we are concerned, who are endowed with adequate allure.

Why is this? They are rough wild country boys for the most part, turf-cutters in summer, migrant workers at other times of the year; not student material, not our type at all. Yet we latch on to them instantly. I suppose it is partly that the sudden freedom, the escape from family pressures, has gone to our heads a little; we're experimenting in waywardness, trying out certain postures, estimating how far we can go. The *muintir na háite*, with their boldness and rumpus, suggest anarchic possibilities to which we respond with an equal measure of attraction and alarm. I am perfectly well aware that I will try to get out of any sticky situations in which I find myself − that a point will be reached at which timidity, prudence, social conformity or whatever will come on strong. Yet my entire being is geared towards inducing just such a sticky situation.

This first ceilidhe is a tremendous success, from my point of view. It is almost the high spot of the holiday. I am amazed at how well things go. Even my terrible dancing, my inability to master the basic dance steps, the sevens and threes which present no difficulty to anyone else, doesn't bother me unduly on this occasion. I shuffle through the complicated sets of 'The Sweets of May' and 'The Haymakers' Jig' – bandaged toe and all – in a state of exhilaration. Since that heightened evening at Coláiste Bhrighde, all that time ago, I've experienced a comparable feeling, I suppose, no more than seven or eight times. You catch someone's eye across a crowded room – say – and instantly you are flooded with intense expectancy and wellbeing. It leaves you bubbling over with jubilation – and never mind if the reaction, the downside, is certain to be equally overpowering.

Picture us then, dolled up and strung up, in that makeshift dance hall on the very verge of nowhere – just as Irish, but otherwise bearing no resemblance at all to William Trevor's desperate Ballroom of Romance – picture us revelling in the hullabaloo, the hearty fiddles and accordions, the talk in Irish, only half understood, the whoops and foot-stampings and other flourishes of the native population; and evading, as far as possible, the watchful eyes of priests. Most of the boys I dance with are schoolboys, starting with sixteen-year-old John Reid from Omagh who later develops a friendship with Angela Magill; but there comes a moment – a truly stirring moment – when I am singled out by the newly arrived Maghnas Bell, who marches straight across the room to where I am sitting, with arm outstretched to draw me on to the dance floor. He doesn't even need to ask if I will dance with him. Well, why should he? I am sure a besotted expression is fixed on my face.

We have that dance together, and the next one; and then he explains to me the rule about varying one's partners. (It's a wonder the local boys are allowed to attend the college dances at all; I suppose it would look like an abuse of hospitality, a slight on the people of Rannafast, to try to exclude them.) I must have looked at him in some bewilderment. '*Cad chuighe?*' I ask: 'Why?' But it's too complicated to grasp in Irish. What I do grasp is that he's suggesting a jaunt in a car on our next free afternoon, with himself and his cousin, whose name is Dinny or Danny or something of that sort; and do I have a compliant friend, he asks, someone who won't object to a bit of rule-breaking? I nod at once, thinking of Olivia. They'll pick us up, he says, along the road by the turning towards Annaghry, at two o'clock.

I rejoin my friends in something of a daze. Another dance is announced, and this time my partner – by another miracle, it seems to me – is our teacher Martin Henderson, the second most attractive man at present in the townland, in my opinion. (It's only much later, when I've acquired a better understanding of the Irish college rules, that I wonder if he hasn't been dispatched by Father So-and-So to get me out of the clutches of a predatory native speaker. The priests notice everything: they have their work cut out to quell any impulse towards impropriety and don't scruple as to how they go about it.) To entertain my friends, following these attentions from heart-throbs, I mime a state of idiotic bliss; but it isn't too far from what I'm actually feeling. I am filled to the brim with exaltation.

Around two in the morning we are wakened by a series of knocks, some scuffling and a sort of muted commotion going on outside our bedroom window. I make a move to investigate, but Angela Magill, with whom I'm sleeping, catches hold of my blue cotton nightdress, at the same time threatening to hit me over the head with my own torch if I put a toe outside the bed.

In a cross whisper, she enjoins on me a titter of wit. Do I want to be sent home before I've been five minutes in the Gaeltacht? It's a group of local boys, we know, doing the rounds of likely houses; looking to winkle out those among us who aren't averse to a spot of naughtiness in the night. 'All right, all right,' I mutter, half asleep. The noise outside recedes, then dies away. I'd have been interested to see who was there, but I haven't yet quite got the hang of this form of bad behaviour. That comes later. In the meantime, I am filled with buoyant anticipation for the promised excursion with the Bells.

The days go by and an unaccustomed heat wave settles over the Gaeltacht. Sleeveless, full-skirted frocks are sorted out, a lot of puffing and blowing is indulged in and sales of ice-cream soar. The incomparable beaches stretch pearly-white and inviting. This is one kind of absolute weather. The countryside, which is most like itself in rain and desolation, has turned as colourful and decorative as a Paul Henry painting. Everyone makes jokes about the Riviera. Copies of the republican newspaper, the *United Irishman*, come in handy to fan our sweating brows. Some of my free time I spend lying in marram grass among the sand dunes – well, the weather encourages it – or just behind some convenient turf stack or furze bush, in the arms of Maghnas Pheadair Bhig or some other sexual opportunist (but never Martin Henderson – well, he is a teacher, after all, not on our level; and besides, I learn from one of his pupils at Garron Tower that he's engaged to be married). I'm not alone in this try-out wantonness. If you know where to look you will find the whole countryside dotted with cross-purposed couples: one insisting, the other resisting (to varying degrees). We are definitely ignorant girls from school, the whole lot of us.

The prearranged car trip for our first half holiday duly takes place, and occasions a lot of surreptitiousness and hilarity. For example, it is necessary for the two of us, myself and Olivia, to scramble down below window level every five minutes or so.

Any passing vehicle might contain a teacher from the college, and for us to be spotted would mean the end of our holiday. In fact a college priest, a Father O'Friel, does pass us at one point in a car travelling back towards Rannafast; we are out of sight, as it happens, hunkered down on the floor and jammed up against the boys' legs, but the incident rams home the need for caution. What doesn't cross our minds is the thought that, observed in that peculiar position, we'd have been convicted of sexual practices we had never even heard of.

It's an unclouded afternoon. The Rannafast cousins drive us into Dungloe – in Irish *An Clochan Liath*, The Grey Stone – where we risk getting out of the car to stretch our legs, allow ourselves to be treated to an ice or two at a dingy café in the town's main street, and listen to the Slim Whitman recording of 'Danny Boy' on a juke-box. It's an elating business, breaking the rules and getting away with it – let alone being escorted by boys whom half our friends would give their eye-teeth to be seen with. (We don't yet understand, or at least I don't, that that is a fairly easy outcome for anyone at least half-way presentable to bring about. 'Chasing the daft holiday bitches', in the poet James Simmons's phrase: that's what Maghnas and the others are up to, and I don't think it makes much difference to them which one of us they end up with. The more compliant, the better; that's all.)

On the way back we stop again, this time to visit a chapel – on whose suggestion I can't remember. The occasion, anyhow, enables me to inscribe a priggish remark in my schoolgirl diary some months later – something to the effect that, knowing these boys as I do now, I wonder at their effrontery in presenting themselves before a tabernacle (this is the kind of self-righteous character I'm cultivating at the time). I suppose, on that August afternoon in a corner of the Rosses, we must have dipped our fingers in the holy-water font before making the sign of the cross – even gone down on our knees in the holy hush inside and muttered a prayer or two. Who exactly is trying to impress whom? Envisaging the scene, I can only dub us an anomalous bunch of worshippers – the two youths sexually on the make, the future apologist for political expediency and the embryo apostate.

The daft holiday bitches. It isn't long before the car is parked along a boreen (*boíthrín*: byroad) for the kissing session which is the primary purpose of the afternoon. This is something I can enter into with enthusiasm, knowing full well the limits beyond which I'm not prepared to go. These are very clearly delineated, in my head. Looking back, I am sometimes amazed that my actions, or non-actions, never provoked more unpleasantness; that my obstinate withdrawal of my person at one crucial moment or another didn't cause my co-experimenter, whoever he was, to cut up rough. Still, it's true that I can call on widely held notions of goodness to back me up – that the whole weight of religion, social usage, even intrinsic Irishness is on the side of abstinence, as much abstinence as can be mustered. Who, without renouncing their birthright, could argue all that out of existence? 'But it's nice' doesn't amount to much of a countervailing assertion against the brick-wall pronouncement 'It's a sin.'

Decent Catholic Ireland. 'The term was vague and yet had meaning: the emergent nation, seeking pillars on which to build itself, had plumped for holiness and the Irish language – natural choices in the circumstances.' Thus William Trevor in the story 'Paradise Lounge', evoking one of the breed of fierce old priests who held dance halls and make-up to be an abomination. From Yeats's Father Rosicross on, Irish literature is full of them, denouncers and distorters to a man. John Montague knows the type – in 'A Change of Management' we get a bishop fixated on the licentiousness of modern life. (The story was published in 1964.) 'On all sides we are wooed by the sirens of lax living, but – remember this – if Ireland holds a special place in God's plan it will be due to the purity of her men and the modesty of her women.'

This – to me – rings fearfully true. We were constantly being subjected to exhortations along those lines, and, given the age we

97

were, some of it was bound to get engrained into our psyches. We were shown no means of reconciling self-respect and an untrammelled attitude to sexual relationships. Girls who 'did it' – those few we knew about, or had listened to rumours concerning – were somehow surrounded by an atmosphere of seediness and inferiority. They were likely to be unwholesome and weak in the head. Far from free spirits, they were a disgrace; unable to grasp or abide by the rules of social behaviour. The verdicts 'cheap' and 'damaged goods' were the appropriate clichés, and clichés we were adamant would never be applied to *us*. No lust-ridden adolescent, parading his libido in front of us with rather more energy than ability, was going to get the chance to lose respect for *us*, thank you very much.

On top of the ethical aspect (though the two were intertwined) that social axiom was the thing implanted most implacably in our heads: that respect *would* be lost, following any lapse from chastity, as sure as night follows day. Many sensible older women, all our mothers and aunts and family friends (though not nuns, for whom Church teaching, rather than social expediency, was the primary concern) had assured us that this was so. The whole idea of sexual terrain was conveyed to us as a clash of wills. Men were only after one thing, and it was up to us – forewarned – to keep them from getting it. The alternative, from our point of view, was to forfeit our place in the marriage market. Having once given in, we'd be relegated thereafter to some sort of sexual dust-heap. And probably impregnated as well as denigrated. An odd implication, for the men themselves, was that the sexual act was somehow not repeatable – or not, at any rate, with the type of third-rate female who'd go along with it in the first place. Belief in all this nonsense probably helped to perpetuate it. Primed for post-coital revulsion, many straying Catholics (and not only Catholics) must have felt just that.

I've overstated the case, of course, just to outline the deterrents faced by would-be free spirits among the girls of my generation studying Irish in the Gaeltacht. A homegrown version of the sexual double standard which prevailed nearly everywhere (and only began to be eroded in the 1960s) held us fast in its grip. With our insufficient experience of life, and deficient clarity of vision, we weren't in any position to pose a challenge to it.

I'm not suggesting that Irish boys, whether our contemporaries or those of an earlier generation, fared any better. The testimonies of such experts in repression as John McGahern and Patrick Kavanagh (to take those examples) leave us in no doubt about the sexual misery, guilt, waste or distortion fostered with such vehemence all over the country. 'A nation of masturbators under priestly instruction,' wrote Brian Moore in one of his novels: since no other sexual outlet was available, this practice was bound to flourish. It's a bitter comment on the way things were. And some boys, I'm aware, puritanical by conviction if not by nature, were denied even that. Those were the ones for whom indoctrination had struck deep. They gritted their teeth and did without.

It's true, as well, that we're not all endowed with the sexual instinct to the same degree (not even in adolescence, with hormones in overdrive and emotions all over the place). Some of us are puritanical, or indifferent, or frankly antagonistic, by nature. I'm acquainted with a good many girls so devoutly Catholic that they've renounced make-up and go about with rows of holy medals pinned to their clothes. And boys of the same stamp, usually dowdy and dull, who wear Pioneer 'total abstinence' pins in their lapels and spend half their lives on their knees in the chapel. Station Island material.

Cal McCrystal (again), who attended St Brigid's College a few years before we did, recalls spending a lot of time chasing girls from an Enniskillen school and actually getting one of them into a tiny turf shed, where 'a certain amount of molestation' took place, stopping short 'at a point where most girls in those days stopped short'. When word of this exiguous exploit got around, he was treated as a pariah – by his contemporaries, no less, who had swallowed the guff about 'self-respect' and 'an occasion of sin'. Well! It would seem that some – though not many – of the Gaeltacht aficionados were genuinely there to improve their minds. Perhaps McCrystal's school, St Malachy's in Belfast, was particularly proficient in breeding an attitude of stainlessness and gravity – though it's hard to estimate how tongue-in-cheek the following account of a trip to Rannafast in 1933 actually is. It was written (in Irish) by a senior St Malachy's pupil for the centenary issue of the school magazine, the *Collegian*.

He praises the

> ... Gaelic spirit that transcends all the hardship. Every family has at least one cow, and it's the job of the children to tend the cows after school is over ... wet or fine, they have to go about this business, and you'd often see them sitting on a rock, half-drenched with rain, and not even a pair of shoes on their feet.
>
> It's a wonder to see how peaceful, patient and happy are the people of Rannafast despite every hardship. An outbreak of laughter will overcome any bout of low spirits that comes upon them ... They can tell thousands of stories, and recite reams of poetry ... As with work, they're accustomed to storytelling from an early age.
>
> You'd find old women telling stories as a pastime in the long winter evenings. In Rannafast at present there's an Irish college which is doing great work on behalf of the language ... Coláiste Bhrighde is a children's college, but teachers and parents attend it too. There are ceilidhes nearly every night, and great revelry and excitement goes on in the company of the young Gaels of Ireland. The name of one dance or another is called out, and before you can clap your hands together, the floor is full of dancers impatiently waiting for it to start. It's great to see this large crowd in one another's company in a Gaelic district, and the English of England a long way away. The nights there isn't a ceilidhe in the college, there'll be one in some house in which there's a good storyteller, and it's usual for a crowd to be gathered round the fire listening to the stories.
>
> Without any doubt, this is the way to revive the language, to send children to the Gaeltacht, where Irish is still strong and lively. A good many come every year, but more should come, and more again, till Irish spreads up and down throughout the whole of Ireland.

This has all the elements of a true picture, indeed, but given an impossibly bland and Gaelic and wholesome slant, like de Valera's vision of athletic youths and comely maidens diverging to the fullest degree from the English of England, and never demeaning themselves by laying a finger on one another. It embodies a kind of deflected vitality, as if – to quote the Irish Edwardian social commentator and suffragist, Margaret Cousins – 'some more artistic way of continuance of the [human] race' had been vouchsafed to the Irish, or at least the truly Gaelic Irish. And as it filtered down to us, the sanctimonious stance appealed to the cowed, or high-minded, or prudish among us, while affecting others only partially, and indeed almost passing the light-minded by.

Between the pious brigade and the flibbertigibbets – those girls for ever back-combing their hair and applying powder to their faces – I would hope (though I can't be sure) that some of us had the potential, at least, to be sane about sex: to give it its due as one of life's great glories and pleasures.

I am getting into deep water here: deep water with many cross-currents. I'm truly not envisaging some impossible erotic idyll, with couples all over the Gaeltacht enjoying continuous and carefree copulation. I'm all for restraint and discrimination – the former most particularly at the age we were at the time … As for the rest, I am merely trying, I think, to get to grips, however partially, with a complex web of religious pressure, social expectation, nationalist truism, anti-feminist fabrication and all the rest of it – all the bits and pieces of a system which, at some deep level, placed us all in a faulty relation to nature and natural forces. Coming to sexual consciousness, in those days, was fraught with even more abundant anxieties than is normal at the best of times.

But we didn't let it get us down. We're determined to acquire as much practice, as much *savoir faire*, as is available to us, in the circumstances. I remember walks across the fields of Rannafast, away from the college, local boys striding ahead by previous arrangement, and us following after at a distance designed to throw officious teachers and other grown-ups off the scent. It's only when we're well out of range of any possible prying eyes that the two complicit groups first converge, then separate into pairs.

On one of these occasions, I remember, I learn from Maghnas Pheadair Bhig a fact or two about life in the Gaeltacht (and away from it). Nearly all the men and youths of the district leave their homes at intervals for seasonal work on farms and in coal mines, in Glasgow and elsewhere. For this they are paid a high wage which includes danger money, and they're expected (Maghnas says) to tackle tasks beyond the powers, or the inclination, of workers from Scotland or England. He paints a grim picture. It's fearsome work, and the lot of them will go to any lengths to postpone their departure from the Donegal townlands. On top of the sheer hard labour, he goes on, the dockland atmosphere sets his teeth on edge. Prostitution is rife. And Irish girls are nearly the worst of the lot. To see the way they carry on with sailors is enough to make you ashamed of the place you come from.

While Maghnas is telling me these things, he is running the fingers of one hand through my hair, and trying to undo my bra with the other hand. My button-through summer dress is partly unbuttoned. I make noises concurring in his estimate of Irish women's lewdness. Indeed it is worse for them than it is for loose women of other nationalities. They have that much farther to fall.

'The young girls of Donegal come radiantly innocent from their own glens and mountains but often, alas! they fall into sin in a far country.' Thus the unsophisticated Glenties novelist Patrick McGill, echoing William Carleton's tongue-in-cheek comment on the wives and daughters of the Irish peasantry. The observation occurs in McGill's *The Rat Pit* of 1915, a sequel to the better known *Children of the Dead End*. These two novels make a pair, and tell the stories of – respectively – Dermod Flynn and Norah Ryan, both from the (imaginary) Donegal townland of

Glenmornan. The first of these, Dermod Flynn, is sent, at the age of twelve, to a hiring fair at the Lagan, near Strabane, where the children of the Gaeltacht stand up like cattle to be poked and prodded by Planter (i.e. Protestant) farmers in search of cheap labour. ('Ah, the poor Donegals,' Benedict Kiely's grandmother would say, remembering the famine years of the 1840s and barefoot, Irish-speaking labourers coming in droves to the hiring fairs of Omagh and Strabane, 'the poor Donegals'.) After a couple of sessions here, Dermod is ready for the next stage in the deadly economic sequence: digging in the potato fields of Scotland.

The story continues: the boy becomes an itinerant worker who tramps around Scotland in the company of a florid old layabout named Moleskin Joe, working by turns as a digger of sheep drains, a platelayer on the Glasgow–Greenock railway and a labourer on the waterworks at Kinlochleven. 'I looked on life,' he says – or the miscalculating author says on his behalf – 'in all its primordial brutishness and found it loathsome to my soul.' God bless us. It is hard to imagine anyone from the Gaeltacht speaking or thinking like that, in any language.

Patrick McGill's novels are full of arresting social detail, but you have to work hard to extract it from the mass of indistinct but high-flown comment surrounding it. For example, from McGill we learn that Irish and Scottish 'tatie-hokers' were formed into squads, accommodated in disused barns and out-houses where they slept under stinking horse blankets, and set to work at four in the morning. All day, the women crawled through the fields on their hands and knees, dragging heavy baskets. This is terrible for anyone, but worse, perhaps, if you're young and vulnerable. And, in the first novel, among the original members of Dermod Flynn's squad is a young Glenmornan girl who suffers all the worst excesses of Gaelic hardship. The dismal story of Norah Ryan, touched on in *Children of the Dead End*, is recounted fully in *The Rat Pit*.

In McGill's view, the combined forces of religious and commercial extortion are to blame for all the evils in the Irish countryside; and to illustrate the point he creates a diabolical shopkeeper who, on a whim, keeps from the women of Donegal the yarn they need to earn a pittance from knitting. Knitting for profit is an old resource of these women, and it's linked with oppression in the minds of past social critics, such as McGill. *The Rat Pit*, though it arouses exasperation with its departures from authenticity, opens on an electrifying note. The author has assembled a group of women by the sea shore, just before dawn in the dead of winter. The bitter cold hardly breaches their hardihood as they wait to cross the estuary at low tide. These are turn-of-the-century knitters of the Rosses, women who think nothing of tramping sixteen miles, barefoot, to collect a bundle of yarn from a shopkeeper hell-bent on exploitation. It's a bad novel, it's true, full of social and emotional melodrama, but it makes an impact with its opening vignette.

The shopkeeper has a rival in the ill-treatment stakes in the rapacious priest who saddles his parishioners with the building costs for a new mansion for himself to wallow in. 'If yer father doesn't send me the pound ... he'll have no luck in this world and no happiness in the next.' All right, McGill is not the only commentator to be outraged by the excesses of grasping clerics – however, social criticism of this kind tends to be more effective if it's presented with a satirical undertone, rather than the endless sensationalism McGill goes in for. If you turn to the work of Peadar O'Donnell, for instance, you find an equally committed socialism without the hokum and ineptitude.

I know I'm being too hard on Patrick McGill, who passionately spoke out against the wrongs inflicted on the hard-pressed people of the Donegal Gaeltacht, and proclaimed their moral superiority as a kind of counterbalance to the low esteem in which they, as unskilled workers, tended to be held. But it can't be denied that he goes too far.

Glenmornan, for example, the birthplace of Dermod Flynn and Norah Ryan, is every bit as hapless a locality as the mythical Corca Dorcha of Flann O'Brien's *The Poor Mouth*. Here is a description of it: '... nothing ... but rags, poverty and dirt; pigs under the bed, cows in the house, the rain coming through the thatch ... the winds of night raving and roaring through wall and window.' Whew! Here, without a doubt, is the source of all Gaelic misery. It is not an auspicious locality from which to emerge, as Norah Ryan's trials all too clearly show. What happens? In a moment of weakness, Norah, the potato digger, allows herself to be seduced by a Scottish farmer's son; and from this point on, it's a matter of remorse, despair, decline, disaster, blight. The initial wrong turning propels her into pregnancy – what else – destitution and, eventually, prostitution. Her life is as luckless as the observances of pulp fiction can make it.

The whole farrago, indeed, is devised to cry up the labour movement in Ireland; but somewhere along the line the author's ideological bent has got the better of him. There's supposed to be a thread linking Norah Ryan's proliferating tragedies with the priests and shopkeepers sitting at home in Glenmornan ordering an unjust society; but somehow an enormous gulf opens up between cause and effect, into which half the cast is shoved (if they're not beaten up, inflicted with illness or threatened with starvation, they're run over or drowned in a canal – all this to ram home the point about the sufferings of the upright poor).

Norah, as a character, is meant to embody mildness and selflessness as well as standing for undeserved adversity, but unfortunately Patrick McGill only succeeds in presenting her as ignorant and dim-witted. By absolving Norah from all responsibility for her own actions (well, she's to blame for the initial act of unchastity, perhaps, but not very much to blame), he makes her a morally uninteresting heroine. Sex only comes into the picture as a means of degradation and misfortune; the very opposite of a positive force.

Among the other things the Donegal poor are apt to be done out of is the 'radiant innocence' which is their birthright. McGill preaches charity towards the unchaste, indeed, but it never enters his head that chastity itself is a variable concept, or that a woman's 'virtue' may reside in areas other than that of sexual abstinence. Of course, he is writing about the *mores* – the Irish *mores* – of the early part of the twentieth century; but all these attitudes persisted for long enough to affect us, as we came to adolescence at the tail-end of them. Our era was the immaculate 1950s, and the still-to-be-renovated 1960s, when benighted forms of Irishness and Catholicism retained their vice-like grip.

Some new friendships are established in the Gaeltacht, and some old ties begin to wear a bit thin. In *Teach* Eddy Doyle, the sleeping arrangements are revised after a week or so, to enable the bolder spirits among us to leave our beds in the middle of the night, should the fancy take us to do so. The three of us who end up sharing a bed, who are game for anything to stir things up, to create an atmosphere of eventfulness around ourselves, are myself, Maire Maguire, and a late arrival, a short, dark-haired, pretty, voluble and high-spirited girl called Susie Greenwood, from a school on the outskirts of Belfast. (Also attached to our circle, but prevented by modesty, or an uncensorious piety, from joining in our late-night escapades, is the bosomy black-haired County Tyrone girl, Kathleen Shannon, who'd accompanied us on the first walk along the beach when I'd hurt my toe. Kathleen has turned out to be one of the most proficient Irish-speakers among the non-natives, as well as enjoying a good laugh as much as anyone, at a proper time of the day.)

What usually happens in the night-time is this. A rapping on the window-pane occurs in the small hours, and one of us scrambles out of bed and shoves up the window-sash, peering out in the darkness, half-asleep, to try and make out who is there. (I am always hoping it will be Maghnas Bell, but there's only one occasion, towards the end of the month, when this proves to be the case.) Then, if we're in the mood to be daring, we slither or wriggle through the aperture and lower ourselves to the ground (only a foot or so), all the while racked by stifled hysteria and the most frantic cautiousness. Gasps are suppressed, whispers muffled and giggles quashed as we help one another out, and stumble into the arms of whoever has come along on the off-chance of obtaining a bit of sexual gratification – or its equivalent in exhilaration, in derring-do.

Most of those involved in this peculiar transaction understand that it's the fun of the thing, and not uncontrollable lechery, that gets a few of us out of our beds in the night to misbehave moderately by the side of a cow-byre – even if we hadn't signalled as much by swathing ourselves in many layers of clothing before plunging out into the Atlantic night: layers designed to discourage unwanted liberties, to protect our reputations. It's likely, I think, that one or two of these Donegal Lotharios are hoping to fall in with a truly bad girl (according to the ethics of the day); but most, I am sure, approach the business in the same spirit as ourselves. I can vouch for it that the genuine seducers, those serious about sex, have to go further than *Teach* Eddy Doyle to get their purpose fulfilled. We're about as much use to them as sixpence to a spendthrift.

Half the time, it's a lottery whom one ends up with; sometimes we clamber out expecting to be met by boys with whom we've tentatively set up a late-night encounter, only to find ourselves in the clutches of perfect strangers – who must be surprised by the bulkiness of the bodies they're embracing. On one of these occasions, I recall, I am clad in pyjamas, a skirt, a blouse, two jumpers, a cardigan and a borrowed short suede jacket; and my friends have wrapped themselves in equal quantities of garments to safeguard their modesty. People who try to grope their way through one or more of these layers soon give up. No one can accuse us of not doing our best to observe the rules of dress as laid down by the Catholic Truth Society.

Still, if we come out at all, there's a tacit agreement that we won't object to being kissed and indeed we don't, being eager to compare notes later and comment on the performances of those concerned. We pride ourselves on knowing what's what, in this respect, on being able to tell the naturally gifted from those who are either annoyingly perfunctory, or subject to unproductive erotic seizures. We are very full of ourselves and opinionated.

There comes a night when I awaken first as the window is tapped from the outside, poke Maire, then Susie, until she rouses herself, sleepily rubbing her eyes and muttering, '*Tchím* torch'

('I see a torch') and '*Cluinim gluaisteán*' ('I hear a car') – catch-phrases that get themselves repeated sixty times a night with every glimmer of light in the distance, and every noise suggesting a squad of priests patrolling the district on the look-out for delinquents – and somehow propel the three of us out on to the grassy patch beneath the window, as agreed beforehand with a boy named Gallagher and a couple of his friends. However, the trio confronting us outside the window are completely unknown to us – later, we find that they are on the way home from attending a wake in Min na Leice, and just decided to try their luck at a house picked at random. It must have startled them to gain such a quick response – a knock on the window, and there all at once are three stout schoolgirls tumbling out at their feet.

This incident is typical of many others – the most tremendous bustle and hilarity in the night, unpremeditated grapplings in the dark. It may or may not have been the time when one of the three locals is perceived at once to be completely bald – throwing each of us into a frenzy of determination not to be lumbered with him. It's Maire who's unlucky, beaten by Susie and me in the rush to attach ourselves to the two who have hair. None of the three of us can stop laughing, even though it isn't at all wise to create a commotion. If it doesn't bring the *bean a' tí* down on top of us brandishing a rolling pin, it may reach the ears of some fanatical kill-joy among the college authorities – and then the direst repercussions will ensue.

'*Tchím* torch,' Susie keeps on whispering urgently, '*Cluinim gluaisteán.*' It's her imagination, of course – or if it isn't, it's nothing to do with us – but every time she says it, it pulls us up short, to peer and listen for a minute or two. Then, it's a matter of scurrying in pairs over the short springy grass by the side of the house, with its outcrop of stone, towards the back of the empty house next door to ours; when I reach this place, clutching the hand of someone I don't know at all, I find that Susie and the other dark-haired person-from-the-place have got there before us and positioned themselves in a recess in the wall. The next thing I see is Maire scampering past arm-in-arm with the man without hair. (He turns out to be the brother of someone I know slightly, a Mickey Coyle, and only twenty-four years old; I don't know if his premature baldness is an effect of genetics or caused by the drinking water, which is held to blame for the high incidence of toothlessness in the Gaeltacht; if toothlessness, why not hairlessness?)

The sight sets me off into a further fit of giggles; and I hear Susie succumbing in this way too. Also, by this time I've discovered that the person I'm with – though perfectly amiable, and full of chat about the wake they've just been to, a wake for an old woman famous for her singing and soda bread – is no more use at kissing than the gatepost. And neither is his brother, Susie's partner, as it turns out; for after a few minutes she comes striding past, saying she is going home to bed. 'I'll have to go with her,' I whisper to mine, rather glad of a pretext for getting away. Susie and I clamber back in through the window, and subside on the bed in an eruption of laughter. 'Was yours ... ?' 'So was mine ...'

Then it strikes us that perhaps we ought to go back and look for Maire, in case she is getting into difficulties with the third party. So it's out into the blackness of the night once more. (Poor Kathleen, Angela and the rest of our roommates do not get much peace to sleep, on that occasion and others.) Eventually we track down Maire to a hen house, where she's locked in the arms of her man and not very pleased to be interrupted – 'I'll come in a minute,' she says. 'Go back to bed.' It seems, after all, she has had the best of the bargain. But we refuse to be waved away, and drag her bodily back to the house, where a further outbreak of laughter occurs as she describes with relish the bald man's proficiency, saying it serves us right to suffer a let-down in this respect, for allowing ourselves to be mislaid by superficialities such as a good head of hair.

'What a night!' goes the exclamation in my juvenile diary, referring to this episode or one very like it. 'I don't think I've ever laughed so much in my life' – well, I go on, leaving aside a ceilidhe on the previous evening, when Maire (Maire again) finds herself pursued by an avid fat schoolboy about four foot six inches in height, and has to run and hide in the ladies' lavatory every time she sees him coming. *An buachaill ramhar* – the fat boy – and Maire's aghast evasion of him: these fragments, or possibly figments, have a place in the general uproariousness which seemed to characterise our stay in the Gaeltacht – well, the greater part of it at any rate, and before retribution sobered us up. In my diary I note, colloquially, on the subject of Maire's antics: 'We were all in fits at her.'

And what, you might wonder, in the midst of all this jollity, has become of Maghnas Bell and my enthralment with him? Shouldn't this state of mind have kept me from fooling around with anyone else (given that our teacher, handsome Martin Henderson, my second choice among the men in the Gaeltacht that summer, clearly isn't to be diverted away from his fiancée and takes no amorous interest in me or anyone else among his charges)? The truth is that after the first week or so, and greatly to my chagrin, I am paid decreasing attention by Maghnas, who, it seems, has only a limited use for juvenile venery. (His own age is twenty-three or thereabouts.)

A flirtation continues to be carried on between us whenever we meet, but – for whatever reason – we hardly ever do meet. He isn't in Sharkey's shop when I go in there, he stops attending ceilidhes, he's not at home at Peadar Bhig's when I drop in on Olivia. Hanging around at spots where he might be expected to appear produces no result. All that's left to me, in these dispiriting circumstances, is to suffer as flamboyantly as possible. It's not a bit of use for my friends, old and new, to advise me to catch myself on. A lot of energy is expended by me on sighing and groaning over my bereft state.

There's a reason for this: I have taken it into my head that a connection exists between experiencing an emotional crisis and having an interesting personality. Well, I am sixteen; I suppose a bit of silliness and superficiality is in order. And, for all the play-acting, it can't be denied that it's painful, at any age, to find one's dearest longings unreciprocated. I am thankful for all the abundant goings-on, of every sort, which actually leave me very little time to mope. And thankful, too, for the enchantments of the place: the curved bays, dry-stone walls, ferocious breakers, jagged coastline, dramatic headlands, poverty-stricken houses scattered here and there about the rock-strewn territory like clumps of daisies on a lawn.

Maghnas's defection is bad enough, but worse is to follow. A morning comes when I am sitting, as usual, in our classroom at Coláiste Bhríghde, surrounded by talk and laughter, awaiting the arrival of the teacher. Out of the blue, my friend Olivia – the recipient of my most candid confidences about my current infatuation – turns to me and announces blithely that she can hardly keep her eyes open through, she alleges, having been kept awake half the night by Maghnas Bell and his brothers, who'd stolen into the visitors' beds in the small hours, occasioning great excitement and amusement. Not that it's the first time they've behaved like this, she goes on; in fact she and the other girls staying in the house take turns in this manner with the Bell brothers nearly every night – and she, as a matter of choice, prefers the brother named Dermot.

For the moment I am flabbergasted, and unable to comment on these outrageous revelations. I just sit there looking blankly at Olivia. Then, as the class gets going, I start to succumb to puzzlement and dismay, at the same time trying, under the eye of Martin Henderson, to fix my attention on a story about the poet Peadar Ó Doirnín, and then to make sense of some bemusing instruction concerning the subjunctive mood.

All the time, it's as if I've suffered a fearsome blow to the chest. I sit there envisaging the three Bell brothers creeping about the house in the dead of night, turning the handle of the girls' bedroom door and thrusting themselves unceremoniously into one or other of the visitors' beds. How was there room for them? How much of their clothing did they keep on? How far did things go? (As to that – I never do get at the truth of the matter.) Have they all gone mad – the girls incontinently relinquishing every social and moral precept they've grown up with; the boys so desperate they don't give a damn who their bedfellows are, or whether their night-time activities will cause a scandal of such proportions that the whole system of Gaeltacht holidays will be brought to an end?

Good heavens, my thoughts run on, I *know* all the girls who sleep in that room, and some of them are so ill-favoured, gauche and priggish that you'd be within your rights in consigning them to a convent. Yet here they are – if Olivia's report is true, if it's not some ill-conceived tease she's inflicted on me – for all the world carrying on like the inmates of a brothel. It doesn't make any sense. They go to Mass every morning – I know they do – kneeling there before the altar with butter-wouldn't-melt expressions on their horrid faces. It doesn't make any sense.

I am overtaken by anger – anger at Maghnas for ditching me, for deriving more enjoyment from multiple half-baked couplings; anger at Olivia for not repulsing him; but most of all for her incomprehensibly off-hand disclosure of these shocking goings-on at *Teach* Pheadair Bhig. Didn't it occur to her that I would find it upsetting to be put in the picture in this casual way? Has her judgement been impaired in every respect? Has the Gaeltacht atmosphere gone to all our heads?

Somehow I get through the rest of the morning, and then I am gathered up and borne away by Maire, Susie, Kathleen and other friends from *Teach* Eddy Doyle, who do seem to understand the effect Olivia's news has had on me. (Well, I imagine that consternation was plainly imprinted on my face.) 'What's the matter with her?' Susie wants to know, referring to Olivia. 'She couldn't wait to tell you – and to tell everyone else within earshot. I don't think it's anything to boast about.'

Some time later – I am not sure how, or when – I find myself with Olivia, just the two of us, picking our way along a narrow, overgrown pathway, edged by dry-stone walls, heading down towards the beach. It is late afternoon, the air is sultry, bees and butterflies are everywhere. Even now, if I think back, I can hear her voice assuring me that it won't ever happen again, that she's probably exaggerated the whole business anyway, that it's just a bit of sport she thought I'd be interested to hear about. Besides – a slight contradiction creeps in here – besides, it's as well for me to know what Maghnas is *like*. Her motives in telling me were perfectly altruistic; it surprises her that I've taken it amiss. I shouldn't let an ephemeral episode involving an unimportant holiday acquaintance come between us – we, who've been friends, kindred spirits, in and out of one another's houses since the age of eleven. All right, I won't, I'll forget the whole thing, it's nothing to me what Maghnas Bell does; and as for understanding what he's like – that was plain to me from the first moment I laid eyes on him. (This is not strictly true.)

I am recovering. I ask about the plain girls in the bedroom: Maeve McWaters, Frances Quinn, even our friend Colette; surely it can't be true, I say, that these have succeeded in luring men into their beds? Well, says Olivia, it's not exactly a matter of luring; whatever happens, happens in the dark; the Bells take no notice of lumps such as these in the daytime. Probably they, the boys, are not sure who they've been in bed with. There is no romance in the activity at all; it is all expediency. This affords me quite a bit of consolation.

Olivia and I renew our friendship, but things are never quite as intimate between us again.

It's not because of Maghnas, or hardly at all; I'm over that in a week or so, it doesn't go deep, it really doesn't matter at all. What should I expect? *The Waste Land*: 'And if you don't give it him, there's others will, I said.' I'm too young, I know that, I'm not sophisticated enough for a would-be seducer like Maghnas Bell. But I am sophisticated enough to think it likely that, if we met in, say, ten years or so, the positions would be reversed. Somewhere in the back of my head I'm nourishing intimations that Catholicism, and chastity, are concepts I will grow out of. (I'm not mistaken in this; but the process suffers a setback, because of what happens in Rannafast.) But for the time being, a sense of my own worth has been instilled in me far too strongly to allow me to proffer my person as a kind of sexual punchbag. (The tomfoolery round the side of *Teach* Eddy Doyle

113

is different in quality, undertaken in a spirit of merriment only. We're all on the same level, out there in the dark, with no one trying – or not trying seriously – to coerce anyone else.)

I still wonder about those unprepossessing girls, Olivia's Rannafast roommates. Did they shut their mouths and refrain from squealing, abandon piety for the moment, for the sake of being able to confide to cronies, later, that boys, against the odds, had shown an interest in them? ('Look – he came into my bed every night ...') The social and the moral are in conflict here: no one wants to be left outside the glowing circle of boy–girl relationships, intrigues, powerful attractions, social success. One minute all this is in the ascendant; then Catholic teaching. None of us is free from the need to hold the two in some kind of equilibrium.

When I try to get Olivia to be specific about what takes place on the horsehair mattresses of *Teach* Pheadair Bhig, all I get is sidetracking and fudging of the issue. Did they or didn't they? Of course there's nothing *reprehensible* in it, she says; nothing their mothers could object to. (Laughter.) Then the next minute she wishes she hadn't done it, she hopes she won't miss her period. But surely that means ...? She isn't sure. No, of course she's sure; she's only teasing.

Perhaps it is genuinely a case of ignorance. Would I be able to tell, I ask myself, if things had taken their full course? I think so. But I can't be certain. Lessons in the mechanics of repro-duction are some way in the future. The nearest we get to this is biology – but biology isn't one of my subjects.

As for myself and Olivia – it's practical considerations, really, that scupper our inseparability. Though we haven't – naturally – the smallest inkling of it, upheavals are imminent. The new term, only a few weeks away, will see us enrolled, in something of a daze, at different schools. No more waiting, for me, at a cer-tain bus stop in the mornings, until I spot Olivia, who is looking out for me, among the hordes of maroon-clad schoolgirls on a bus heading down the Falls Road. Her relatives, holding me to blame for the catastrophe, will attempt to cut off all communication between us. We will have to meet, clandestinely, after school on certain days of the week, in the city centre, within reach of our respective bus stops; she coming in on the Lisburn bus, I on the bus from Ballynahinch. Winter afternoons, rain or sleet falling at dusk, a doorway in Donegall Square West, gossip exchanged over a hurried cup of coffee, running with our satchels to catch another bus, a bus up the Falls, which enables us to stay together until the last possible minute. For a time, we will write to one another (the letters delivered by a go-between), until her parents find out and put a stop to that too. It isn't a fruitful way to conduct a friendship. And, for both of us, other interests, other alliances, are about to supervene.

Up until this point, the year after our expulsion, it has been utterly taken for granted, by both of us, that school will be followed by university: no other possible course of events has ever entered our heads. We can't pass Queen's, which we do quite often, on our walks about the city, without one or other of us remarking smugly, 'That's where we are going to be –' in three years' time, or two, or whatever. It's not that we mean to kill ourselves with work; we simply assume that, somehow, at the right moment, the transfer to a highly desirable, heady kind of student life will be effected easily. We are good, or at least better than average, at passing exams. (It's true that I have one spectacular failure to my credit, failure in an exam regarded by everyone else as a pushover. Not a public affair: an inner-school test of religious knowledge known as the Bishop's Exam. I am so resentful at having to sit this footling test at all that I do no preparation and consequently end up with something like fifteen marks out of a possible hundred. This is not to be wondered at. Church history induces agonies of boredom in me – even now, a dimly remembered phrase like 'the Edict of Nantes' or 'the Albigensian Heresy' – what is that? – causes my spirits to wilt. I am proud of the notoriety this unprecedented failure confers on me – but of course, in the eyes of the nuns, it's another black mark against me, when my future at the school, or out of it, comes up for discussion.)

What gives us such confidence in our academic abilities? It's not the school, that's for sure; it isn't a good school, its priorities are askew. I remember an occasion when four or five of us, fifth-formers, are positively keen to relinquish most of the free periods we get in a week, in order to sit in at the back of a class which is learning German. We've consulted the timetables and worked out that it can be done. However, when we turn up clutching pens and exercise books, and wearing eager expressions on our faces, we are scolded for presumptiousness – 'How dare you come uninvited into my class, I never heard the like of it' – made to look foolish in front of a lower form and sent away with a flea in our ear. There are only two teachers, sisters, Miss Casement Senior and Miss Casement Junior, in all the years I spent at that school, whose attitude is humane and positive, whom I can recall without flinching. (Instead of watching the clock and trying not to yawn, the state most lessons reduce one to, I hate it when Miss Casement Senior's English classes end.)

No, whatever encouragement I get, I get at home. I am lucky enough to have parents who have never once, throughout my life, withheld approval, complained, or criticised any action I have taken (and many of these actions must have run counter to their expectations for me, their only child). My mother is a Queen's graduate, a scholarship girl, the first member of her family to go beyond elementary education, as far as I know. She doesn't doubt that I will get to Queen's too, in my turn, if I put my mind to it.

Our ambition, mine and my friend Olivia's, now strikes me as unduly modest; we might have aimed higher, as high as Trinity College Dublin even, given the right preliminary conditions. Our liking for gallivanting never precluded a certain scholarly bent – and we'd have got on better, I do believe, in circumstances in which the acquisition of knowledge took precedence over piety and tractability. In other words, as pupils at a normal school. When I read a piece of autobiographical writing such as Margaret Forster's *Hidden Lives* – to take that example – I am overwhelmed by vicarious elation (more elation, in this instance, than the author seems to have experienced herself) at the triumph of this working-class girl, a girl from a council estate in the North of England, in securing scholarships at both Oxford and Cambridge – *embarras de choix*.

I'm astonished, too, when I consider the case of another bright sixteen-year-old, Lorna Sage – my exact contemporary – who found herself pregnant without being altogether sure how it had happened (she tells the story in her vivid memoir, *Bad Blood*), and showed a fierce determination not to let motherhood, or early marriage, be an impediment to academic achievement. It's an astonishing story, to me, chiefly because of the attitude of her Shropshire school: true, she encountered some disapproval, but also a lot of support, in particular from older women teachers imbued with a left-over suffragist spirit, teachers who'd no more have sanctioned a waste of intellectual gifts than they'd have taken to rock-and-roll singing themselves. There was no question of post-parturition Lorna being refused permission to sit her A levels.

She even became something of a heroine among her schoolfellows on account of her predicament, and her handling of it. 'It was my first and last moment of popularity in six years at Whitchurch Girls' High School,' she claims, wryly. The irony is that it wasn't pure lust or social defiance that had got her where she was – more a kind of foolhardy innocence. As for me, it seemed that sex was to be my undoing, even before I'd ever properly engaged in it.

Perhaps this is the moment to record a criticism directed at me, when I was eighteen or nineteen, by an acerbic friend: 'There *are* other things in life, you know.' Well yes, I do know that, as a matter of fact – just as I know that a lot of girls among my contemporaries are resolutely unsusceptible to the lure of the erotic. It's a combination of Catholicism, a no-nonsense disposition and failure to overcome the unease and embarrassment which surrounds the topic. Some of these girls are just late developers, stuck in a juvenile mode of equating sex with silliness, and crossly repudiating an undue interest, or any interest at all, in the sordid business; while for others, it's as if this dimension has been left out of their personalities altogether. For the rest of us, who make no bones about perpetually experiencing what the novelist John Banville has described as 'an elated, twittery state of adolescent expectation and surmise', no doubt the whole thing is intensified by the hush-hush, forbidden garnish imposed on top of it.

Possibly one or two of us have even been lumbered for ever after with a fixation on the illicit. I'm not suggesting that our libidos wouldn't have been activated at full force in a more wholesome social climate but that, on the contrary, without repression, the sexual instinct common to all of us might have developed and flourished more harmoniously.

I am learning a lot of things in the Gaeltacht. I am learning about the strangeness of the West, the remotest part of Ireland; about the unreliability of friends, and communal life, and the Irish song tradition. I am learning – I hope – how to put a good face on things, how to slough off discouragement and disappointment. I am learning how easily adolescent affections may be transferred from one object to another (well, I knew that already). I'm about to learn the truth of the old nursery maxim about an excess of laughter being the prelude to lamentation.

Some events of that interesting August stand out more clearly than others. What else do I recall, in a fair amount of detail? There's a morning at Coláiste Bhrighde, when six or seven names are read out at the end of class – mine included. The pupils specified are instructed to stay behind, while the others stream off in pursuit of various objectives – mostly their midday meal. No, it's not that we've been caught out in some piece of misbehaviour; on the contrary, we're about to be rewarded for the way our Irish is coming along. We're invited to a social gathering due to take place that evening at a local house, the home of a celebrated storyteller called Nelly Sally Phroinsias. It's been judged that our proficiency in Irish is such that we might derive some benefit from the experience.

Nelly Sally is ninety years old, and famous in the district as a *seanchaí*, a teller of tales. 'Lá de na laethibh agus uair de na huairibh,' she'll begin. 'Lá de na laethibh agus uair de na huairibh a raibh Fionn Mac Cumhaill agus a chuid Féinne ag seilg i nGleann an Smóil …' More than one generation of Irish-speakers has been riveted by her stories of Fionn and the Fianna, Conchobhar of the Two Sheep, the Daughter of the King of the Hill of Gold, the King of Norway's Children and Miogach Son of Colgain from the Norse Territories of the Sweet Music.

It's a marvel, even we can see that, that such an activity has persisted up until the present. Here on the western edge of Ireland, the modern world is encroaching only slowly on traditional preserves; though of course there is no doubt that it will win out in the end. Already you get the odd pebble-dashed bungalow and indoor lavatory to herald the coming adulteration of an ancient way of life, along with the juke-box in O'Driscoll's Café where 'The Homes of Donegal' is a popular choice of record. The bulk of the people, one imagines, will put up little or no resistance to alien influences, when it comes to the bit. And why, indeed, should they deny themselves comfort and advancement? (I am torn between the two arguments; one minute I'm all for traditionalism, the next on the side of social mobility.)

There won't be any call for a successor to Nelly Sally, I know that: television will usurp her place. Her like will not be seen again. It's impressed on us that we are very privileged, schoolchildren that we are, to be allowed to sit in on what will surely be among the very last of these age-old performances.

As it turns out, my Irish proves inadequate to grapple with the convoluted events of Nelly Sally's story, and my concentration soon slackens. A talking cat, a blackberry bush, a dead man bundled into a sack and suddenly restored to life … I can't make head or tail of it. It's enough, however, just to sit there and imbibe the Gaelic atmosphere. Knowing this way of life to be on its last legs makes the whole occasion especially poignant. There sits Nelly Sally in front of her audience, black stockings, shawl and cardigan, the glow from the turf fire casting deep shadows on her animated old face and gesticulating hands. '*Maith thú, a* Nelly' ('Good for you, Nelly') comes from one corner of the room or other every five minutes or so: not an interruption, but an accepted means of rallying and applauding a performer.

I can't say I'm happy with the seating arrangements. I am stuck halfway along a row of kitchen chairs, between Kathleen Shannon and Susie Greenwood. The position offers no scope for flirtation. The dozen or so college boys invited to the gathering are bunched together (as we are) at the far side of the room. None of our friends among the locals is present – I've looked in vain for Maghnas, Donal Gallagher, Paddy Boyle and the rest of them. No doubt they prefer more up-to-date entertainment. There are plenty of local men in the audience but they're all, without exception, exceedingly old. The row in front of us is filled with members of the college staff, priests and lay teachers and the odd schoolmistress (though not Martin Henderson, oddly enough, since it's he who's responsible for our presence here, in Nelly Sally's kitchen).

Two seats away, to my left and next to Kathleen Shannon, is a portly old white-haired local celebrity named Joe Peadar Burns. This Joe Peadar (it's been explained to us) has done great work on behalf of the Irish language and culture, collecting and recording forgotten songs of the district and further afield, and broadcasting them on his own special bi-monthly programme on Raidió na Gaeltachta. Introduced to us – or told, at least, that we're Irish-oriented pupils from various city schools – he's greeted us affably enough, but with a slight air of bemusement, as if he can't quite fathom what we're doing here, with our shell-pink lipstick, our crisp cotton dresses and Banlon cardigans.

The applause is vociferous once the story's completed, though just before the end a certain restlessness had crept over the audience, signalled by the creaking of chairs, the clearing of throats, and the pouring of beer into beakers clasped in local farmers' hands. Next on the agenda comes the recitation by Joe Peadar Burns of a poem entitled 'The First Tuesday of Autumn' ('An Céad Mairt de'n Fhomair'). Getting to his feet, he explains for the benefit of the visitors: 'This is a tragedy, a lament for a young man named Padraig O'Donnell who met his death by drowning in the year 1811. The body was washed up on the beach down here; I can show you the exact spot. It was Padraig's father Seamus who wrote the poem; and it achieved a great circulation in the Rosses. When someone congratulated Seamus on its success, he replied: "It's success I'd as lief have done without, for it was dearly bought".'

The poem follows, and once it's over an outburst of stamping, cheering and clapping of hands testifies to the popularity of Joe Peadar. Having resumed his seat, this ponderous old person smiles and nods in all directions in acknowledgement of the audience's approval.

The kitchen door stands hospitably open, summoning all the moths of the district, it seems to me, to meet their end against a light bulb suspended from the ceiling in a fringed crimson shade; I sit in dread lest one should fall on me. I have an aversion to creepy-crawlies. It's pretty late by now – ten o'clock at least – and the summer light has gone. Two or three country-looking people, strangers to me, shamble in through the door and proceed towards the back of the room with its makeshift arrangement of benches and chairs, exchanging greetings with their neighbours as they go. A muddy sheepdog squirms in after them, pokes its nose into Kathleen Shannon's lap, and is promptly shooed out again by Joe Peadar Burns before I can get a chance to stroke it. I have noticed that the locals have a rather callous attitude towards their animals. There are few pampered pets in the townlands.

All the old farmers, as far as I can judge, have craggy Donegal faces and haven't changed their style of dress since Patrick McGill's day: the same serge suits, and, in winter (I imagine) tweed overcoats tied around the middle with bits of string, serve this older generation as well as any previous one. I envisage them expertly slapping cattle on the rump, or travelling the roads with cartloads of turf. 'Clabber to the knee' indeed. Here, in Nelly Sally Phroinsias's stone-floored kitchen, a man in one of the ubiquitous dark crumpled suits has got to his feet – a mite unsteadily – and gone into a full-throated rendering of a song entitled 'Paidín's Wife', which I'm pleased to be able to follow. It goes something like this:

> May you break your legs and your bones
> May you break your bones, Paidín's wife.
> May you break your legs and your bones,
> May you lose both your legs and your life.

I'm sitting there enjoying the bracing ruthlessness of this quatrain (if I've got it right) when all of a sudden the room is plunged into blackness. Taken completely by surprise, we require a minute or two to figure out that a power failure has occurred – I find myself turning futilely towards Susie Greenwood and asking for an explanation, amid the confused babble that's arisen in the darkness. A minute later, I'm aware of my arm on the other side being clutched and shaken, and an agitated voice – Kathleen's – demanding that I accompany her outside. 'Yes, all right,' I mutter, 'I'm coming' – still trying to get my bearings. 'What is it? The lavatory's round the back of the house; you have to turn right and be careful not to trip over the turf-stack.'

Some people by now have gathered their wits sufficiently to retrieve torches from their pockets and switch them on, and one man is working away at a fuse-box in the corner. The light comes back on as Kathleen and I are blundering towards the door. Kathleen continues to barge ahead with uncharacteristic determination. Is she bursting to get to the lavatory, or what is wrong with her? Once we're outside, it's plain to see that Kathleen is undergoing an emotional upset. She slumps against the windowsill and bursts into tears, while behind us the sound of fiddling indicates that the entertainment has resumed. All I can do is stand there helplessly looking at her. 'What is it, are you ill or something? I'll get one of the others. I don't know anything about first aid.'

At this suggestion, Kathleen's distress visibly increases. She manages to indicate that the last thing she wants is an audience. Finally, calming down a bit, she fishes a hanky out of her pocket and gives her nose a good blow. 'Ugh,' she shudders.

'What was all that about?' I ask. 'Did something happen when the light went out?'

Kathleen confides to me, in a whisper, that her modesty has been outraged. She felt, in the dark, a hand being inserted into the front of her blouse. She and I peer in unison at the place where, sure enough, a button has come undone. Acting instinctively, Kathleen says, she grasped the hand and thrust it away from her. Then the horror of the thing overcame her. 'Whose hand?' I wonder, stifling an urge to giggle, trying to figure out to whom Kathleen's ample bosom would have proved irresistible. There is definitely a tinge of absurdity about the incident.

'Joe Peadar's.' This information is divulged in a dire tone. 'Oh God, it was awful,' Kathleen moans. She adds that she'll never be able to look anyone in the face again.

'Joe Peadar Burns? That old man? Kathleen, are you sure you didn't imagine it?'

Kathleen is quite definite on this point. Good heavens, she's not the sort of person to make a fuss about nothing. She demands that I should give her credit for knowing an assault from an accidental caress. Besides, there's the evidence of the opened button, which at this moment she hurriedly fastens as a latecomer turns into the pathway and strides towards us, whistling. It is Martin Henderson, our very personable teacher. 'Well, girls,' he starts, 'how's it going?' But it only takes a closer look at the two of us standing there speechless to alert him to the fact that something is amiss. Kathleen starts to say something and then bursts out crying, perhaps fearing that Martin himself may be impelled to repeat Joe Peadar's performance. There really isn't any danger of it.

'Whatever is the matter?' cries Martin.

It's left to me to explain, as best I can, that Kathleen is the victim of an unfortunate experience. I don't mean to be coy, but between deficiency in Irish, and embarrassment both at the incomprehensible act, and Kathleen's excessive reaction to it, I'm reduced to a fair amount of stumbling and stuttering. Martin has to press us to go into detail. Eventually the name of Joe Peadar Burns is dragged out of us. At this point, Martin frowns and looks terribly serious. 'Joe Peadar is an old friend of mine, a most respectable man. Joe Peadar would never do a thing like that!'

'Well, he did,' mumbles Kathleen. I can't resist adding, probably through nervousness, 'We're never going to be able to look him in the face again.'

'Now, look here,' says Martin, every inch the schoolmaster, 'come round the side of the house for a bit, both of you.' It's clear that cracks are going to be papered over – also, I can't help considering it extremely ironic that it should be in these circumstances that Martin Henderson, on whom several of us have a schoolgirl crush, at last invites me round the side of a house …With an arm around the shoulder of each of us, Martin explains at some length that Joe Peadar is a poor old man, a luminary of the language movement, the victim of a repressed life, and a person against whom a solitary piece of bad conduct should not be held. 'It must have been a sudden impulse,' he decides. 'Joe Peadar has never done anything like that before, that I know of.'

He urges the two of us not to let it go any further. It is certain that Joe Peadar is deeply ashamed of himself at this moment. We don't want to bring trouble on him, do we? A poor old man – and after all his good work on behalf of the Irish language. 'He never married, you know. And men can't help themselves sometimes – not nice, I know, but there it is.'

It crosses my mind that that depends very much on the man concerned, that I could bear it without flinching if a similar impulse came over Martin, for instance, in relation to myself – though I understand that it isn't going to happen. He must be wishing he'd kept us well away from Nelly Sally's kitchen with its scope for outrage. All I can do is agree to screen out the incident of the groping hand, as Martin so intensely desires; and Kathleen too says she'd much rather the whole thing was forgotten. She'd hate to be associated with a scandal in the Gaeltacht. She will try to put it out of her head, and act normally towards Joe Peadar Burns if she should encounter him doddering along a *bóithrín* – though if she does, it's possible that mortification may get the better of her. His action was so unexpected and revolting! A person of his age.

Martin makes soothing noises, and praises the pair of us for being able to see the thing in such a sensible light. Of course he knows we are reasonable girls and incapable of harbouring ill feeling towards anyone over the head of an isolated lapse from propriety. A good night's sleep is what Kathleen, in particular, needs as an aid to dismissing the whole unpleasant business from her mind. We've a lot to look forward to over the next few days – a ceilidhe, and a treasure hunt, and a picnic at the Point, all arranged for our delectation. He, Martin, is relying on our discretion; he knows he can trust us. And look at the time it is – there is no point in rejoining the revellers indoors. Everyone will be leaving shortly. He accompanies us down to the roadway, helping us to negotiate the rough track in the dark, and sends us on our way back to *Teach* Eddy Doyle. If anyone should ask where we got to, we're to say that Kathleen suddenly developed a headache and had to leave early. And we mustn't forget our promise of secrecy. We assure him that our lips are sealed.

Oddly enough – in view of my relish for gossip – I don't have any difficulty in sticking to this promise. There are several reasons for it. First, I've given my word to Martin; and it's nice to be involved in a small conspiracy with him. Then, the aberrant act, when I think about it, fills me with queasiness rather than glee. It would have been a different matter, indeed, if a contemporary's hand had strayed towards Kathleen; sexual behaviour of any kind seems the prerogative of our age-group (well, give or take a few years up or down). On reflection, I still consider her reaction overdone; but I can see why anyone would feel violated, in the circumstances. Grandfatherly concupiscence is outside the ken of all of us.

And Martin is right, of course: with an abundance of goings-on to divert us and occupy our thoughts, the impression of an upset at the storytelling soon fades. And, if only we'd known it, a far more annihilating occurrence has already been set in motion; at this very moment, forces are massing which will overturn the brighter prospects of one or two of us. Joe Peadar's reputation is safe; we are not vindictive girls, and the incident has no sequel beyond an outbreak or two of hysterical laughter, on the part of Kathleen, whenever she chances to catch my eye across the dinner table.

'Livin' in Drumlister,' as W.F. Marshall has it, 'in clabber to the knee.' Irish repression is responsible for the hordes of seedy old celibates dotted about the countryside, most of whom do not have the Gaelic language and its upkeep as a resource. ('The Irish towns and Irish countryside have an astonishing number of bachelors and old maids,' wrote an American observer, Paul Blanchard, in 1953.) *Great Hunger* territory: Kavanagh's Patrick Maguire and his ilk leading lives as meagre as a Presbyterian's Sunday revelry – and as remote from our experience as an upbringing in an igloo. We belong to a world of streets, parks, cinemas, back alleys, double-decker buses, milk bars and Saturday afternoon browsing among the treasure trove of Smithfield Market. We relish the atmosphere of libraries and student dance halls. Rannafast, as far as we're concerned, is only an idea, a version of romantic Ireland. It isn't our natural habitat. None of us is keen on solitude. The stony fields and *bóithríns* of the Gaeltacht wouldn't be half as agreeable to us if the place wasn't crammed to bursting with a whole range of new friends and contemporaries.

At home in Belfast I have a boyfriend in whom I'm losing interest: in my eyes he stands convicted of a timid and conventional nature, very much at odds with his appearance. I suppose I'd really like to tangle with something more intense and dangerous (well, sixteen is probably the age when the Heathcliff figure looms largest in romantic girls' imaginations). Looking back, trying to impose a pattern of sorts on these distant events, I'd have to place Maghnas Bell in a line of wayward, debonair, disruptive men, men with no respect for suburban proprieties, who hold a certain fascination for me – and for whom sex is clearly the driving force in life. Not that this is the only type I'm drawn to: by my mid-teens I've indulged in temporary, absurd and more-or-less fruitless passions for everyone from a blond-haired, unemployed teenage wastrel from the Whiterock Road, to a visiting art master at St Dominic's School. But it is a distinct type, I think, and it's cropped up in my life from time to time.

Its next embodiment that I recall is a fellow student at art school, a person of considerable charm and aplomb, who can't believe I'll go on resisting his sexual advances – and God knows it goes against the grain to do so – but finally understands he's up against invincible, if unnatural, prudishness. That episode ends in tears at an end-of-term barbecue, when he tells me point blank that he is rejecting me in favour of a girl who takes a more adult line about these matters. (I'm put in mind of the early Simmons poem, 'Protestant courts Catholic', which homes in on the dedicated pursuer, and the nervous but adamant repudiator of undue liberties.) It is a fearful blow to my self-esteem. I spend the rest of that ruined evening howling on the shoulder of one long-suffering friend after another, assuring them all that the one thing I'm glad about is the fact that I never did give in to the bugger (or words to that effect). Within a year, though, that's a major regret – that all that inestimable ardour should have gone to waste.

But that's some way in the future. In the meantime, in the Gaeltacht, we heed the plaintive and insidious voices speaking to us out of the past: '*Bheirim comhairle do mahná óga dá nglacfadh siad uaim í gan a bheith ag ól le fir óga ná ag creidbheáil a scéil …'* ('Here's advice for young women, if they'll accept it from me, / Don't be drinking with young men or believe a word they say …'). Seduction and betrayal, Gaelic fashion. The substance of a good many songs. The promises unfulfilled, the baby wrapped in a shawl in the crook of its young mother's arm. We're frightfully susceptible to the glamour and illicitness of it all, even while mapping out very different futures for ourselves. They are irresistibly romantic, the wronged eighteenth-century heroines with the blood spattering down over their little buckled shoes, taking loss and misery in their stride or exacting a supernatural revenge. We'd like to go wrong with equal style, if it weren't laughable to think we might go wrong at all.

What else can I extract from the somewhat blurred events of the Rannafast summer? I remember Martin Henderson being accosted by a tinker woman – this must have happened in one of the two local shops, or outside the college where a crowd of us has congregated – who goes to great lengths to persuade him that his life's happiness depends on the immediate purchase, from her, of four piebald donkeys. Describing the animals' great virtues, she insists they're a gift at the price. Poor Martin can do nothing but laugh nervously, make helpless gestures with his hands, and plead a lack of suitable accommodation. He lives in a terrace house in Ballymena, he explains; and how would he even get them home? Everyone within earshot is rolling about in an ecstasy of mirth.

The absurd woman, no doubt encouraged by all the laughter, becomes increasingly theatrical in her manner. She's an exceedingly wild-looking tinker, with head and shoulders wrapped in a tartan shawl. To make matters worse she hasn't a word of Irish. We have no idea why she has singled out our teacher as a possible collaborator in the odd transaction. Is she having him on? No one has ever heard tell of a piebald donkey.

Eventually she takes herself off, with instructions to Martin to stand where he is while she leads one of the animals into Sharkey's shop – it is probably Sharkey's shop – for his close inspection. He waits until she is out of sight before taking to his heels – and spends the rest of the day, by all accounts, on tenterhooks lest she should reappear leading a donkey on a string like something out of a farce. As for us – we're left clutching our sides and mopping the tears from our cheeks. How wonderful that such a performance should take place for our benefit!

There's a girl in our house named Breda, very podgy and unappealing, who fills the role of sneak and goody-goody without which no gathering of schoolgirls can be complete. When a car draws up alongside us one day, and its occupants – strangers to us, though one of them identifies himself as a cousin of a boy we know – offer to drive us to a Sinn Féin ceilidhe in Gweedore the following evening, and we accept, Breda promptly runs off bearing this intelligence to the *bean a' tí*, who of course forbids us to do anything of the sort.

She, the *bean a' tí*, has already cottoned on to the nightly activity in and out of the house, and one afternoon we arrive home to find our bedroom windows nailed shut. She won't report us to the college authorities, the daughter of the house assures us, but she'll take other measures to curb misbehaviour. It's not the first time she's had to deal with this sort of thing – we didn't imagine, did we, that we were among the first lot of summer visitors to indulge in such excitements in the night? It's an annual hazard for landladies. (Even back in pre-war days, I learn from a friend years later, a Rannafast rashness routinely overtook about half of Coláiste Bhrighde pupils. Among those affected, or infected, was the future novelist and short-story writer Benedict Kiely, who, with another boy, broke out of his bedroom to meet up with a pair of similarly moonstruck Dominican girls – at which point, I am assured, actual congress took place. Wild nights, wild beyond *our* imaginings.) It is as well she isn't running off to Father O'Friel and the others to lay complaints before them. A few of us do not have unblemished records – including, oddly enough, my upright classmate Angela Magill, who's had a black mark placed against her name for sitting out a dance at a ceilidhe with a boy she'd previously been on the floor with: if it happens again, she is warned, she'll be on the first bus home.

I note in my diary, amid the usual embarrassing gush and guff, that they are terribly strict in Rannafast. Some naughtier girls (myself among them), spotted standing by the wayside in conversation with a group of locals, are instructed by a college official, Francis Cassidy or something I think his name was, to take care lest something untoward should befall us: these boys work tremendously hard in Scotland, we are told, and as a consequence run wild whenever they come home. We'd do better to stick to our own kind, fifth- and sixth-formers like ourselves attending the college. (If he'd been a priest he'd have told us to stay away from boys altogether.) We stand there meekly and attentively while filled to the brim with unspoken insubordination.

Breda the sneak, in charge of *Teach* Eddy Doyle's food supplies for a picnic, unwraps a bundle of thick jam sandwiches at which the more fastidious among us turn up our noses. We prefer to go hungry. To reach the spot chosen for the picnic, the Point, we've had to traverse miles of silvery sand, wading knee-deep in sea-water at one moment – did the men all get the bottoms of their trousers wet? And how did the priests and older teachers manage, without jeopardising their dignity? I can't remember. It's no trouble to us, though, to tuck our skirts into our knickers and forge ahead.

I am enchanted by the paleness of the sand, which stretches away on all sides, and the blueness of hills beyond the horizon. It seems to me a paradisal place. Even the absence of our friends among the locals – departed en masse, it seems, to a football match in Letterkenny – hardly diminishes the perfection of the day. Swimming and paddling in the sea, lolling about among the sand dunes, an impromptu ceilidhe on the beach …

Going home, we're transported in relays by boat across the estuary, where the tide has come in. It's one of those airy, scented, gold-tinged summer evenings, the sky still cloudless, a hazy light blue at this hour about to turn pink. 'Girls, girls!' some teacher calls to us in Irish, 'No dawdling on the way home!' Scrambling out of the boat, we find the sand loose and warm beyond the reach of the tide, as we sink into it ankle-deep. A few red poppies are in bloom along the edge of a cliff where grass grows short and springy. We pass the hollow underneath a furze bush which used to accommodate an illegal *poitín* still (more recently it's accommodated myself and Maghnas Bell during one of our restricted kissing sessions). The luckier ones among us have got themselves beautifully tanned, while others – myself included – are freckled and scorched in patches. My knees, nose and shoulders are actually burnt – but never mind, I'm sure the glow will have faded in a day or two.

Though our holiday coincides with an unusual heat wave, as I've said, the days aren't uniformly sunny. I remember a couple of thunderstorms, rain and drizzle early on in the month, an overcast evening or two – one in particular, during which an official entertainment, a treasure hunt, is in progress. Looking at my notes concerning this activity, I find it hard to make head or tail of it. On the way there, I've written, we meet a boy who tells us he has fallen off his bicycle and can't come. This seems something of a non sequitur. A lot of bustle appears to be going on in the vicinity of Coláiste Bhrighde, I next observe. Another boy, clearly a native speaker, stands poring over a list of clues which he then translates for our benefit (we must have been issued with a printed sheet), while someone else runs around stealing various items to pass on to us, including a skipping-rope – from two young children who don't appear to have had any say in the matter – and a hen. (A hen?)

Paidí Mící Rua, I note, allows us to borrow his driving licence, another item on the list. I then digress to comment on the attractiveness of this person's appearance – black curly hair and the rest of it – plus his peculiar penchant for making overtures to plain girls in glasses. We have got the measure (or so we think) of a great many of the locals. Despite all the help bestowed on us (I record) we lose the contest. It is probable that we have failed to approach the thing in the right spirit. No prize on offer from the college is among our objectives. The treasure hunt, like everything else, is judged according to the scope it offers for setting up assignations.

Despite the setbacks my heart-strings have been subjected to, I still find my breath quickening whenever a figure with reddish brown hair, wearing jeans and an open-necked American check shirt, hoves into view. Maghnas Bell. It happens again on the evening of the treasure hunt. We're on the way home when he detaches himself from a group assembled outside Sharkey's shop, and saunters over to us. After more or less ignoring me for days on end, he has now (it transpires) taken a fancy to participate – with my cooperation – in our nightly fun and games. Specifically, he is asking to make a date with me for 2 a.m. Well! I ought to get on my high horse, I know, over the business of being dropped and taken up at Maghnas's whim. But naturally I'm far too weak-willed to do anything of the sort.

For the moment – once again – all I'm conscious of is elation. There's a problem, though: I can't get out, I tell him. The *bean a' tí* has taken steps to pin us down in our beds at night by securing the windows. No matter – he'll bring a pair of pliers. He'll also come bolstered up by as much company as he can gather (he doesn't put it like that). A group of *muintir na háite* will come knocking on our window, to the delectation – he implies – of those among us who are up for a final episode of unorthodox egress. (We are due to go home in a day or two.) My friends have gone on in front, leaving myself and Maghnas standing together like a pair of conspirators, hoping no censorious eye is falling on us. I say – out of the side of my mouth – I can't be certain how many of us will be awake, and willing. But I'll be ready to hop outside myself, I whisper, once the *bean a' tí*'s defences have been breached.

A pitch dark night in the Gaeltacht, and four adventurers banging cautiously on our windowpane, as agreed. Maghnas, his brother, his cousin, and a noisy young roustabout by the name of Feda. Anticipation having kept us from falling deeply asleep, we stumble out of bed wearing the usual precautionary wrappings, and grope our way towards the muted hullabaloo outside. One of our visitors clambers up on the windowsill wielding a pair of pliers, and we all wait anxiously while the *bean a' tf*'s imprisoning nails are dealt with. Eventually the bottom pane shoots up, enabling us to tumble out. I am first through the aperture, my hand is grabbed by Maghnas, and we take off at a run across the grass beyond the clothes-line to the rocks ahead.

All goes well for about ten minutes or so before Ulster puritanism, or prudence, needs to assert itself. 'No,' I mumble; then more firmly: 'No, no, *no*.' There's a bit of argument, some attempt at persuasion – I'm the only girl that summer who's refused to go the whole hog, all my friends are doing it, Maghnas tells me, which I don't believe for a moment, even lying there in the dark I don't believe it; then comes the belated assurance that he'd never force me to do anything I might be sorry for, since he likes me so much. I am clearly a person of great integrity and moral fortitude – or words to that effect. It is possible that the layers of buttoned-up cardigan, blouse, pyjama-top and petticoat have bred in him a compulsion to end the whole unprofitable business. 'Blow this,' he may have murmured to himself, at one with the worried young hero of Beryl Bainbridge's *A Quiet Life*, whose sexual exploration is stymied by a woolly vest.

Ambivalent as ever, I am half grateful for his forbearance, and half regretful – not that I'd had any doubts about the outcome of the episode. And that's it; we get to our feet and head back towards the bedroom window, no longer having anything much to say to one another. Once I'm inside the house, Maghnas tries to follow; he gets one leg across the sill and thrusts his torso into the bedroom, taking me by surprise. Perhaps he hopes he may light on someone more compliant, snoring away in one of the big iron double beds.

When I realise what he is up to, I gesture frantically towards Susie Greenwood, who rises up out of a tangle of sheets and blankets in her baby-doll pyjamas and joins me in shoving Maghnas out backwards; she gets a grip on his shoulders and pushes him out, all the while threatening, in a furious whisper, to 'wreck' everyone within reach (this is one of her expressions). Between us we force him back on to the ground outside – he doesn't put up much of a struggle – just as Maire and her escort loom up out of the darkness. Maire, breathless, is through the window in a jiffy, and then the other two (whose identities are lost to me); and some hysterical confidences are exchanged in whispers before we settle down for what remains of the night.

And that is the end of my association with Maghnas Bell. I only see him once again, at the final ceilidhe of the season, two nights later; arriving around eight-thirty or nine, he finds a seat by the wall and spends the entire evening there, never getting up to dance or speak to anyone, as far as I can see. I'm still sufficiently interested to keep an eye on him, though more concerned to present an imperturbable face: an objective which, as it happens, is about to be severely tested, in a totally unexpected manner.

A ridiculous and vicious drama is brewing up about us – a drama of little consequence, indeed a source of pleasurable interest, for anyone not at the centre of it; but for three of us at least, a pickle of unprecedented dimensions. We've succeeded beyond anyone's expectations in getting into our school's black books. Our lives, in fact, are about to be wrenched off-course – whether happily or unhappily in the long run, it is hard to say. What's beyond dispute is that things would have fallen out differently, if a summons, via a loud-speaker, hadn't boomed into that fuggy room, on that August evening, as the last strains of music for the Sixteen-Hand Reel died away, and we stood there smoothing our hair and regaining our breath after the exertions of the dance ...

A tense silence comes over the room as everyone is asked to pay attention to what's about to follow. Two local houses are specified, *Teach* Pheadair Bhig and *Teach* Eddy Doyle; all St Dominic's pupils staying in either of these houses are requested to make their way immediately to the secretary's office. No other school is mentioned. The tone of the announcement suggests that something serious is afoot; but, looking at one another open-mouthed, we haven't a clue what it's to do with.

Summoned to the office, I note in my schoolgirl diary, 'We went, quaking.' Olivia, Colette, Doreen Hurley, Frances Quinn, myself, Angela Magill, my bedfellow Maire and several others whose names I've forgotten. That sentence from my diary has, I suppose, the merit of being laconic. As for the rest of my on-the-spot impressions – I am not very forthcoming about what took place that evening, or later: whether out of a wish to minimise the whole thing, the need to preserve a certain amount of secrecy, or through narrative incompetence, I cannot be certain. To make anything of it, at present, I have to read between my own lines, as well as trying to dredge up the effect of the contretemps on my state of mind – or rather, successive states of mind, as confidence gives way to apprehension, and security about the future is succeeded by disbelief.

I didn't think I was in it up to the neck. In the rúnaí's office, that evening, we are lined up in front of a kind of tribunal, consisting of some severe priests, the secretary himself, a grim lay teacher or two, and our own Miss Boyle, whose expression suggests we've come in with dung on our shoes. (Whatever we've done, it has let the side down.)

The chief priest, Father O'Friel I think, begins straight away to harangue us mightily: 'I have to tell you you're all in bad trouble. A call has just come through from St Dominic's School on the Falls Road in Belfast. I don't know the ins and outs of it: the nun I spoke to told me it was far too shocking to repeat over the telephone. But I gather there's been some carry-on with boys here. I have the names of the boys concerned. My advice to you all is to make a good confession at the earliest opportunity. I hate to think of the state of your immortal souls. I'm disgusted with you. I'd have thought girls with your advantages, a good

135

education and all the rest of it, would know how to behave. It doesn't say much for the way you've been brought up. The only thing you can do is pray to the good Lord for forgiveness. I don't know what put such filth in your heads, girls of your age! I can tell you, if you weren't going home anyway first thing in the morning, you'd have been sent away from the Gaeltacht in two shakes of a duck's tail; we don't want girls of your stamp here. I don't know which of you' – surveying us sternly over the rims of his glasses – 'is the most to blame, but my understanding of the matter is that the whole lot of you are going to be expelled from your school. And serve you right. Now get out of my sight. Pah!' – or words to that effect. It is all in Irish, so I may have missed some salient bits.

We are dumbfounded. Another of the adults in the room, I forget which one, explains to us in elementary Irish that a letter, written by one of us to a classmate in Belfast, and detailing our unspeakable transgressions, came into the hands of that girl's parents, who were so appalled by its contents that they bore it straight away, probably at the end of a pair of tongs, to the nuns in charge of our moral welfare. Hence the diatribe above. The only other piece of positive information we can glean is that the indiscreet letter-writer is an inhabitant of *Teach* Pheadair Bhig, not Eddy Doyle.

Released from the office, we fly to the cloakroom, where the majority of us break down in tears. (But not me; I'm not aware of having anything to cry about. The terrible letter, whatever it is, can't be laid at my door; I've been far too busy having an eventful time to do more than dispatch the odd innocuous post-card; and I find it hard to take the notion of a mass expulsion seriously. I'm still pretty strung-up and agitated, though, affected by the general dismay, and understanding that the outcome for some of us may well prove calamitous. And I'm thankful – selfishly – that I never succeeded in effecting the wished-for transfer to Olivia's house, the house seemingly at the centre of the row.)

All our friends from other schools crowd in on top of us, agog to hear the details of the disaster. Whatever can have happened to overturn the carefree spirit of the place, and threaten to bring down the direst retribution on our heads! *Excitements at the Chalet School* aren't in it. We are not normally tearful girls, yet the whole cloakroom is filled with sobbing and snivelling, along with choked disclosures about our horrendous plight – word of which circulates very quickly through the dance floor.

Everyone, I note in my diary, is tremendously concerned and sympathetic – even Maghnas Bell, who finally rises from his bench to enable me to sit down, although we seem no longer to be on speaking terms. I do sit down, smiling gratefully at him, though in fact it's the last thing I want to do; I want to be in the thick of the throng, discussing this newest crisis with all and sundry and securing reassurance that it's a storm in a teacup (or an envelope). *Cogadh na sífíní* is the Irish expression: war of the wisps.

Who is to blame for the current debacle? We narrow it down to two, my friends Olivia McAloon and Colette Buckley, both of whom admit to foolhardy insinuations in letters to classmates. Cross-questioned by me, each denies having mentioned me at all in any of her spicy communications. So I am pretty well convinced I'm in the clear – more concerned, in fact, for my friends than for myself. I've geared myself, however, to undergo a degree of fuss and reproof, since the evidence in black and white damning one or two is certain to brush off on the lot of us.

(The evidence is more damning than I understand at the time. The thrilling letter, posted off by Olivia – it seems it *was* Olivia and not Colette, as I indicated in my *Observer* article, though she never exactly admitted as much to me, no doubt preferring to keep the thing enshrined in vagueness and mystification – the letter contained some lurid announcement to the effect that, if she were to have a child, she'd be at a loss to identify the father. What the earliest shocked readers of this letter fail to realise, I think, is that Olivia is quoting from one of her favourite authors, John Steinbeck: though whether this improves matters at all or not, I cannot say.)

We are up at six-thirty the following morning, take our leave of the *bean a' tí* and the others, and lug our cases down to Coláiste Bhrighde, where a fleet of buses is waiting. Some of us manage to get our belongings stowed on one bus, and ourselves on another, but it all gets sorted out at Derry. Our heads are still in a whirl from the previous evening's upset. There's already been a prodigious exchange of addresses and promises to keep in touch – and for those of us from St Dominic's facing trouble at home, reiterated good wishes: it mayn't be as bad as we fear.

My attention is focused on getting a copy of the banned republican newspaper, the *United Irishman*, smuggled across the border – which, in fact, I accomplish with such ease that it's something of a let-down. What is the point of defying a deplorable regime – the Stormont government – if its representatives can't even be bothered carrying out the simplest checks against acts of insubordination! Once we're safely past the customs' post, I say as much to Susie Greenwood, who turns on me a look of exasperation: am I not in enough trouble already, she snorts, without trying to get myself arrested on top of being expelled from school? (This is a joke.) The seditious paper, which is wrapped around my waist with my school blazer buttoned over it, holds an immense significance for me at that moment. The shop in Rannafast had sold out when I'd tried to buy it, and what I've now got is Maghnas Bell's own personal copy, which he kindly sorted out for me, and allowed me to keep. It's my last link with the Gaeltacht – for the time being – and a twofold trophy.

(In the 1970s, when I am staying with my parents in Belfast, I return home one day from a shopping expedition to find my mother with a box of matches in the back yard frantically setting fire to that actual, long forgotten copy of the *United Irishman*, which she's come across in a tea-chest in the back bedroom containing such relics of my childhood as bygone issues of the *School Friend*, *Eagle*, *Lion*, some battered *Rupert* annuals and my postcard collection from 1955. In those dangerous years it's not expedient to keep anything remotely dicey about the place.

People driving to work with a copy of the morning paper tend to stow it out of sight beneath a seat, lest possession of the *Irish News*, or the *News Letter*, should identify them lethally with one side or the other.)

It is strange to be back in Belfast after a month in Donegal, whose place-names are still ringing in my ears: Falcarragh, Burtonport, Dungloe, Bloody Foreland, Loughanure. Normally, I'd have savoured the return to a familiar routine, and the inspiriting prospect of a new school year, just a week or two away: the coming-on of autumn, a great smell of dead leaves burning, a bracing coldness in the air, smoke and fog, reunion with classmates, gossip, a different classroom and position in the school, new teachers, timetable, school books to be sorted out … all the bustle and exhilaration peculiar to the moment of reassembling. But this year, things are askew – to an extent to which I'm not yet aware.

On my first morning home I'm awakened at about 8.30 a.m. by the arrival on our doorstep of Olivia and her aunt. They remain closeted in the front room with my mother for some time. I've already warned my mother to expect some trouble, telling her what has happened (stressing my own peripheral involvement in it). Olivia too, it seems, has confessed all. The aunt, summoned from across the town to deal with the crisis, hadn't wasted a moment but had rushed to the school the previous evening. Word still was that the lot of us were up for expulsion. So I am hurried out of bed and hustled on to a bus going down the Falls Road. (Most houses in those days, ours included, are not equipped with telephones.) My mother and I wind up in the nuns' parlour at St Dominic's waiting to be interviewed by Mother Helena.

The role of this nun, whom I recall as the prime mover in the business, puzzles me. She wasn't the Dominican headmistress, though she had been previously, and would fill the post again in the late 1960s. *My* last headmistress at the school was a Mother Ailbe, very ugly and neurotic as I remember her; and she, at that moment, was about to be succeeded by a Sister Urban (whom I never knew). But all our dealings are with this Mother Helena, who pronounces my fate as she enters the room: I'm not to be allowed back at the start of the new term. When my mother remonstrates with her, however, she turns to me and demands a full account of my stay in the Gaeltacht. I do my best to give her what she wants – at least in a censored version, omitting any mention of illicit revelry, and denying I've ever done anything with Maghnas Bell other than walk along the road between his house and ours discussing the economic position of the Gaeltacht vis-à-vis the Republic's government (in Irish, naturally). Mother Helena listens to all this without comment, and then requests my mother to return to the school – alone – on the following Sunday.

(All I can think of is an occasion during my first year at St Dominic's, when Mother Helena – then headmistress – came into our basement classroom to talk to us eleven- and twelve-year-olds about piety, grace, the sacraments and the probable state of our immortal souls. 'Your souls,' she meant to say – always providing we hadn't committed any mortal sins – 'your souls, the souls of all good children, are all bright and shiny'; unfortunately the last phrase came out as 'shite and briny'. A number of us, those deficient in goodness, nearly wet ourselves in the effort not to give way to hilarity.)

That evening, I've arranged to visit the Ritz Cinema in Fisherwick Place, to see what turns out to be an unmemorable film called *Rio Bravo*, with my new friend Maire Maguire, who lives in Derby Street near St Peter's Pro-Cathedral, with its twin spires dominating the whole of the Lower Falls. Maire tells me she's already been summoned up to the school by a Sister Philippa, a nun with whom I've had the odd run-in in the past, though recently we've got on better terms due to my interest in the Irish language and culture. I'm fairly confident that Philippa, if necessary, would speak on my behalf. And Maire's account of our Gaeltacht goings-on, as reported to me, seems to tally with mine. '*And* I told her how good you were – going to Mass every morning, and all.' This makes us laugh. It's true, though, that we've attended early morning Mass in Rannafast on a number of occasions when we didn't have to – for what reason I can't now imagine, unless it was (in my case at least) to demonstrate an affirmation of virtues I thought it right to subscribe to. My confidence, which was at a low ebb earlier in the day, begins to build up again.

The nuns' decision, relayed to my mother on the Sunday, is in my favour: I may, after all, return to the school. ('The beast' – i.e. Mother Helena – 'said I was to be allowed back', my diary has it.) Olivia and Colette are not so lucky. The verdict of expulsion stands, in their case. And Olivia immediately confides to me that her aunt is adamant about my role as ringleader. All she can do is shrug, when I ask for an explanation of this rancorous bee in Aunt Ita's bonnet. There is clearly something here that I am missing. But I'm too relieved at escaping the role of outcast to devote much time to pondering an old aunt's crotchet. I am sorry about the other two, of course – especially Olivia; sorry they've been caught out and had this desperate sentence pronounced on them (and all over the head of a bit of fun). But I don't feel that I have got away with murder – or the next worst thing, indecency – not unless Maire, Angela Magill and the other occupants of *Teach* Eddy Doyle who joined in the rollicks admit to harbouring the same misgivings.

Olivia and Colette are accepted as pupils at the single (non-Dominican) convent on the outskirts of the city: Rathmore. This entails a change of uniform from maroon to dark navy.

Three or four days go by. Another summons to the school arrives for my mother, possibly conveyed by the terrible games mistress, who lives not far from us on the Falls Road, near St John's Chapel. It's a Friday, I remember, and I have a friend to tea: a prim sixth-former from the other Dominican Convent, Fortwilliam on the Antrim Road, a girl whom I like without considering in any way a kindred spirit. It's not until she, Pauline Something-or-Other, has gone home that the news is broken to me: the expulsion is on again.

What has happened? Someone, it appears, has identified me as the owner of a dirty book which went the rounds of Form 5A, and provoked some previously chaste girls to assume an uncharacteristic licentiousness in the back end of Donegal. So the whole rumpus can, after all, be laid at my door. Never mind that I, myself, found the book in question – the lethal *Peyton Place* – so dispiriting that I couldn't read it to the end, and had warned would-be borrowers that it wasn't enjoyable, only bringing it into the school under extreme pressure, and then washing my hands of it. (It disappeared; and I never saw it again.)

I sometimes wonder if the lesson I received at that point about the destructive power of bad literature wasn't among the factors responsible for my eventual choice of profession – to be a literary critic, you need to hold strong views on the merits or demerits of any given work, and care about upholding literary standards. If I'd been asked to review *Peyton Place* for the nuns, they'd have understood that I didn't regard it highly, either as work of fiction or a guidebook to the ways of lust.

This time, there's no redress. And various complications are about to heighten the blow. (I am not, at this stage or for many years into the future, aware of those behind-the-scenes machinations of the Clonard confederate of Olivia's aunt.) Mother Helena's first action after dismissing my mother is to get on the telephone to Rathmore, whom she directs to keep their doors closed tight against me, describing me as a corrupting influence. (I learn this much from Olivia, whose aunt has assured her parents that she's best separated from me – the aunt no doubt having got the details from the Clonard priest who instructed Mother Helena in the steps she should take.) So, when my beleaguered mother rings that school from a public call box, she is told that the sixth form there is already crammed to bursting, and cannot accommodate a single further pupil.

Ejected and dejected. Belfast at the time contains only three Catholic (convent) grammar schools, those I've mentioned above; and I am now barred from all of them, on the principle that '*Salóidh aon chaora chlamhach tréad*', a single scabby sheep will infect a flock. 'Disaster'd me'. In a social climate of less inflexibility the obvious course would be to apply at once for admission to a Protestant, or non-denominational, school; but this resource is not available to me. Apart from the scandal it would cause in the neighbourhood, it happens that my mother is a full-time employee of another order of nuns, the Sisters of Charity, also based on the Falls Road, whose Secondary Intermediate School, St Louise's, has recently opened on what used to be part of the Bog Meadows near our house. It's only in the last year or so that she's been eligible for full-time employment, with the lifting of the Bishop's ban on married women teachers. Before that time, her Queen's degree had netted her nothing but a series of bits and pieces, private tutoring or filling in for someone off sick; to add to the ironies piling up around us, she has at various periods been a valued, though necessarily temporary, member of the St Dominic's staff itself – and incidentally a source of deep embarrassment to me, when I'd meet her in a corridor striding along with a child behind her carrying her books. (She has even taught my year, though fortunately not my class: a circumstance too excruciating to contemplate.)

Her cherished teaching post, for all I know, may already be in jeopardy due to her daughter's disgrace (and my father's wages aren't sufficient to maintain the middle-class comforts to which we're all growing accustomed) – but to step outside the line of Church regulations would make the thing a certainty. So, a Protestant school such as Belfast Royal Academy or Grosvenor High is not an option. But neither is applying to join the civil service or seeking a job as a shop assistant. With the new term now only a week away, the situation is dire.

At this juncture, my mother recalls a school at which she'd once taught, briefly, a good many years ago; further urgent telephone calls are made, the upshot of which is the presence of my mother and myself in a different convent parlour, awaiting inspection. The school, Ballynahinch, an Assumption Convent, is – just – within travelling distance from Belfast. (This is important; there is no question of installing me anywhere as a boarder.) About half its pupils are boarders, while the rest travel in each day on buses from Belfast and various locations in County Down. It's a small school – a hundred-odd pupils compared to St Dominic's five hundred – and old-fashioned; just how old-fashioned I don't yet understand. We've concocted a story to explain my departure from St Dominic's – something to do with the failure of the O-Level curriculum to meet my particular needs. It's unlikely that this story fools anyone at all, but that's another thing I don't understand at the time. A vast amount of talk and speculation must have gone on behind our backs, my mother's and mine, but we have our revised account – revised in the interests of expediency – and stick to it.

It is probable that the nuns of Ballynahinch would have found themselves unable to embrace a pupil who came proclaiming her expulsion from a different convent (however unjust); as it is, they swallow the nonsense about the timetable – or pretend to – and enroll me as a new girl in the Lower Sixth. (*Rachel Changes Schools*; *The New Girl at Greychurch*; *Her Second Chance* ... the next title in this series should be something like *Leslie Wins Through* or *Sybil Makes Good*, but I'm not sure that these are appropriate.) For myself, I'd very much rather have broadcast the facts about the Rannafast business and its aftermath, but I've taken in the reasons for not doing so.

Throughout the drama, I haven't had a single bit of crossness or word of recrimination from my saintly mother, who knows the truth of the matter (as I see it anyway), and is completely on my side ... Didn't she ever give way to a spurt of anger at me personally, for all the trouble and perturbation I'd brought hurtling down on both our heads? Did such a mutinous thought ever cross her mind? Of course it must have done, she must have wanted to take me by the hair of the head and give me a good shaking, or pummel me into a penitent frame of mind for all the worry I'd caused her, showing her up in front of her friends and relations, enabling those who'd pronounced me spoilt to nod their heads sagely at the arrival of the outcome anticipated by them. So much, they'd have agreed in avid whispers, for my mother's benevolent child-rearing strategies. She'd have been blamed and held up to ridicule for the way I had turned out.

144

Well, it could hardly have been otherwise: having a daughter at the centre of a juvenile sex scandal could only reflect appallingly on her. Expelled from school! Cast into the wilderness! What extremes of depravity were thereby blazoned!

My mother's faith in me might well have wavered at this fraught moment. But she had invested too much in my upbringing to modify her partisanship now. Indeed, it would have torn her apart to have separated herself from my interests or point of view, even to the extent of criticising any headstrong or asinine carry-on on my part leading to a crisis. In her eyes, the school and the nuns were the villains of the expulsion drama, while I – if not entirely blameless – was merely unfortunate enough to be unfairly implicated.

It was all a tremendous disaster and botheration. But facts, even the abysmal fact of my dismissal from St Dominic's, could have an alleviating slant imposed on them, my mother thought, once the shock of the nuns' decree had worn off, gathering up the shattered pieces of her equanimity and setting about the business of rehabilitation. As I say, the episode fuelled neighbourhood gossip for years and years, but my mother persuaded herself that this was not the case. She thought she had quelled speculation by gritting her teeth and displaying a resolute aplomb ...

In her opinion, I have suffered a disproportionate punishment, and she is every bit as incensed with the Dominican authorities as I am. At the same time, it is not agreeable to consider oneself or one's family as fodder for scandalmongers; and her entire being is focused on keeping the truth from as many people as possible, and – in damage-limitation mode – steering clear of the topic with everyone else, until it all dies down and is forgotten ...

God knows how she squared things with my father and grandmother, how much of the truth was relayed to them. Possibly she produced some acceptable version of what was happening at the end of that difficult summer. I was leaving the school, she might have announced – implying there was something voluntary about it – because the nuns persisted in blaming me for something I hadn't done. Besides, Ballynahinch would suit me better. (My God!) Or perhaps my parents and grandmother sat up to all hours discussing the situation in depth and from every angle while I was in bed. I don't think this is likely, but I simply don't know. I was lying low and keeping quiet, myself, until my life should get back on to some kind of even keel. Certainly the distress and tension afflicting our home must have been apparent to everyone in it, but (as I remember it) my father and grandmother stayed in the background at the time. Neither of them, I think, subjected me to very much in the way of either backing up or dressing down.

It's part of my mother's strategy for getting back to normal that the wretched topic of my expulsion is relegated to a zone as far away as possible from everyday activity. For many years, the circumstances surrounding my change of schools is a taboo subject in our home – with my mother, eyes agleam with sparkling malice, only allowing herself a flicker of satisfaction on hearing of any misfortune befalling the Dominican nuns. *An ní nach bhfeictear nó nach gcluintear, cha bhíonn trácht air*, when a thing is neither seen nor heard of, there is no gossip about it. Well, maybe.

In truth, there is nothing glamorous or beguiling about being an expelled girl – although probably, in my mind, in retrospect, the role has taken on a tinge of those qualities (backed up by the reactions of people who, hearing about the business for the first time, are immediately intrigued. 'What did you do?' they ask; meaning, 'How bad were you?' – uttered with a measure of admiration). No – for me, the emotions of fear and rage, plus the sense of guilt and rejection, combined in my psyche to produce goodness knows what areas of malfunctioning.

The fictional expulsion is something else. There's a very funny scene in Edna O'Brien's first novel, *The Country Girls*, when bumptious Baba makes up her mind to get sent away from her Limerick convent and forces Cait (the narrator) to go along with her. They put their names to a rude rhyme concerning a Sister

Mary and the School Chaplain and leave it lying about. It achieves its end.

> As we walked past her [a prefect] she withdrew in close to the wall, because now we were filthy and loathsome; and no one would speak to us. In the hallway girls looked at us as if we had some terrible disease, and even girls who had stolen watches and things gave us a hateful, superior look.

'Your mind is so despicable that I cannot conceive how you have gone unnoticed all these years,' poor Cait is told. '… This afternoon you did a disgusting thing, and now you have done something outrageous …' Cait is cowed, while Baba, the dare-devil, is bursting with glee and filled with aplomb. It's a standard comic situation with the narrator casting herself as stooge and ingénue – and the convent is shown up wonderfully as back-waterish and shivery. Unfortunately we, in our predicament, have no one among us to match Baba's insouciance. We'd all, given half a chance, slink back to the red-brick fortress on the Falls with our tails between our legs.

Nanda Grey (the alter ego of Antonia White) is another quasi-fictional heroine who suffers from an overreaction on the part of nuns. Nanda's Ouida-type manuscript, her attempt at writing a full-blown romance, which she keeps in her desk while she goes on composing it, falls into the wrong hands and gets her convicted of depravity. The year of this disaster is 1912 or '13, the setting a swanky English boarding school, the Convent of the Five Wounds, Lippington (in reality, the Sacred Heart Convent in Roehampton). There are complications here, as it turns out: it is in fact Nanda's father who insists on the proposed sentence of expulsion being carried out, comparing his daughter's mind to a sink of filth and impurity. (People confronted with juvenile expellées tend to lose their sense of humour.) The nuns might even have been willing to reinstate her. But White's portrayal of the school is effectively chilling, with its atmosphere at once repressive and lurid. The nuns' declared objective is to break the will of each and every pupil, and especially the more recalcitrant, for the purpose of resetting it, as if it were an arm or a leg, 'in God's own way'. There are, you soon realise, extremely disturbing undercurrents to Lippington's idealisation of order and sanctity.

Frost in May, the autobiographical novel of which Nanda's expulsion forms the climax, was followed by a couple of sequels in which the heroine's singular misfortunes seem geared to suggest that anyone subjected to the rigours of a convent schooling is in some way disabled and unfitted for ordinary life thereafter. (The sexual impotence of a couple of husbands and recurrent bouts of insanity are only a few of the woes in store for White's unlucky central character, now called Clara Batchelor.)

A morning comes in early September when I have to leave the house at an unearthly hour and board a bus going down the Donegall Road, alighting at Ormeau Avenue where the starting point for Ballynahinch is located. My new school uniform has not yet arrived, so I am wearing ordinary clothes: well, a tartan pleated skirt and my St Dominic's blazer. I have permission to attend classes in this get-up. The Ballynahinch colour is royal

PC during her Ballynahinch year

blue, and the uniform – to my horror – includes black lisle stockings and black laced shoes, items discarded by St Dominic's as far back as the 1940s. This is a real worry to me; I dread having to appear in the street looking a fright or an oddity. Indeed, it is possible that all the misery, apprehension and incomprehension surrounding my expulsion got itself focused, for the moment at least, on those impending lisle stockings, which assumed something of the character of a bugbear in my mind.

I have only a week's respite before this torture is inflicted on me. In the meantime – on this first morning – I nerve myself to accost a stocky blue-uniformed figure standing at the bus stop, introducing myself as a new girl. She has the look of a hockey-player or form-captain about her. I am taken under her wing, once she understands I'm not a retarded first-former, but someone going straight into the Lower Sixth. Friends in the same blue uniform swarming up to join her are informed of this phenomenon, i.e. me. I resign myself to being an object of curiosity – friendless, for the moment, wearing the wrong blazer and joining the school at an absurdly late stage.

Ballynahinch is a rather dismal market town (or so it seems to me at the time), and the Assumption Convent is a countrified school with a deranged headmistress and the bulk of the pupils either furtive or hysterical. The building itself glowers over the town at the Belfast end of the main street; it's approached via an upwardly curving drive. Disgruntled pupils inch their way along this drive, spirits plummeting as the hideous entrance looms in sight. (I may be exaggerating; but I really don't remember the least jolly thing about Ballynahinch.) To be a boarder here, I soon understand, is to undergo a systematic quenching. (Lippington without the starchy and snooty tone.) One friend who did board, up until the second term of her final year (my only year), when her family's move to Belfast enabled her to travel in on the bus with the rest of us, cannot, even now, hear the word 'Ballynahinch' uttered in any context whatever, without flinching. The word reverberates as 'Lowood' must have sounded in the ears of Jane Eyre.

I'm sure I have an unfair view of Ballynahinch. If one had gone there from the start (as a day pupil anyway), no doubt one would have fitted in and absorbed the school spirit. As it is, I never do get the hang of it. Well, I am not there by choice; and no unexpected largesse about the place occurs to modify my view of it. As far as I can judge, the school is crabbed and dull, full of unnerving corridors and imprisoning classrooms. It seems in desperate need of Peadar O'Donnell's big windows (in his novel of that title) as an aid to enlightenment. It does not foster charm or bonhomie. Every pupil is on her own, and any deviation is apt to be picked on.

Not long after I arrive there, I find myself the butt of intemperate jeers on the part of a small group of my new classmates. My face doesn't please them – as they're for ever telling me – being covered in revolting freckles and further disfigured by albino eyebrows. My hair is peculiar. 'Wouldn't you just hate to look like that?' – this, as likely as not, addressed to someone with a snub nose and permed curls.

Once they've exhausted my appearance as a topic, they start in on my character. Someone knows someone else whose friend at home goes to St Dominic's. (Oddly, no one ever taxes me to my face with having been thrown out of that school.) Significant looks are exchanged. I'm the disgusting sexpot who flaunted her bust at the senior ceilidhe by turning up in a see-through blouse with a neckline down around the waist. (What exactly I was hoping to achieve by this unimaginable attire at an all-female event is not explained.) Incorrigible dirty-mindedness is my predominant trait. And so on, and so on. All accompanied by nudges and sniggers.

The only way I can deal with this is to affect an air of amused superiority, which is probably very exasperating. I don't even bother to contradict the nonsense, but serenely eat my cheese-and-tomato sandwiches while turning the pages of an Agatha Christie novel – these baiting sessions usually take place during the lunch hour. At the same time, some highly coloured storybook titles – *That Detestable New Girl*, *The Outcast of the School*, *The Troubles of Tazy* – spring into my mind. (I must be fair – it was only a small minority of Ballynahinch girls who behaved with this kind of almost statutory hostility; and once they'd tired of their new lunchtime amusement, which happened fairly quickly, they didn't expect me to make anything of it. Which I didn't. But it didn't help to create a happy impression of the school in my mind.)

My enemies' allegations have a soupçon – but only a soupçon – of authenticity. These are the facts. It's happened that, during my last Dominican year, I've been summoned one morning to the office of our scraggy headmistress, Mother Ailbe, and there taxed with having been improperly clad at the senior school ceilidhe. The charge actually does relate to a low-cut neckline and it leaves me totally perplexed, the blouse in question having been plain white cotton, and buttoned nearly up to the throat. (The nuns' obsession with keeping their charges modestly dressed seems to have persisted up until the 1970s at least, by which time the school had one or two male teachers on its staff. One of these remembers hearing a fluttery nun admonish her pupils every time he appeared in a corridor: 'Girls! Button up your blouses quick! It's that man again.')

While I stand there regarding Mother Ailbe with some bewilderment, she shouts at me that I'm the boldest girl in the school – a reprimand heard by nearly every pupil at one time or another; and then – as a grand climax – snatches a piece of black satin ribbon from the pocket of her Dominican habit and flings it at me: 'Here! Go away and tie your hair back in a decent fashion with this. If your parents can't afford to buy you a hair ribbon, you'll have to have this at the expense of the school. I'm not having you walking about the place looking like – like –' she spits out the comparison as if it is the most tremendous insult '– like a film star!' At that moment, I gain an inkling of how Mary McCarthy (as recalled in *Memories of a Catholic Girlhood*) must have felt when told, as a reprimand, that her mind is like Keats's: 'Brilliant but unsound.' Nevertheless, Mother Ailbe's crackpot insinuation rankles. I complain bitterly to my friends about all aspects of the incident.

(Scrutinising the 125th anniversary magazine of St Dominic's High School, 1870–1995, I'm amused to observe that the great majority of pupils in the class photos wear their hair tumbling about their shoulders or streaming down their backs as mine did in the past, falling simply as it grew, without artifice or restraint.

Clearly, looseness of morals and looseness of hair are no longer identical in the eyes of nuns.)

By the end of my first term at Ballynahinch I'm accepted by my peers as a more or less normal member of the Lower Sixth, with archetypal schoolgirl characteristics and foibles which enable me to settle – if insecurely – into a niche in the class. But I only make two proper friends from that year. One is the traumatised boarder alluded to above (Sheila McMahon by name). An ironical attitude to her troubles gets her through the school, with only minimal scarring. As far as appearance goes, Sheila is by far the best looking girl in the class, with thick auburn hair and an attractive face: a circumstance that appears to gain her no plaudits at all. She takes some getting to know, being something of a dissenter by nature, and not entirely open to friendly overtures, or not, at least, in that fraught setting. A common interest in detective fiction and hostility to the school environment draw us together. (We are still friends.)

The other kindred spirit I encounter in the class is the dark-haired, scholarly May McMullan from Raholp, near Down-patrick – a girl who subsequently becomes famous in the school for pointing out an error in one of our Irish language textbooks. (The whole class bursts out laughing as she performs this feat.) The minute I arrive at Ballynahinch, May tells me we've already shared a classroom – Martin Henderson's, at Coláiste Bhrighde. Since *she* never made herself conspicuous there, I don't remember her at all. It's a shock to have that fateful place brought up so quickly. May is kind enough, however, not to make any comment at all concerning my change of schools. (She and I keep up a kind of friendship over the next few years, but finally lose touch with one another. I'm pleased to note, however, that May's latest achievement is to translate the entire *Harry Potter* sequence into Irish.)

Nothing about the Assumption Convent suggests to me that I might prosper there; and I don't. As far as school work goes, I am able to hold my own, nothing more. Being wrenched from my O-Level course at St Dominic's naturally does me no good. The lessons at Ballynahinch on the whole do not interest me. No nun or lay mistress there shows much flair for teaching. Some of them go about the business in an odd way. I am not accustomed to being taught (for example) while kneeling on the floor: this is a punishment sometimes meted out to the whole class following an infinitesimal instance of misbehaviour on the part of a single pupil. There's one nun in particular whose idiosyncrasy is to fly into a paddy and take it out on a girl who sits in the row behind me, comparing her (among other things) to 'an ugly plant growing up the school wall'. This child, Rose Something-or-Other, is so intimidated as a consequence that she seems unable to speak – at least, I never hear her volunteer a single remark during the entire year. Her voice, whenever she's addressed by a teacher and forced to respond, comes out in a strangled and hesitant manner which is painful to hear.

Ballynahinch furnishes plenty of material for the obnoxious-school story, but I don't think anyone there had diabolical intentions; it was just that the whole place was awash in heavy-handedness and religiosity. My own sense of the school is biased and incomplete: I'd never have chosen to attend so backward an institution, and I stayed there for the shortest time possible. In my own view, I'm as out of place as a pony in a hen-coop. Half the girls in my class have crushes on *nuns*, for heaven's sake; one of them actually goes away to be a nun; and some years later I learn that our French mistress too has joined the Assumption Order, swopping her *Gasc's Concise Dictionary* for a missal.

It's that kind of place. Exposed for too long to its feverish Catholic imperatives, you might find your resistance to irrationalism endangered. You might swallow the whole package, prayer book, priests and precepts. St Dominic's, for all its shortcomings, offers far more scope for stimulation: not that it's any less authoritarian, but its size, and its situation in the heart of the city, mean a certain worldliness can't be excluded from its precincts. Interaction between the pupils themselves, and between certain pupils and one or two teachers, carries at least the possibility of productive disputation, an exhilarating give-and-take. Though we're miles removed from the confident heroines of the school stories we all devoured at eleven or twelve, something of that self-possessed spirit has brushed off on us; we're not, unlike the bulk of the Ballynahinch girls, all of a lumpen piece.

At Ballynahinch, one or two lighter moments occur in the classroom – as when someone is required to give the Irish word for 'stomach' (it is *bolg*), hesitates for a second and then comes out with 'bulge': a felicitous approximation. Art and English lessons here are tolerable – though the latter aren't a patch on Miss Maire Casement's at St Dominic's, Miss Casement who once nearly caused me to fall off my chair when she berated the class for something or other: 'You're all a bunch of idlers and dunderheads,' she cried; and then, after a pause, 'Except for Patricia Craig.' This has stayed in my mind since it's the only time I remember being singled out for approval rather than censure. At Ballynahinch I'm not subjected to an extreme of either. I don't make an impact on the school. I am threatened with being sent down to a lower form if my maths doesn't improve, and praised for my parrot memory (being able to recite yards of verse) and slight flair for drawing.

The year goes by. The lunchtime taunting fades away as that measly contingent in the form grows accustomed to me. I apply my wits to solving a major cause of distress: having to appear in public wearing black lisle stockings like the inmate of a bygone orphanage. It occurs to me quite early on that there's nothing to stop me leaving the house in ordinary nylons, carrying the antiquated garments in my school case and somehow wriggling into them in the upstairs back seat of the Ballynahinch bus, suspenders and all – and reversing the process on the homeward journey. It works – with some unavoidable exposure of thighs and knickers. However, to begin with, the partial dressing and undressing procedure scandalises my fellow sixth-formers on the bus, one or two of whom threaten to report me to the nuns. I tell them to go ahead. They don't actually go to these lengths, as it happens; and by the start of the spring term they're all at it – changing into and out of their black uniform stockings on the top deck of the Ballynahinch bus. I account this my prime contribution to progress at the school. (Within a couple of years Ballynahinch has discarded black stockings or tights as part of its uniform and I have taken to wearing them. So the wheels of the outmoded/avant-garde go round and round.)

The year goes by, and more and more I am conscious that a further year in this prison-house is too excruciating to contemplate. My moderate proficiency in the art class offers an escape route. I apply to, and am accepted by, the Belfast College of Art, then housed on the top floor of the massive College of Technology – a building dating from the early years of the twentieth century, which one would be sorry to see disappear from Belfast, even though it couldn't be more unfortunately placed: right bang in front of the classical façade of Inst, whose full effect is consequently undone.

The 'Tech', as it is known, in accordance with the local flair for abbreviation – the Tech, with its marble floors, its great stone staircase, and, from the topmost storey, its tremendous views out over the surviving remnants of the Georgian city, is the site of my next three years of education: a wrong decision for everyone concerned, myself and the college authorities; though it seemed at the time, and still seems in retrospect, a tremendously enjoyable interlude. I'm no longer reluctant to get out of bed in the mornings, nor do I have to grit my teeth before stepping on the bus which transports me down the Donegall Road, past the quaint Carnegie library near the railway line where all those delectable adventure stories were borrowed by me from the age of six on, along Great Victoria Street, which still contains the Great Northern Railway terminus, to alight near the famous landmark statue known as the Black Man.

It's a heartening short journey in all weathers: louring overcast mornings with the rain sweeping down in sheets from Divis Mountain, alluring sybaritic sunshine, the nip and chill of autumn. Best of all is the rare thick snowfall working its mysterious transformations – the closest ordinary weather can come to a storybook ambience, a setting rife with possibilities. Look sideways through a mass of swirling snowflakes, and you can nearly see the Little Match Girl bravely holding up a tiny flickering flame; or the jolly boys of Greyfriars, in scarves and overcoats, tramping through the wintry countryside towards some occasion of seasonal chicanery to which they will put a stop. You can think yourself back to an imaginary New England Christmas in Civil War days, in particularly glistening and festive form.

But I'm getting too far away from the Black Man and its surroundings. The original occupier of the pedestal was the young Earl of Belfast (dead at twenty-five), cast in bronze but then for some reason painted black; this statue, the first in Belfast, was on its plinth by 1855, but twenty-odd years later it came down to make way for an effigy of the Revd Dr Henry Cooke, 'the framer of sectarianism in the politics of Ulster', as one unimpressed commentator put it. Cooke, every bit as black as he's painted, still stands on the spot, appropriately positioned with his back turned to Inst and all its liberal traditions – and later to the even more permissive Art College – for ever gazing down Wellington Place in Presbyterian disdain for the unconverted. (Actually, though it's still known as the Black Man, Cooke's statue is plainly green, the green of verdigris.)

For some of us, he might stand as a reminder of the pass to which we're brought, partly as a consequence of the theological certainties he embodied: one version of them anyway. Antipopery or Ultramontanism, you can take your pick. Cooke's elevated position is appropriate in another sense. From boyhood, it seems – if we're to credit a story told by his biographer – he was accustomed to raising himself (quite literally) above the ruck. Having mastered the stunt of walking on stilts, he would sometimes frighten the life out of the Georgian (George IV, that is) matrons of Maghera by striding, apparently on air, past their upper windows. Well, it was a suitable exercise in thaumaturgy for a future roaring divine.

When I became an art student in 1960, the area around the Black Man was still dominated by Georgian terraces – not yet replaced by stretches of waste ground and brutal featureless constructions: old tall houses allowed to get damp and rickety, but nevertheless redolent of a defunct grandeur which is very piquant. The Kensington Hotel, or its successor, is still there in College Square East; and underneath it, on the ground floor, or in the same block, is a café (I seem to remember) where we take our morning coffee and discuss the dramas of the day. Further along, towards the GNR, is the house once inhabited by Robert MacAdam and his brother James; but my awareness, at the time, of the history of Irish-speaking in Belfast doesn't extend to its Presbyterian initiators (in particular MacAdam, a counterpart of Cooke, if you like – though Cooke himself, it has to be said, understood the odd phrase in Irish and wasn't opposed to the acquisition of the language among his co-religionists, if only for proselytising purposes. Right down to the present time, the Presbyterian Church in Ireland can count Irish-speakers among its ministers – just to confound all those for whom sectarianism signifies a monolithic consistency, and to act as a warning to all of us about making sectarian assumptions).

That July, between school and art school, I'm back among the gorse and turf-fumes of Donegal, in a different Gaeltacht, Loughanure instead of Rannafast (*Loch-an-Iubhair*, the Lake of the Yew Tree), with different companions and different social expectations, Rannafast – for the moment – having deactivated my urge to misbehave. This is a more sedate sojourn than the previous year's. No one comes knocking on our bedroom windows at midnight; no full-blown infatuations suggest to us the possibility of Catholic morals going by the board. Boisterousness and hilarity are kept to a minimum. True, we make friends with one or two of the boys-from-the-place and join them for the odd walk across heathery fields, but this is a very low-key affair, these are nondescript characters in comparison with the tearaways of Rannafast.

This is as it should be. Part of my purpose in being here is to demonstrate (to myself as well as others) that the Donegal

Gaeltacht is not out of bounds as far as I am concerned, whatever restrictions may prevail for the pupils of St Dominic's High School. I'm divesting the Gaeltacht of its damaging associations. And Loughanure, untouched by scandal or mystique, is attuned to this anodyne imperative. Later, there'd be other cut-off Gaeltachts in which to enact a quintessential Irishness and embrace the holiday spirit to the full – all the way down the west coast from Teelin to the Dingle Peninsula, places in which I'd come up against the all but impenetrable Gaelic of provinces other than Ulster.

And Rannafast itself would be revisited in due course, and not only in the summer; there'd be frozen landscapes to revel in, happed-up excursions into the countryside with frost imposing a wintry frivolity on the austere townlands, moments of despair and fatigue on the Cloughaneelly road with an Arctic wind whipping hailstones into our faces as we totter along with suitcases trying to thumb a lift. Once, picked up in such circumstances by a kind-hearted couple, I'm surprised to be singled out as the chief object of commiseration: '*Níl mórán aoise aicise,*' they exclaim: 'She's not very old,' meaning, 'Dear, dear, what is she doing out in this weather in the middle of nowhere when she should be at home tucked up in bed.' To which I can only retort, 'Oh – but – *tá fiche bliain agam.*' ('I'm twenty.')

I am twenty, and only a few months away from completing my Tech course (graphic design/illustration). I'll be sorry to leave the predominantly zestful place: which, looking back on it, strikes me as constituting a kind of halfway house between the past and the future – my future, with all its troughs and fillips undreamt of by the nuns of St Dominic's (though the one who predicted a future for me as a pavement artist, and *never* a nun, perhaps wasn't too wide of the mark). The Tech embodies all the tentativeness, along with the 'charmed circle' aspect, of provincial student life. It is rooted in its locality in ways I don't fully appreciate at the time. I'm not terribly familiar with its traditions, or indeed with the tradition of art in Belfast – though I've often been, with pleasure, to the Ulster Museum on the Stranmillis Road, where I've graduated from admiring Rosamund Praeger's chubby sculptures of infants and elves to an appreciation of the jaunty street scenes of William Conor and the allegorical romanticism of John Luke. I have a lot to learn ...

I'm not aware, for example, of the Art College's early connection with Inst, going back to 1849, when it opened in the North Wing of the famous Belfast boys' school. It had a short existence there, in fact, since inadequate funding led to its closure in 1854. Then it reappeared in 1870 in the same place as a Government School of Art. Thirty-odd years later, it was shifted into temporary accommodation in Lower North Street, while the monumental College of Technology, its ultimate destination, was rising up in solid Portland stone to obliterate the harmonious aspect of Sir John Soane's Inst ... And there it stayed, on the top floor of the Tech, with its thirty mellow workrooms, for nearly sixty years, before its next removal to bleak new quarters – newly built – in York Street, where it still is.

I'm thankful to have been among the last intake of Tech art students, with the whole top floor and its build-up of a uniquely creative atmosphere to relish. The importance of accretion in establishing a sense of purpose and integrity cannot be overstated. And even if, in our ignorance, we were hardly aware of so much as the names of former prominent students, we might have grasped at some level that the place was alive with the aura of these students and others who'd bequeathed to it something of their own dynamic approach to things.

For myself – despite my general lack of knowledge at seventeen or eighteen, I do have a strong awareness of the art school as an inestimable agency of enlightenment. It stands four-square as a countervailing force to the philistinism and puritanism of the North. For me, as a place of learning, it's enriching and bewitching – well, it could hardly be otherwise, after the withering atmosphere of Ballynahinch. It's as if I've been let out into the clear air after long confinement in a coal cellar ... I'm still on the edge, though, observing rather than participating. It will take the even more exorbitant excitements of 1960s London to get me fully into line with the more advanced *mores* of the day.

There's a lot to take in all at once, it seems to me: easels and paint-stained overalls, an aroma of clay and linseed oil, life-drawing from naked male models (well, almost naked), eccentric pipe-smoking lecturers wearing tweed jackets (including the wonderfully named Romeo Toogood), the enormous inspired canvases of top-notch students, incredibly glamorous and knowing third-years thronging the corridors between classes. The last, I feel, are as far beyond me in matters of *style* as I considered myself to be beyond the frumps of Ballynahinch. But I'm not above picking up a tip or two – for instance, plaiting a few strands of hair at each side of my face while the rest hangs loose; or wearing a pendant on a black velvet ribbon round my neck. And I'm beginning to be aware of the affirmative possibilities of opaque black stockings, under the influence of a new friend who wore them with a certain panache, long before it was fashionable, or even acceptable, to do so.

This friend, Eunice McClelland, is actually a one-time classmate from St Dominic's; on our first morning at the Tech, diffident newcomers, we latch on to one another with a surge of relief at spotting a familiar face amid a sea of unknowns, unknowns, moreover, with names like D'Arcy, Gregory and Cooper-Chadwick, which are clearly Protestant, and toffee-nosed Protestant at that. But that same morning we join forces with another new arrival, a confident ex-pupil of Belfast Royal Academy, and drop any tribal biases we might be harbouring. This is the place for disembarrassing yourself of sectarian pre-suppositions. Art-school friendships are not formed along religious lines, and this is a revelation to me. Not that Protestants, indeed, were ever an alien species as far as I was concerned, with half my first cousins, not to mention grandparents, uncles and aunts, being fully subscribing members of the Church of Ireland. But in the segregated circumstances of our upbringing, it was hard to have much sustained contact with the other lot (though some of us managed a little). They inhabited a parallel universe, with schools, churches and social activities all their own. It's only at art school that an inspiriting integration becomes a normal mode of existence.

Our tripartite alliance, formed on our first day as art students, lasts until the following summer, when one of us leaves to go in for nursing and another is held back to repeat her first year, while I – who shouldn't – progress more or less smoothly through the course (and then compound the career error by embarking on a further three-year course at the Central School in London: all of which leaves me well, or at least extensively, trained in a subject which has no relevance to my subsequent professional life. But that's another story.). My principal friend at the time, however, is still the redhead from Derby Street on the Falls Road, Maire Maguire, a fellow Irish-speaker and Gaeltacht enthusiast, who has left St Dominic's without completing her A level course and taken a job in a bookshop called Ambrose Serridge in Castle Street. This is not far from the Tech and during a lot of my free time I rush around there to fill her in on the latest item of art school gossip and the current state of my own – generally multiple – infatuations.

The immediate psychological effect of my expulsion from school was to reinforce an acceptance of Catholic morality. I am out to demonstrate to the fullest extent how mistaken the nuns of St Dominic's were to convict me of unchastity. I go about grimly subscribing to the sixth and ninth commandments of the Catholic Church. I might, indeed, have taken a contrary position, deciding to have the libidinous game as well as the name; but, as yet, all those tremendous pressures, social, moral and nationalistic, are firmly keeping my libido in order, in common with most other people's. As for the name (*Ainm gan tábhacht*, the name without the substance) – that was harder to discard than I'd realised. As recently as 1998 I was assured by a male Belfast contemporary that the real reason behind my ejection from St Dominic's had to do with the prominence of my chest; and he added that the same chest had been something of an icon of local masturbators – a fact that may amuse me *now*, though I'd have been truly appalled at the time.

Decent Catholic Ireland. I cannot be certain how far my upholding of this concept was taken seriously at the Assumption Convent, since the place already abounded in those who were, by nature, rather more sympathetic to it. (One girl was said to have taken a saw to the heels of her shoes, in order not to be thought a prey to vanity or worldliness.) Much of my idle talk between lessons has to do with boys, the Saturday night student hop at Queen's University and the spiritual dangers divertingly evaded there, or embraced only partially.

(Spiritual danger is a real bugbear for the Catholic clergy, far more than physical danger of any kind. It's not that long since the Bishop of Derry, a Dr Farren, worried himself sick about teenagers frequenting irreligious dance halls where the standard of purity would fall far short of the Catholic ideal. He's quoted in an *Irish Times* of 1951 posing a rhetorical question: could young people be expected to emerge from such halls 'as good as they went into them'? His answer is a resounding no, but I don't really think attendance at inter-denominational dances made much difference to anyone's morals. Most people's morals – in the Catholic sense – are either inflexibly in place by this stage in their lives, or potentially so corruptible that the point of recusancy will be reached sooner or later, even if they sit at home and embroider cushions. But it's true that those who venture beyond their parish halls get the name of bad Catholics.)

Contemplating the priggish element in the school drives me to scorn and bemusement, even though I believe my grasp on morality to be as tenacious as anyone's. Half the Ballynahinch pupils look and act like convent-fodder: negators and renouncers to a man (or a girl). They, for their part, are disgusted by me and my quasi-erotic antics, which include fending off the advances of an Indian in a turban – very exotic for Belfast – and not coming to grief after accepting a lift from five strange boys in a car. (An extravagant imprudence, on the 'fool's luck' principle, sees me through.)

When I get to art school it's a different matter. Acting the prude here, against the ethos of the place, provokes exasperation in a good many of my fellow students and earns me a dismally strait-laced reputation (strange that I remember going through the whole course in a kind of stupor of eroticism). I have to be good, since I've elected myself a representative of Irish-Ireland with its lofty cultural and moral tone. To bolster up this attitude I have before me at art school the spectacle of a fellow Catholic gone to the bad: a thin, blonde, good-natured giggly girl from a broken home who's forever broadcasting her totally undiscriminating sexual exploits: she doesn't, it seems, draw the line at *anyone*. Well! I should loathe to get myself similarly disrespected.

What I don't quite grasp, because it's far more subtle, is the degree of sexual sophistication prevailing here – an opposing force to the constituents of the decent Catholic, or for that matter Protestant, North. And I am more susceptible to the effects of this force than I understand at the time. Looking back, I don't present an alluring image to myself as a first, second, even third-year art student: virginal, teetotal and unadventurously dressed. I see myself at student parties, an incongruous presence in a twinset amid a lot of Juliette Greco look-alikes, while girls with harshly melodious voices sing non-Gaelic songs containing lines like, 'Cocaine, cocaine, all around my brain.'

But the basis for these and other dismal traits is getting increasingly shaky, as a prelude to being overtoppled altogether.

PART THREE
Tuilleadh Salachair

PC wearing a dress from Maggie Moore's

raised in a northern land of rain and murk ...

DEREK MAHON, 'Death and the Sun'

I was still twenty when I went to live in London, in September 1963, moving further away from a charmed childhood and a world of indigenous preoccupations and steady objectives. It went to my head a little. One of the ways in which the frivolous side of my nature came out was in an enhanced obsession with clothes. If Belfast bred an abhorrence of conspicuousness or eccentricity – hence the woolly jumpers and pleated skirts of my adolescence – London embraced and upheld non-conformity in the matter of self-presentation. It was enormously stimulating. First there were wonderful, newfangled shops such as Mary Quant and Biba, with an atmosphere which cancelled the old idea of buying for practicality. And then came the antique clothing boom which made me an instantaneous devotee of Victorian striped petticoats and 1930s chiffons and voiles. I wore tailored costumes from before the First World War, and skimpy 1940s patterned crepe dresses with puff sleeves. The Portobello Road became my stamping ground. I skittered about like the madcap shopper in Elizabeth Bowen's essay on dress, 'relentlessly driven ... by the exactions of her particular whim'. With my soon-developed, finely honed instinct for 'Utility' survivals or knickers purported to come from Queen Victoria, I was able – wherever I was – to make a beeline for the nearest supply of intoxicating cast-offs.

167

Back home in Belfast, for example, my connoisseur's nose took me straight to Sandy Row and a two-roomed, stone-floored huckster's shop, presided over by a garrulous old body in a blue nylon overall. This was the well-known Maggie Moore's, an old clothes shop and one-time exclusive resort of tramps and washerwomen. It was long a byword in Belfast for rock-bottom shabbiness or demented finery. 'Did you see what she had on? She must have got it in Maggie Moore's!' Thus the respectably clad, in gleefully derisive mode. Maggie Moore's: if its fame was great, it was not good. Locals dubbed it a flea circus, according to Robert Harbinson in *No Surrender*, his lively account of growing up in a street off Sandy Row in the 1930s. He renames the shop Aggie Moore's, possibly to avoid litigation – though who was likely to take him up on his description of the place, I can't imagine.

By the time I discovered it, the original owner with her crystal ball and addiction to red biddy was long gone. Her successor was a relative, a niece I think, who'd inherited the whole terrible package of rotting and frowzy discards of the pre-war era. Some of these garments had clearly been hanging in the same spot under a skylight in the back room for fifty years. Many were unsalvageable, crumbling to dust if you laid a finger on them. But others – ah! others, like Briar Rose surrounded by the dust and cobwebbed accumulation of ages, might emerge intact from their mouldy cocoon. Wonderful, unmarked pure silk antique dresses, exotic chiffons, smart 1940s suits with padded shoulders, even, on one occasion, a dusty blue bouclé wool coat that shouted Schiaparelli. It wasn't authentic of course, but even an imitation Schiaparelli was sufficient reward for braving the filth of ages and the utter bemusement of the proprietor who might have been seen making faces at a crony behind my back, while touching a finger to her head.

Doolally I was not; I knew exactly what I was looking for, and I knew I might find it here, and at an affordable price. But I had to grit my teeth, hold my nose and enter the premises as cautiously as the Revd O'Hanlon setting foot in some shocking habitation in 1850s Millfield. If I was lucky, and some new treasure had been added to the stock of old clothes since my last visit, or if something in the back room had miraculously resisted decay, I had to bear it off at arm's length to the nearest dry cleaner's, and expose myself to further Belfast ridicule while trying to save face by muttering something unconvincing about a theatrical production. Actually, the theatrical production was myself, as I went about looking like a London working girl of the 1890s, a British Far Eastern wartime refugee in my 'Tenko' dresses, or a Connemara fisherman's wife from the era of J.M. Synge. It all added to the gaiety of life.

After a downbeat girlhood as far as daily wear was concerned, I suppose it was natural enough that a reaction should set in; and it was just luck that it coincided with an exhilarating upgrading of the second-hand tradition in clothes buying. Of course, there was second-hand, with its drab and poverty-stricken associations, and then there was vintage; but no frequenter of Maggie Moore's, I am sure, would have known the difference. In London, I was precipitated into the middle of a costume extravaganza, and whatever of its impetus I assimilated, I carried with me back to sober-suited Belfast. It was as if the opposite of a Pandora's Box, a treasure chest filled with limitless possibilities, had got itself opened and imbued the city streets with a carnival colouring.

Of course, survivals from the past in every area – reading, architecture, interior decoration, mugs and jugs and what-have-you, had always answered to some requirement of my nature, and it wasn't surprising that clothes should be added to the list. I had long been an addict of evocation. But, at the same time, my allegiance to the vogue for piquant pyjamas and Tess-of-the-d'Urbervilles sun bonnets no doubt had about it an element of a belated riposte to the antediluvian death's-heads in charge of my schooling. These, nuns and priests and all, believed the closer a young girl's clothing approximated to a straitjacket, the better.

Well, they were people who'd been nurtured themselves in the cult of the hair shirt and the fetter-like wimple. If they couldn't get us into actual straitjackets, the next best thing was to clamp down on any out-of-school style-consciousness that

came to their notice. Anyone suspected of an interest in adorn-
ment would have to endure an onslaught of sarcasm … Did she
really think, with her desperate looks, that a spot of lipstick or a
frilly blouse would cause anyone in their senses to give her a
second glance? If this was so – then more fool she. Better to
accept, with due humility, the face and figure God had lumbered
her with. Or words to that effect. For the rest of the class, the
nun's tirade would have us squirming in our seats in embarrassment and sympathy for the latest victim of sledge-hammer
castigation. The nun, of course, would have thought she was
doing her duty, nothing more. Nuns in those days were adamant
in adhering to guidelines laid down by Irish church fathers a long
time ago, church fathers whose lives in some crazy instances
were governed by an immense devotion to the concept of purity
in dress.

It is, indeed, both amusing and amazing to consider those
pronouncements which issued, in the early part of the twentieth
century, from the mouths of especially zealous priests such as
Father James Cullen S.J. (This specimen of barmy purity has
come into my hands via a dusty old book recovered from an
attic.) Father Cullen's biographer, a fellow cleric, laments at one
point in his narrative: 'In his efforts to start a Campaign for
Modesty in Dress, he did not achieve much success.' Father
Cullen, it seems, spent a lot of his time looking askance at contemporary fashion, or pagan apparel, as he dubbed it; what really
got his goat was the spectacle of Irish women having the gall to
approach the altar for Holy Communion wearing all kinds of
'repulsive attire'. Since he died in 1921, the year of the founding
of the Legion of Mary, it's hard to envisage exactly what caused
him so much agitation: hobble skirts? Tea-rose tea gowns? Arts
and Crafts dresses of the type worn by Lily and Lolly Yeats at the
Cuala Press? Land girls' breeches imported from England? The
sight of ankles? Whatever it was that got his dander up, you
might have thought – with the country in an uproar, as the Land
War was followed by illicit drilling of Volunteers in the North
and the South – you might have thought he'd have better things
to do than interfere with people's freedom to dress as they

pleased. But no. It gets worse. What's likely to instil the greatest alarm in present-day readers of Father Cullen's life story is his strictures on the practice of putting insufficient clothing on *little girls* (his italics): the short skirts and bare legs of little – and worse, big – girls are an abomination to him.

The *Irish Messenger of the Sacred Heart*, founded by Father Cullen himself back in 1888 along with other periodicals such as the *Irish Catholic*, kept the subject well to the fore in devout readers' minds as the flighty 1920s, with their plentiful temptations for the clothes-conscious, got under way. The onus was on true Irishwomen 'to stem the tide of immoral fashions'. Failure to go about buttoned up to the chin was tantamount to proclaiming an indifference to Irishness – at any rate, in the eyes of priests and nuns and their followers. It was, indeed, a fairly futile proscription: these people were up against an instinct more fundamental than erotophobia, the instinct to achieve an appearance as pleasing as possible.

But the fear of fashion and its implications for immorality: this force, by dint of incessant trumpeting, *did* work an effect on Irish social life of the mid-twentieth century. Its more egregious out-lets are pretty well documented. Frank O'Connor, in his travel book of 1947, *Irish Miles*, is rendered speechless by the tendency of Catholic activists to go about pasting strips of brown paper over images of women's chests on advertisement hoardings in cities and towns. And then you got odd members of the laity appointing themselves a scourge of the bedizened. Women and girls in the streets of Dublin, according to Austin Clarke in his autobiography *A Penny in the Clouds*, used to take to their heels – their high heels – in droves, at the approach of an eccentric person named Philip Francis Little, whose mission it was to denounce in a loud voice any shortcomings he spotted with regard to neck- or hemlines.

There's a priest in Brian Moore's novel *Fergus*, a master at St Michan's College in Belfast (a fictionalised St Malachy's), who, the rumour goes, marches off every now and then to the school dentist's office bearing a pair of scissors to excise certain advertisements from magazines distributed about the waiting room. It's to spare the boys exposure to corsets and brassieres, or anything else likely to have an inflaming effect. (Things have changed. On a recent – 1998 – visit to St Malachy's, I was amused to spot in the reception area an *Ulster Tatler* with a picture of 'Christmas Lingerie' all over the cover.)

The scissors as an emblem of expurgators crops up again in a real-life anecdote about Brian Moore. When his first novel, *Judith Hearne*, was published in 1955, his mother in Belfast sent a copy of the book to her youngest daughter, Eilis, a nun in a convent in England. But first she took a pair of scissors and went through the book cutting out anything overtly sexual or blasphemous, leaving Eilis – Sister Anne – with a severely mutilated text. Like the mother of the Leeds poet Tony Harrison, Mrs Moore must have had the thought go sorrowfully through her head, 'You weren't brought up to write such mucky books.'

It was a different world. Of course it's unfair to apply the standards of the present to the ills of the past; change is a built-in factor of the human condition, and attitudes taken for granted at one moment are apt to be strongly repudiated the next. We are *all* enlightened now – or so it seems, until the next exposure of current misbeliefs comes into being. However, the Ireland of the mid-twentieth century, de Valera's Ireland, presents such an extreme case of backwardness that it seems fair game. At the height of its churchly monomania, it was out of kilter with the rest of the world, especially the post-war world. Where else but in Ireland would you find an edict going out from an archbishop ordering members of a Girl Pipers Band to lengthen the hems of their kilts, lest the sight of knees marching smartly in unison should induce affront, or arousal, in spectators in the streets?

Poking their noses into girls' bare legs is only a sample of the ways in which the Archbishop of Dublin, Father Cullen and their ilk assert an unassailable power over their congregations. There is more to their scope for outrage than the cut of their flocks' frocks. No aspect of life goes unregulated by them. 'In Ireland,' notes the American Paul Blanchard, in his 1953 account of the conflict between Catholic policy and modern democracy, *The Irish and Catholic Power* – 'In Ireland ... courtship is the business of the Irish priest, and petting is the business of the Irish priest, and even the etiquette of the marriage bed is the business of the Irish priest' – along with birth control, mixed marriage, illegitimacy, sodomy, masturbation, divorce, separation, sex education, the kind of sanitary protection permitted to women, and 'keeping company'.

Well! To get the population into a tractable state with regard to all this it's necessary to catch them early – and indeed, the guideline for teachers is set out unambiguously. Their aim should be to foster in every pupil 'a true Catholic outlook on human life as planned by God'. Dissenters from full-blown religiosity need not apply. As the case of the novelist John McGahern illustrates, Church control over the employment of teachers extended until well into the 1960s. In the mid-century, fearsome Catholic groups came into being to sabotage 'Protestant' or liberal influences in the professions. In 1944, the edict placing Trinity College out of bounds for Catholic students was reinforced by Archbishop McQuaid in his Lenten Regulations. Catholics were segregated at University College Dublin, where their doings could be monitored by the archbishop and his henchmen. All this was vastly over the top. No one can reasonably disagree with Paul Blanchard when he deplores the Church's 'tendency ... to represent all modern, non-Catholic progress as decadence'.

Blanchard finds himself at a loss to explain the docility of Irish people in the face of all this priestly coercion and interference in their daily lives. It's not a new perception. Around the turn of the twentieth century, you get George Moore attributing the malaise of western Ireland to the strong-arm tactics of fanatical priests – priests whose moral development is often in excess of their intellects. And for a rational commentator like Michael J. McCarthy (author of *Priests and People in Ireland*, 1902), acceptance of the Church's 'perplexing and interfering with our adult population in every sphere of secular affairs' is a cause of surprised dismay.

Why was it that scant attention was paid to these voices of reason, while the ludicrous pronouncements of bishops and archbishops were swallowed without a qualm? To even begin to answer that question, you'd need to take historical circumstances, ideas of national identity and other large matters into consideration. For certain critics of Catholic submissiveness, though, it was pretty simple: the people had had the spirit bludgeoned out of them by a barrage of spirituality. Or at least, they'd allowed themselves to be deprived of some vital impulse: as Blanchard has it, 'the total sexual expression of the Irish people is much less than it is in other countries ... The Catholic crusade against normal sexual life has actually created a nation of men and women who try to drown their fundamental instincts.' It's wrong, he says, to blame the moist damp climate for eroding Irish ardour, as some have tried to do. Rain is not the primary constraining factor here.

Elizabeth Bowen puts her finger on something fundamental about Irish writing before the 1950s, when she alludes to its sexlessness: by implication, the point she is making about Sheridan le Fanu's *Uncle Silas* – that 'no force from any one of the main characters runs into the channel of sexual feeling' – this point may be extended to apply to the whole genre of Irish writing, traditional Irish writing. In its pages, the sexual act is simply edited out altogether (the more usual course), or presented as a feat, as in one of Benedict Kiely's stories when he has someone applaud a pair of lovers in a field who ruin a half acre of turnips in their enthusiasm.

Though it wasn't peculiar to Ireland, of course, censorship operated here a long time before it was officially imposed. In a book which sets out, as far as possible, to defend the Catholic Church and its achievements (*Goodbye to Catholic Ireland*, 1997), Mary Kenny mentions George Orwell's singling out of 1917 as the year in which literature took an unbridled turn. Before that date (she agrees) 'mainstream literature maintained a certain decorum. It did not describe sexual acts in detail, and it seldom challenged established religion or morality.' This is true as far as it goes. However – there's a difference between those *English* classics of the nineteenth century, in which an erotic dimension is palpable, if subterranean, and equivalent Irish works, in which the point made by Elizabeth Bowen (above) is amply borne out.

There are, of course, many reasons why the Irish novel, for all its liveliness, failed to reach a level of sophistication displayed by its counterparts elsewhere – not least, the abandonment of the native language, allied to poverty and instability. But an endemic prudery seems to have marked it from the start, a prudery that escalated as the Ireland of Cardinal Cullen (another Cullen) gained its defining – Catholic – characteristics. (Paul Cullen, 1803–78, one-time rector of the Irish College in Rome, set out to impose a definite – a Roman – shape over Irish church affairs, thereby opening the way for the eventual constitutional alignment of church and state, as well as fostering illiberalism in every area: inter-denominational relations, policies of education, sexual morality and what-have-you.)

The Gaelic League, though its aims were different, was at one with the Catholic Church in putting up a stiff resistance to any moral contagion speading in from England. In fact the Church took over the League's stern views about the worthlessness and vulgarity of English commercial culture. It's rather ironic, then, to find a priest in Portarlington (in 1905) getting into his pulpit to rant against the Gaelic League's Irish language classes for mixed students (i.e. male and female). Such classes, he claimed, 'were not conducive to the good morals of his flock' (quoted by Mary Kenny). It was feared – and indeed the same fear persisted right down to our day – that enthusiasm for the language among the young was only a pretext for try-out dissipation. I'm not suggesting that this fear was ill-founded – only that a disproportionate importance was attached to it.

There were good reasons why the Gaelic League came into being when it did (in 1893). By the end of the Victorian era, a demoralised populace was badly in need of something to reinforce the sense of national worth and distinctiveness. Misgovernment, famine, emigration, poverty, land wars, evictions … every imaginable abuse had been inflicted on the Irish, and to cap it all they were fed up with being portrayed, in the pages of *Punch* and elsewhere, as assassins or buffoons. The Gaelic League, and subsequent Irish-Ireland movement, offered a means of retrieving dignity and cultural respectability. 'Not only Gaelic, but free as well; not only free, but Gaelic as well': this dictum became its watchword – a stance, as many social historians have pointed out, underpinning 1916 and its aftermath. The thing was to cry up every particular in which Irishness differed from Englishness – and religion, and by extension a specific type of spiritual soundness, loomed large here, and got itself grafted on to the language movement (notwithstanding the Protestantism of the Gaelic League's founder, Douglas Hyde, along with a good many of its adherents).

The whole field of Irish-Irishness is fraught with anomalies and complications. Everyone is familiar (to cite a famous example) with the *Playboy* riots of 1907, which saw *Gaeilgeoirí* up in arms over the supposed aspersion cast by Synge on the morals of Mayo women. 'It's Pegeen I'm seeking only,' Christy Mahon declares at one moment in the play, 'and what'd I care if you brought me a drift of chosen females, standing in their shifts itself, maybe, from this place to the Eastern world?' 'Shifts' was the last straw; perhaps this is the only occasion when Irish belligerence erupted over an issue concerning bodice and soul. Gaelic League members who took part in the protest did so, presumably, in ignorance of the fact that the national language had produced a literature in which references to this particular item of underclothing weren't unknown; as an example, we have the folk song, 'Eadar Caiseal agus ÚrChoill' (Between Cashel and the Greenwood) in which a girl rejected by one man announces that there are plenty of others who would be happy to take her in her shift (*léine*) if that was all she had. Synge, understandably annoyed by the whole furore – 'Did you hear that we had to have fifty-seven peelers in to keep the stage from being rushed, and that for four nights not a word could be heard for booing?' – got off to his friend Stephen McKenna an entertaining account of Lady Gregory's first action in the crisis. She went backstage to consult the Abbey Theatre charwoman about whether or not a breach of decorum had been committed. The verdict was that 'chemise' was the only acceptable word for the garment.

The outcry provoked by Synge's plays was modulated gradually until it had turned into an ovation; by 1910 the Gaelic League, or one of its representatives, had proclaimed a reversal of opinion in a magazine article which included the work of Synge, along with the *Táin Bó Cuailgne* (*Cattle Raid of Cooley*) and the anonymous ballad, 'Slán le Pádraig Sairséal' ('Farewell to Patrick Sarsfield'), among the glories of the Gaelic tradition. The recantation came too late to gratify the playwright, who'd been dead for a year. It's also, you might argue, an assessment scarcely more judicious than the earlier nationalist denunciations. There are those who believe that Synge's literary impulse was satiric, reading into his creation of Christy Mahon, for example, an intention to deflate the heroic Cuchulain figure of Irish romance. This is a plausible and illuminating speculation. What's certain, though, is that Synge's own writings provide for the satirist or parodist a target even more conspicuous than anything contained in the Irish sagas. Here is Flann O'Brien: 'I have personally met in the streets of Ireland persons who are clearly out of Synge's plays. They talk and dress like that, and damn the drink they'll swally but the mug of porter in the long nights after Samhain.'

The sagas and other Irish writings were not at all mealy-mouthed, but it's true that translators of Gaelic material, from Charlotte Brooke on, had tended to tamper with any robustness of expression they found therein. It wasn't until the middle of the twentieth century that a few – a very few – collectors had the gumption to take down the bawdier portions of songs and recitations along with the rest. Pádraigín Ní Uallacháin, in her monumental study of the song tradition of South Armagh (taking in parts of Louth and Monaghan), *A Hidden Ulster* (2003), mentions her father Pádraig Ó hUallacháin's familiarity with the Rabelaisian aspect of Rannafast culture which quietly flourished alongside more seemly features. Some previously censored lines were retrieved by him and passed on to his daughters, including those in which you get a sexual braggart alluding unabashedly to his *seanbhríste mór*, his 'big old trousers', and the maidens' delight they're concealing. Among the friends and acquaintances of Ó hUallacháin, his daughter tells us, were many of the older women singers of Rannafast between the 1920s and '40s, and he used to take great pleasure in the hearty laughter they broke into during the singing of such risqué songs. Pádraig Ó hUallacháin, incidentally, was the *rúnaí* – secretary – of Coláiste Bhríghde in Rannafast between 1937 and 1947, a role filled in our day by a George McAdam who was present during the diatribe delivered to us caught-out debauchees on the last night of our Rannafast stay.

This is not the place to go into the vicissitudes of the Irish language – but, in brief, it was all but obliterated as a living tongue before Douglas Hyde's call for 'de-anglicisation', in 1892, brought about a measure of resuscitation. Throughout the nineteenth century, at least in the more accessible parts of the country, the language had been mainly in the keeping of scholars and antiquaries like Robert MacAdam (see above): safe enough, as far as it went, but not exactly alive and burgeoning. And most of the fragments of Gaelic literature that reached the public (in translation) had already been through the hands of bowdlerisers. (Breandan Breathnach, in his authoritative 1989 study of Irish music and dancing, *Ceol agus Rince na hÉireann*, mentions George Petrie's reaction to certain words and phrases in Gaelic manuscripts which struck him unpleasantly. 'Of such a nature as will not allow even a specimen of it to be translated,' was his outraged attitude.)

This bowdlerising had something to do with the sedateness of the age – but more, I think, with a wish to present antique Gaelic culture as unimpeachable in every respect. Whatever required prettifying or purifying was heartily attended to. No one was going to get the chance to say that those old Gaels, Fionn, Oisin, Goll Mac Morna and the rest of them, were a lecherous lot. And the more Gaeldom and Catholicism converged, the more it seemed that people should be kept well away from any circumstance or conjecture at odds with the Church, for all the world like a crowd of unruly infants denied access to a dangerous play area. Irish grown-ups – i.e. the church fathers – reserved to themselves the right to make judgements about what was, or was not, suitable fodder for their dependants. So it was inevitable that censorship should become an expedient of the Free State government, after the State came into being in 1923 and entered into an unspoken competition with its counterpart in the North to produce a society as rebarbative as possible. If you'd wanted to award the palm for bigotry, it would have been hard to decide which of the two – North or South – to fix it on.

Those of us enrolled at Catholic primary and secondary schools in the North in the 1950s were at the mercy of educators who'd inherited the Church's whole package of pietistic hogwash. What was clear to Michael F.J. McCarthy in 1902 – that 'we have allowed the education of our children to become a branch of theological administration' – still held true over half a century later. Most Six-Counties Catholics felt themselves to be adrift, politically; but as far as religion was concerned, the same structures and devices operated throughout the whole of Ireland. As for the liberal ethic – it is difficult to judge whether we in the North were in a worse position, with a clashing form of bigotry constantly before us to reinforce our own; or whether the proximity of a different system of values and beliefs actually worked, willy-nilly, to lighten the moral air. Ghettoes or religious enclaves certainly existed, but it was impossible to ensure that segregation would be total. Some of us had non-Catholic friends, despite the Church's – or the churches' – disapproval.

The Church's – or the churches' – disapproval. Given such an attitude, any movement towards integration was suspect. Integration equalled adulteration, or at least dilution: dilution of faith and morals which could only be safeguarded in a (selectively) devotional atmosphere. So we underwent our separate forms of spoon-feeding. Of course, while our education was in progress, we were hardly aware of its larger implications: we just enjoyed, or chafed at, appropriate parts of it. We were fortunate, getting a kick out of companionship and juvenile intrigues, doing our best to re-enact the experiences of our favourite story-book characters, mystery girls brought up by gypsies, *School Friend* crusaders against colourful breaches of justice. We had summer meadows to lie around in in our white cotton blouses, chewing blades of grass and gossiping; and the thrill of fog-bound classrooms with the lights full on at midday and the prospect of having to grope our way home.

Our school is strict, but in the battles between pupils and nuns we sometimes come out on top, evade punishment, 'get away' with things. And strictness is relative, anyway. I hear tales of children at Catholic schools being made to crawl on bare knees along gravel paths, having mutton or semolina pudding – whatever nauseates them – forced down their throats, of getting their hair whacked off. 'Charitable institution' tales, like those concerning the now infamous Magdalen Homes, those supposed refuges which embody the dark satanic side of Irish provincial Catholicism. To undergo a normal convent education, even at a school such as Ballynahinch – this was, by comparison, a bracing and congenial business, especially if you enjoyed being one of a crowd, immersed yourself in school activities and avoided a reputation for misbehaviour, as some found easy to do. Some pupils took so enthusiastically to school life that they left their alma mater only for the length of time it took to gain a teaching qualification, whereupon they were back again and involved in the reassuring routine of classrooms, timetables, school lore, inter-house competitiveness, rallying one's charges, apportioning encouragement and censure, upholding and enlarging the school tradition. These are the ones who have the history of the school at their fingertips, who can name the prominent members of any class in any year going back to 1926, who applaud the achievement of distinguished old girls, such as Mary McAleese. For them, the school is a community in itself, a haven, and a source of emotional sustenance – never a place where harm is done.

A couple of years ago I went back to St Dominic's. I took a taxi from Rugby Road in Belfast, where I was staying; down Botanic

Avenue, along Great Victoria Street, up the Grosvenor Road – or what remains of it; and then I had to direct the driver. Turn left, I said; then right – into the school grounds. It's a winter's day towards the end of term. The drive is crammed with teachers' cars. Otherwise, it's just as I remember it – the enormous twin brick buildings joined at ground level by a passageway; the imposing entrance to the convent part; the modified gothic detail. Good heavens, there is even a nun, in proper Dominican habit, standing in the opened doorway – or am I seeing things? I thought the habit was a thing of the past. The scene in front of me – the red of the brickwork, the green, nearly oval-shaped patch of grass with flower beds in the middle, the bare trees, the lull during lessons, the little gateway I know to be let into the school wall round to the right – all this strikes deep into my seven senses.

I was four when I first came here. The school had a kindergarten department in those days, in which I spent a year before being transferred to Aquinas Hall on the Malone Road, as a shake-up of the system occurred with the implementation of the 1947 Education Act (the start of the Eleven-Plus). I was four, and desperate to get to school, as an only child with a yearning for playmates. However, I hadn't quite understood that the new experience would entail parting from my mother and taking my place among a crowd of strangers, in a strange setting. In the

St Dominic's school buildings photographed by Robert French, early twentieth century

181

event, I was dragged kicking and bawling into St Dominic's on my first day there, hauled and pulled along by a hefty nun in a habit, while I tried my hardest to keep a hold of my mother, my anchor. Coercion seems to have marked both my coming and my going. The nun won, as was inevitable, and I was left to my fate: parked in a room full of toddlers doing peculiar things with chalk and plasticine. I made the best of it, having no alternative. I ceased to snivel – though I met with no particular kindness or understanding – took a scornful line about some contemporary wetting the floor and having to be hustled out of the classroom by a tut-tutting teacher, and gained a bit of credit for being able to write my name.

Soon there were tears in the morning if I *couldn't* go to school, through running a temperature or some such. Like everyone else, I wore a small box-pleated maroon-coloured tunic and sash, with the school crest emblazoned on the left-hand side, and regulation white Viyella blouse. These garments were purchased from a school outfitter's near Dunville Park on the Falls Road. In the classroom, we learned things by rote – 'Four ones are four, four twos are eight'; 'Who made the world? God made the world.' This led to some misunderstandings. One child for years declaimed the line from the Apostles' Creed, 'Suffered under Pontius Pilate', as 'Suffered under a bunch of violets'. To her, one version made as much sense as the other. (Years later, I remember hearing about a similar misapprehension on the part of a non-comprehending pupil. The Secondary Intermediate school where my mother taught, St Louise's, has a school song in praise of its patron saint, which goes something like, 'Hail, St Louise, something, something / Captain and guardian of our school ...' This stuck in one person's head as, 'Kept in the garden of our school', which actually did make sense, since the school grounds contained a statue of St Louise.)

Some of the big girls about the place made a pet of me and brought me sweets and did up my shoe laces for me, while others – teasers – went in for pinching and hair-pulling. Once, when I turned on one of the latter and bit her, I was put to sit on a high stool in a corner to contemplate my wickedness. I was prepared for my First Holy Communion in this place. Photographs show a group of us smirking for the camera, our parents standing proudly behind us wearing their choicest suits and hats. We communicants are dressed up to the nines in nasty little fussy white art-silk frocks and veils, clutching mother-of-pearl-backed missals in our kid-gloved hands: Margaret Dornan, Margot Farrell, Fiona Devlin, Sally Smith.

My first return to St Dominic's was at the age of eleven, happy to be a grammar-school pupil, an eleven-plusser. Since leaving it five years later under that fearsome Gaeltacht cloud, I'd tended to look the other way while passing the place on the top deck of a Falls Road bus. Certainly the time has come to quell any residual antipathy I may still be harbouring. The first thing is to learn whatever I can about the history of the school – hence my current visit, to pick up a hundred-and-twenty-fifth anniversary booklet. Dominican nuns, I find, existed in Ireland seven hundred years ago; Penal Laws in the seventeenth century drove them into exile in Spain and Portugal, before a motherhouse was established at Cabra, County Dublin, in 1818. Fifty years after that date, a communication went out from the Bishop of Down and Connor to these Cabra nuns, inviting them to Belfast to found a school. This is it. Opened on the Falls Road in 1870, with four day pupils and a boarder, the convent, according to a contemporary report in the *Ulster Examiner*, 'occupies an elevated and agreeable position in the environs of Belfast and commands an extensive view of the surrounding country ... Unremitting attention is given to the health and comfort of the Young Ladies ... No efforts are spared to train the Pupils in habits of obedience, industry and neatness ... During the summer months the pupils are permitted to take long walks in the country.' We're in L.T. Meade territory here, accompanied by a whiff of peculiarly Irish Catholic innocence and decorum.

Whatever the realities of the situation for these early Belfast convent girls, they are now irretrievable, absorbed into an idealised, holy haze. However, judging by the numbers of them who went on to become nuns themselves, there can't have been

183

too much insubordination. Early photographs show small girls in pinafores, strolling arm-in-arm through the extensive grounds, or sitting in the long grass making daisy-chains. You get no sense of things being fraught or disagreeable – though no doubt they sometimes were. Reminiscences of St Dominic's earlier days, mostly written by nuns, are uniformly jolly in tone, as though to suggest that eventual assumption of the veil needn't entail a goody-goody girlhood.

By 1914, St Dominic's had 161 pupils, all of whom would have come from well-to-do families; most children at the time didn't receive secondary education at all, and in the Falls Road area you would have had 'half-timers' (i.e. those whose days were divided between the classroom and the mill) learning the rudiments of English, arithmetic and so forth, in a school such as St Vincent's, run by the Sisters of Charity and accommodating up to five hundred pupils in four classrooms.

We're all appalled nowadays by enormities of the past, insupportable living conditions, hair-raising ills, unimaginable deprivations. In compensation, though, we might note the tendency to applaud the spirit of people who tholed all these, and more, and more – and the Falls district, in particular, entertains the strongest possible sense of its industrial and political past, charged with culturally assertive energies. The cluster of red-brick streets, some named topically after battles of the Crimean War (Sevastapol, Omar, Balaclava) nurtured all kinds of insurrectionary affiliations. There was more to the Falls than men in duncher caps discussing greyhound racing at street corners, shawlies scurrying towards the local pawn shop, exuberant young mill-workers taunting stodgy looking passers-by, street games involving lamp posts and paving stones, loquacious grandmothers and brazen youngsters hitching dangerous rides on the back ends of lorries, or defrauding the management of the Clonard Cinema – though these ingredients of Falls Road life were far from being figments. Parts of the road were semi-suburban, though its core was anything but; it was rich in local lore and indigenous repartee, and harboured a fraternity of the self-taught whose spiritual home was the fusty public library on the corner of Sevastapol Street. Catholicism and nationalism pervaded the air it generated – with the odd gust of socialism just to keep things polemical. Religion and its rituals shaped the life of the area: Sunday masses, Holidays of Obligation, evening devotions, weekly confessions, Men's Confraternity meetings, Children of Mary, May altars, Corpus Christi processions, the family rosary and what-have-you. The Dominican convent was only one of a score of religious buildings dotted along the road, though its elevated position – *pace* the *Ulster Examiner* – enabled it to take a haughty view of itself.

The further you penetrated into the Falls's hinterland, the narrower the streets became, the rougher the brickwork; flat paving stones gave way to cobbles, with ruts in the roadway where the wheels of tradesmen's handcarts trundled through. Front doors were dingier and windows constructed to let in only the smallest shafts of light. Families living here either clung with desperation to the remnants of an imagined respectability, or had given up altogether and thought nothing of sticking their knickers and petticoats out through a front-room window to dry in the tainted air. Photographs from the early part of the last century suggest that about half the children from these areas went barefoot.

In the Lower Falls. Photograph by Alexander Hogg, c. 1912

I think of the Falls as distilling its strongest back-street flavour between the 1890s (say) and the late 1940s: sixty-odd years of fearsome privations, raucousness, clan solidarity and disaffection. It would be an interesting cinematic exercise to show its built-up areas dwindling bit by bit as you go backwards in time, until nothing was left but the original fields and ponds. *Bóthar na bhFál*: the road of the hedges. Before 1840, indeed, as we've seen, the buildings beyond Townsend Street could nearly be counted on the fingers of one hand: a linen factory, a flax mill, a bleach works, two houses and a pub. Closer to the town centre, however, there were plenty of built-up, run-down localities to outrage the sensibilities of a social commentator such as the Minister of the Congregationalist Church in Upper Donegall Street, the Revd W.M. O'Hanlon, whose *Walks Among the Poor of Belfast* was published in 1853. 'We advanced along Durham Street,' writes O'Hanlon in his study of Belfast's nineteenth-century riff-raff, 'peering … into all manner of courts and entries.' You get the sense that he and his companions, in this rough area, advanced very gingerly indeed. Possibly its inhabitants weren't beguiled by the clergyman's shock-horror exposé of their living conditions. O'Hanlon made no bones about telling them what was what. As far as he was concerned, poverty and debauchery went hand-in-hand; and he'd have liked nothing better than to effect a cleaning-up of morals along with living quarters. Drunkenness is O'Hanlon's chief horror; counting no fewer than twenty-two public houses in the vicinity of North Queen Street, he succumbs to an appalled disbelief. Prostitution, sodomy, incest, not to mention feckless procreation … all these, and worse, he believes, can be laid at the door of drink. No wonder the strains of a lewd song issuing from a slum makes his hair stand on end.

I can't resist poking fun at O'Hanlon – however, as a would-be reformer, he was more in the Mayhew than the temperance-propaganda tradition. What he recommended as a lower-class modus operandi was simply an industrious, orderly, sober, well-scrubbed routine. It's just that the practice of obtruding his sniffy clerical nose into all manner of hovels makes him a target for moderate ridicule. He's not at all akin to MacNeice's mad preacher (for example) who embodies the sour, black, rebarbative, life-withering aspect of Ulster religious practice:

> Among old iron, cinders, sizzling dumps,
> A world castrated, amputated, trepanned,
> He walked in the lost acres crying 'Repent
> For the Kingdom of Death is at hand'.

We Catholics, secure in the rationality of our own brands of denial, don't scruple to point the finger at such potty forms of Protestantism; but in truth – as we've seen – there are pleasure-quashers of equal intensity on both sides of the religious split, who together add up to a demented fraction on the edge of normal life. And how you react in the end to the restrictions of your upbringing is as much a matter of temperament as indoctrination. Most sensible grown-up people, all along, would have worked out some personal compromise between churchly obligation and worldly inclination.

It's only in the last decade or so that we have really grasped the extent to which the religious edifice in Ireland was a superstructure imposed over a basis of ordinary laxity. Even priests, it seems, were never as holy en masse as we once assumed. Some Church dignitaries allowed themselves more leeway than they meted out to their flocks – or so the spate of scandals flummoxing Irish Catholicism would suggest. One lurid misdemeanour after another has come to light: we've had bonking bishops popping up all over the place, clerical brothel-haunters, priests and nuns running off in droves, and revelations of the sexual abuse of children by clerics on such a scale that the thing has become a commonplace. The randy Christian Brother has all but succeeded the Scout Master as a joke sexual predator.

I suppose all these, and other transgressions, have been going on all the time, only kept very carefully under wraps. (Even

Paul Blanchard, for all his investigator's nose, accepted that church fathers practised what they preached, and that their parishioners gave them credit for their abstinence.) They can't be peculiar to the present – though no doubt the current moral climate makes it easier for celibates to step out of line. Well, you've only to take the name Taggart, or McTaggart, to understand that priests didn't always stick to celibacy (*Mac an tSagairt*, the priest's son). But it still seems strange to me to envisage those in religious orders as sexual beings in any sense. In my experience, they'd so surrounded themselves with an aura of fortitude and holiness and ascetic segregation that it seemed an impertinence to suspect them of bodily functions at all. They were a group apart, and in a self-elected monitoring relation to the rest of us.

Possibly the most brutal, rancorous and disagreeable of the nuns I remember were actually taking their sexual frustrations out on us, their charges; but fortunately no overt sexual molestation was ever inflicted on us alongside the other vexations of the school day. Indeed, such a thing is utterly unimaginable. No lesbian or lecherous nuns ever crossed our paths to scare the wits out of us. The aim of our Dominicans was to keep their nubile pupils out of men's clutches, never to get them into their own. (A ludicrous and revolting thought.)

As for priests – they celebrated Mass and heard confessions, and that was all I knew of them. I didn't come from one of those church-besotted families who had them constantly in the house. No priest whatever had any personal contact with me. In fact, I never met a priest socially until 1998, when the Jesuit brother of a friend came to visit us at Blackheath. I only saw them in their full regalia performing some ritual or other. Of course, like everyone else above the age of fourteen, I was cross-questioned in the confession box about minor sexual delinquencies; but if my embarrassed disclosures were having an arousing effect on the pastor in question, I'd never have noticed. I wasn't very observant. Indeed, extremes of self-abuse could have been going on under my nose; and if I'd been aware of anything out-of-the-way at all, I'd have attributed it to some

innocuous cause such as trouble with undergarments or a flea in
the cassock.

> It must be tough on a priest who, while trying to abstain from
> fleshly pleasures himself, has to sit in a darkened confessional,
> hand cupped to his ear, as half his congregation sorrowfully
> parades its fumblings, erections and ejaculations before him.

This observation comes from Cal McCrystal's spirited memoir of
1997, *Reflections on a Quiet Rebel* — one of the recent auto-
biographies which alert us to the fact that Catholic schoolboys in
the middle part of the last century actually had it worse than girls,
when it came to a confrontation with unbefitting sexual conduct
(well, unless you were a Magdalen inmate and consequently fair
game for any rapacious priest). They do, however, seem better
equipped to make light of these matters. For the memoirists at
least, sexual eccentricities were hardly more alarming than other
teachers' foibles. It was almost de rigueur for boys' establishments
to include a weird bod or two among the teaching staff. Pupils
soon grasped the identities of those it was best to steer clear of,
outside lessons:

> He was in his early thirties and affable enough, but the boys
> tended to give him a wide berth, fearing a call to his room ...
> This was the priest who seemed to enjoy thrashing boys with a
> cane while in their pyjamas, and had strange nocturnal
> wanderings ... One night I was awakened by a slight movement
> of my bed ... He seemed to have trouble with his breathing.
> What appeared to be a white handkerchief fluttered in the
> vicinity of his waistband. I squeezed my eyes shut, pretending
> to be asleep.

Cal McCrystal, at the time, was a boarder with the Marist
Fathers of Dundalk; this, *c.* 1950, was the school from which a
boy named Daly was expelled 'for climbing a wall to kiss a town
girl'. I have a lot of sympathy for this unknown boy called Daly.
And for Tom Campbell, who, some years earlier, left St Patrick's

College, Armagh, in similar circumstances. Campbell's innocent jingle,

> I have a dainty girlfriend
> And this you'll comprehend,
> Every time she bends her knee
> I see the Promised Land,

transcribed in a friend's album and spotted by a ravening Dean, got him expelled from the school for indecency. This incident is recalled in John Montague's biting sequence of poems about his years at the college – 'a harsh, boorish, ignorant' regime – pointedly called *Time in Armagh*:

> Endless games designed to keep us pure –
> 'Keep your hands out of your pockets, boys' –
> We wore togs even in the showers.

Daly, Campbell: I wonder how many of us, thirty, forty, fifty-odd years ago, were given the boot at the behest of some puritanical maniac?

By the 1960s, things were changing; or perhaps it was just that some boys' schools accommodated an unusual degree of oddness in their employees. An unabashed sexual enthusiast, for example, slaked his lusts quite openly at the Christian Brothers school attended by the novelist and short-story writer Dermot Healy. (Again, recalling our decorous classrooms, I find it hard to envisage such smutty goings-on.) Healy's illuminating memoir, *The Bend for Home* (1996), saddles the town of Cavan with a merry sexual ferment. Joining in, with his own mode of hanky-panky, is a Brother Felim who turns his roll-calling duties to his own ends:

> … he brought you in behind his desk and felt your mickey as you called out the names … He undid a button, then another, and curled a finger round your member …. You could feel through his dress the hump of his erection against your thigh … He suddenly let you go like a bad thing. Did your buttons up …

The cheery tone suggests that no lasting damage was done to

the objects of this lewd quirk. It was only a minor annoyance of school life. And yet – one can't help wondering if clerics all along, while upholding chastity with one hand, were actually undermining it with the other. It is possible that a schizophrenic approach to life, either overtly or subliminally, has been bred in those of us exposed to such contradictions.

All the different forms of blight afflicting Northern Ireland might suggest to the onlooker a society spectacularly lacking in resources for tranquillity or civility. It's one way of looking at it, indeed, but not the only way. There are others who've portrayed things differently. The province has never been short of verses (for example) to keep the spirits up. 'I take my stand by the Ulster names,' wrote John Hewitt,

> each clean hard name like a weathered stone;
> Tyrella, Rostrevor, are flickering flames:
> the names I mean are the Moy, Malone,
> Strabane, Slieve Gullion and Portglenone.

And there are other ways of naming names in order to strike an affirmative note. There's Tom Paulin: 'I lay claim to those marshes, / The Lagan, the shipyards, / The Ormeau Road in winter.' Heaney's Toome and Moyola, Mahon's north coast, Longley's Lisburn Road or Portavogie with its prawn fishermen, Ciaran Carson's obliterated Falls: all these, and more, add up to a kind of communal exercise in re-creation, or appreciation, betokening the strongest understanding of a community about which there is more, much more, to be singled out than its savageries and miseries.

Most people of Healy's [Dermot Healy; see above] generation will remember summer trips to colleges in the Gaeltachta, the Irish-speaking regions of the country, which were supposed to inculcate a reverence for the Irish language and the rural way of life, the twin obsessions of Eamonn de Valera. Of course, they became occasions for explosions of adolescent hormones and doomed love affairs with people otherwise impossible to meet. In a strange way they probably achieved a connection between the Irish language and sexuality, which could only be good for the language.

The above passage, from Catriona Crowe's review of Dermot Healy's *The Bend for Home* in the *London Review of Books* (31 July 1997) neatly sums up both the ideological colouring of these extramural courses, and the actual subtext. Of course the Irish language summer school goes back some way before de Valera. The practice was initiated under the auspices of the Gaelic League, and to begin with, the schools were attended by adults; it was only after Padraig Pearse and St Enda's had identified the potential benefits to a younger contingent that senior pupils got in on the act.

Ballinageary, County Cork, started the whole thing going back in 1904: a time when convent schools still taught deportment to their girls, when 'patriotic dress', complete with embroidery copied from the Book of Kells, drew jeers from Dublin fishwives in the streets ('Them Irishers are going daft'), when Springfield in Belfast was described as an old, old, stone-built hamlet and optimists in the North believed that bigotry was on its last, though still strongly kicking, legs. Tourmakeady, County Mayo, Spiddal, County Galway, Cloughaneeley, County Donegal, and Omeath near Carlingford in County Louth were other early venues for summer-school high-mindedness and conviviality.

Rannafast was a late addition to these prestigious localities, with its Coláiste Bhrighde coming into existence in 1926 as a replacement for Omeath, whose Irish-speaking populace had dwindled to the point where the place could hardly be termed a Gaeltacht at all. One of Omeath's directors, Father Lorcan Ó Muirí (Larry Murray), decided to move the enterprise to Donegal's Atlantic coast, where the language waxed eloquent and undiminished. Ó Muirí, priest, folklorist and indefatigable song-collector, could count among his attributes the distinction of having been expelled from Maynooth, after his superiors took

it on themselves to brand him as a bad influence. (He was subsequently ordained in America.) The Rannafast undertaking did
not get off to a painless start. Funding was obtained – after
prodigious efforts on the part of Ó Muirí – a site was chosen and
the college buildings slowly went up. Coláiste Bhríghde was
about to open its doors to students when a huge wind suddenly
blew up and swept the whole thing out into the Atlantic Ocean,
as an eagle might have carried off a baby in a blanket. Father
Murray's second brainchild must have had stronger foundations,
for it is still there (as far as I know), dispensing Irish and amusement to those enrolled in its courses, though perhaps not so
enticingly as in the past.

Not every commentator, though, is attuned to that bygone
Gaeltacht ambience. According to Michael Tierney, biographer
of one of the Gaelic League's founders, Eoin MacNéill, 'it is
difficult now to recapture even in imagination the spirit of the
summer schools with their plain living amid beautiful surroundings, their open-air classes, their students living in Irish-speaking
homes, their ceilis, their excursions, often by the sea, to visit
historic monuments and places of antiquarian interest, their endless discussions and the deep and lasting friendships to which they
so readily gave rise ...' Well, he makes it all sound fearfully
decorous and antiquated: it wasn't like that in our day, and even
in the distant past it's unlikely to have been so staid – though
you can't quarrel with his list of Gaeltacht pursuits. Tierney's
po-faced prose is simply not equipped to communicate the
uniquely exhilarating atmosphere he touches on.

To get a real sense of summer-school bedazzlement you have
to turn to a writer like Sean O'Faolain, to whom the act of
evocation comes as naturally as sneezing:

> In groups we spent the livelong days together. We spent half the
> day down in the village studying the language in the corrugated
> tin shed grandiosely called the College. The rest of the day we
> spent swimming in the rock pools, or climbing the mountains,
> or cycling to the farther glens, or dancing informally by the
> roadside at night, or more formally in the College, or boating
> on the lake if the moon was up, or simply sitting in the kitchen

listening to some local boy or girl singing a traditional Irish song or playing old tunes on the fiddle, or we merely sat and conversed. Late hours were the common rule. I was always so pleasantly tired, so full of oxygen, that I could have slept soundly under a hedge or on a stone floor. On hot nights I often slept, in the clothes in which I stood, high up in the hay of the outdoor hay barn, waking only when I heard a horse's hooves on the road or somebody working in the stone byre below.

Nowadays, the learning of Irish has lost this magical power to bind hearts together ...

Well, maybe; but something of that first buoyant spirit persisted, though – as O'Faolain implies – compulsory Irish did a lot to stifle it. Irish was never compulsory for us in the North – indeed, its powerful connections with defiance and dissent were a part of its allure.

The group I belonged to in the early 1960s, Cumann Cluan Ard, was fuelled by a wish to reinstate Irish as a medium of everyday communication. Its ambitions were unprecedented but not unattainable. By the middle of the decade, a lot of its members had paired off, moved into newly-built houses all close together, and established the nucleus of what became known as Belfast's Gaelic colony. The next, inevitable, step was the setting up of nursery schools to accommodate their Irish-speaking infants. Then, as required, middle schools and grammar schools came into being, followed by radio programmes in Irish, shops selling Irish books and magazines, and other amenities to boost the undertaking.

I was not personally involved in any of this. Shortly before these remarkable developments got under way, myself and my friend Maire, once keen members of Cluan Ard, had scarpered to England, respectively to London and Manchester, to further our own ambitions which had gradually diverged from *fíor*-Gael-dom. Nevertheless, the achievements of our one-time associates impressed us strongly. They had brought Irish out of the private, and into the public, domain. Their polite determination to speak their own language in all possible circumstances had tremendous implications for the future of the language, as a cultural survival wrested out of complexity and deadlock. Though the Shaw's Road Gaeltacht was a place apart, its singularity had to do with conservation, not exclusiveness. Its inhabitants didn't proselytise on the whole, but liked to show by their own example the relevance of Irish to contemporary life. They were, and are, idealists, but none the less practical for that.

The setting up of this urban Gaeltacht coincided with the arrival of agitation in other parts of West Belfast, and the two in conjunction gave rise to a new version of an old question: were these Gaelic-speakers more, or less, Irish than their daredevil contemporaries who carried on the tradition of fighting, killing and dying for Ireland and never letting ordinary humanitarian reservations affect that grandiose resolve? No one ever came up with an adequate answer (all answers were partisan), but at the same time, terms like 'cultural identity' began to be bandied about, with emphasis (in liberal circles anyway) placed on the need to accord esteem to as many varieties of 'cultural identity' as could be pinpointed. It wasn't long before the Irish language got itself counted among the resources of militant republicanism – a circumstance to which the Shaw's Road *Gaeiligoirí* and others reacted with a measure of wryness. This wryness could hardly be contained following the appearance of political slogans framed in a version of Irish guaranteed to raise the ire of an old linguistic purist such as Flann O'Brien (say). 'Tiochfaidh ár lá', mar shampla.

The summer after the Rannafast debacle – as I've said – I am back for a month in the Donegal Gaeltacht, in Loughanure on the other side of Annaghry, where I keep out of harm's way and engage in no momentous misbehaviour. I am seventeen, and happy to have done with school (since the school is miserable Ballynahinch). I remember visiting a local house at Loughanure where one of the daughters sings '*Buachaill ón Éirne*' in an enthralling manner. I remember, too, that my room-mates here are all demure girls with shiny hair and great proficiency in needlework. It is clear from the start that Loughanure is not quite so lively a centre of Irish studies as Rannafast.

Further visits to Irish-speaking districts, over the next five years or so, take place in the company of delegates from an inter-University Gaelic Society which I have joined. On one of these occasions I get to know a couple of people from Dublin, a father and daughter called Thornberry – Ó Droighneáin in Irish – and it isn't long before we're on pretty companionable terms. A kind of holiday friendship springs up between the three of us in the course of walks and charabanc trips into the countryside of South Donegal, West Galway and the Dingle peninsula, and sociable evenings at ceilidhes or in some sort of makeshift concert hall on a hillside or in the middle of a bog with the wind howling outside and drowning out the current performance of *Charlie's Aunt* – *Aintín Searlais* in Irish. Well, actually, it's the father and I who are on the same wavelength, though it's his pleasant daughter Joan – Siobán Ní Droighneáin – who is my con-temporary. At least, we are on it with regard to literature: a common enthusiasm for the poems of Louis MacNeice, for example, is among the things that keep us sitting up until quite late in the evening before a succession of turf fires in different localities of the west, avidly exchanging opinions and making literary recommendations to one another. The elder Thornberry (Pádraig Mór) is a teacher at a Christian Brothers' School in Dublin; but not at all hidebound or mealy-mouthed in spite of it. Nothing is out of bounds in our discussions – not Henry Miller (whom I abhor), *Billy Bunter* (a childhood favourite of both of us) or *Lady Chatterley* (which I haven't yet read).

It's Pádraig Mór who introduces me to *Ulysses*, entrusting me with his own copy of the book, and stressing his confidence in my ability to approach it in the right spirit (i.e. not to go poking around for salacious passages). I do read it, with some difficulty – it's not for another couple of years that I'm in anything like a position to grapple with the magnitude of Joyce's undertaking, or succumb to the power of the narrative. But – at the time – I'm pleased to have struggled through this key item of Irish literature, however much of it is over my head.

But – but – Pádraig Mór himself is subsequently overtaken by severe qualms of conscience at having foisted this supposedly titillating work on a juvenile (I think I was eighteen). The thing preys on his mind to the point where he comes to call at our house in the Donegall Road (he is visiting relatives in Belfast). His mission is to explain to my parents why he believed *Ulysses* would do me no harm, would, indeed, encourage an already strongly developed appreciation of literature, and make me into a more rounded-off person. He also wants to apologise if they feel he's behaved inappropriately towards a teenage girl he isn't related to.

He needn't have worried. No censorship ever operated in our house – I'd have been at liberty to read every page of the *Kama Sutra* or *Under the Hill* if I'd so desired. Besides, my mother would have known *Ulysses* as a literary work, nothing else; while as far as my father was concerned, the book would have seemed to him on a par with *Oliver Twist* ... Pádraig Mór, all six feet of him, is ushered into the kitchen, given a cup of tea and put at his ease. At least, he's beginning to relax and dismiss Joyce and all his works from his mind, when it's suddenly borne in on him that my grandmother, from her accustomed armchair beneath the window, is subjecting him to a more than mannerly scrutiny. Finally, having thoroughly assessed his face and bearing, she can contain herself no longer but bursts out with, 'This may seem like a strange question – but – did you ever know someone called Minnie Cochrane?' I did indeed, he replies, she was my mother. Well! That's the rest of us excluded from the conversation.

Minnie Cochrane, long dead, was my grandmother's best friend in Lurgan when they were both young girls wearing dresses with leg-o'-mutton sleeves, before they and their descendants were scattered far and wide, to Belfast, Dublin, England and beyond. What's survived of their friendship resolves itself into an image from 1899 or 1900. It's a spring day, very early in the morning, before almost anyone is awake, and three figures are hastening towards the railway station in William Street and a train bound for Belfast. They are Minnie Cochrane and the boy she's eloping with, whose name is Thornberry, and Minnie's friend Sarah, a co-conspirator in the momentous escapade, who's come to see off the runaway pair and carry one of their suitcases. Why the two couldn't marry in the normal way with Sarah as a bridesmaid I have no idea; but as it is the vignette smacks of secrecy and drama and gets my grandmother in at the centre of the action. Girls and boys in Queen Victoria's reign, it appears, were no less devious or headstrong than they were in our day. This was a colourful moment in my grandmother's personal history. In our family lore it's 'I carried Minnie Cochrane's suitcase when she eloped with Arthur Thornberry.'

Another way in which I keep in contact with the Gaeltacht is in conjunction with friends from Cumann Cluan Ard. The spiritual home of Cluan Ard is Rannafast, and so my association with this wild place continues for a time, though on freer terms than those prevailing during the first disastrous summer. It isn't at all the same. We Irish enthusiasts tend to go there at odd times of the year – April, October – travelling from Belfast in a hired minibus, or hitch-hiking whenever we can get away for a couple of days and are feeling energetic. And even during the months of July and August, when the College is functioning and the place awash in schoolchildren, there are houses set aside for club members who've established relationships with many of the local families. You can stay in these houses and not be answerable to any extraneous authority. Of course, by now we are old enough to accept the rules of behaviour governing the visit to someone else's home, and to take a tolerantly exasperated view of schoolchildren's antics. There is no call for our later landladies to nail up the windows to keep us in our beds at night. Oddly, I don't remember, in these later years, running across any of the Rannafast boys who so preoccupied us during our first heady days in the Gaeltacht – or wanting to, for that matter, newer infatuations having supervened, to be fostered in their turn by the intoxicating locality.

Once I'd left art school in Belfast and moved away from home these excursions tailed off, then stopped altogether, like my correspondence with the Thornberrys, father and daughter, which continued for a bit while I established myself as an expatriate with more than half my mind in Ireland, but then in due course ceased. I haven't set foot in the Donegal Gaeltacht for a good many years. But the sense of a kind of Atlantic idyll remains implanted in my consciousness. The outcome of that first visit didn't destroy the place for me. Rannafast and its goings-on may have landed us in a pickle, a pickle with weighty consequences; but the place itself never ceased to embody the spirit of a vibrant and pristine Ireland.

What really were the consequences of Rannafast? There are certain moments in everyone's life when the future begins to assume one configuration rather than another: if so-and-so happens, then such-and-such will follow on, as surely as the pale buds on the tree will turn to profuse green leaves. (Well, as long as they're not wrenched off, or subjected to frost in May.) And whatever happens, you can't help thinking about alternative lives, roads not taken, fantasies never acted out. Penelope Lively has a whole book of imaginary life-stories, or confabulations: an anti-memoir, she calls it. The title is *Making It Up*. It's appropriate to describe this book as the opposite of a memoir, and not simply as a work of fiction, because the episodes envisaged would have required the merest twitch of reality, the most apparently inconsequential step in one direction rather than another, to make them true.

Sometimes, in the made-up version, the imagined outcome is extreme. The entire Lively oeuvre would have been lost to the world of literature, for example, had the event described in the opening story of *Making It Up*, 'Mozambique Channel', come to pass. The author kills herself off as a young child fleeing Egypt with her mother and nanny, in 1942. A Japanese U-boat sinks the ship in which she is travelling, and then she is struck on the head by an oar in the scramble to find a place on a lifeboat. A later story has her – under her actual name, Penelope – wiped out again, this time in a air disaster of 1956. 'Comets did fall out of the sky,' she explains in a paragraph set in italic type, commenting on her own exercise in confabulation, and claiming its own kind of authenticity for the made-up event ...

It's not my purpose here to imagine any of the courses my life might have taken, had things fallen out as expected in 1950s and '60s Belfast – if I'd studied at university rather than art school, for example, and come of age in Belfast rather than London. But it's certain that every major event in my life since 1959 has come about because of that decisive summer. Well, it may have been a stroke of luck despite appearances, I don't know. Friends assure me I'd have been intolerable as an academic know-all, which was one possible outcome of the way I was heading. And I can't really see myself as a grandmother of six, something that's happened to a number of my contemporaries. The role would not have suited me. I have a lot to be thankful for, and perhaps a tiny portion of gratitude is due to those pestilential nuns of the mid-twentieth century Dominican Order, and their cack-handed administrations.

We moved to Antrim in 1999. Our house is still in need of restoration, though the rot has been treated, central heating installed and plumbing and electricity brought up to date. Three or four years of neglect, before we came, had caused blocked gutters and all the other aggravations householders dread. Some domestic vandal of the late twentieth century took away the original lime-mortar pointing and inserted an inappropriate, supposedly durable, material: now it's all to do again. At some point not too far ahead, the roof – the famous Irish roof, bemoaned by novelists from Maria Edgeworth to Caroline Blackwood – will need to be replaced. (Though we don't have vast quantities of buckets, like those arranged along the corridors of Blackwood's Dunmartin Hall – or indeed the corridors – a bucket or two is necessary to catch occasional drips.)

The house feels as if it ought to be haunted, especially when you see it from a distance through a haze of fog or snow; and indeed perhaps there are lingering presences about the place, for those susceptible to such phenomena. It was built, around 1840, for a young Presbyterian minister, the Revd Charles Morrison, and his wife Margaret Oliphant – who shares a name, and possibly an ancestry, with the Victorian author of *The Chronicles of Carlingford* and many other books. Both Margaret Oliphants came from Edinburgh and had connections with the publishing firm of the same name (which ended in the 1950s as a publisher of girls' school stories with a religious bias). The works of the writing Oliphant include some good ghost stories featuring sombre stone houses, not unlike this one, flanked by churchyard yews. But are there ghosts here? Some who know about these things have detected the presence of a sprite – and we know of at least two children, sons of the Morrison family, who died on the spot: one as an infant in 1846, and the other eleven years later, at eleven years. They are buried in the old Presbyterian graveyard nearby, with its sparse and faintly desolate air. As for my own view – I'd go along with Brigid Brophy on Shakespeare's fairies: to be believed in utterly, but strictly in the realm of the imagination.

Three years after the second pathetic death, the family washed its hands of Antrim and moved to North London, where the Revd Morrison had secured a post as principal of Hackney Theological College. The house was sold, in 1860, to a Mr Thomas Hugh Adams of Rokeel, near Ballymena, and another young family (I imagine) had a whale of a time climbing trees in the garden and running wild among the adjoining fields and woods. (I'm sure there was an old nurse like Alice Milligan's in the poem 'When I Was a Little Girl' using a topical threat to control her charges: 'Come in! Or when it's dark, / The Fenians will get ye.') At any rate, one of the Adams sons was so attached to the house that he stayed in it for the rest of his life; a doctor, and unmarried, John James Adams was still here in 1941, when an accident on the front door steps in icy weather brought about his death.

I'm interested in the first owner, the Revd Morrison, who was born in Belfast and educated at Inst, a few years after

Robert MacAdam got his grounding in Irish at the same school. Morrison came to Antrim as minister of the First Presbyterian Church in 1840, and he – or his wife's family – set about building the house, which was later called Ashville. We would like to think that Lanyon had a hand in its construction (Charles Lanyon, the architect of Victorian Belfast); he was working in the area at that time, and certain features of the house suggest the idea may not be unduly far-fetched. (It can't be verified, unfortunately, since the whereabouts of the Lanyon papers is at present a mystery.) The grey stone house, not large, with subdued Gothic touches, built of local materials, must have exercised a considerable fascination even then; it was right out in the country and had a romantic aura about it.

However, Antrim, as it turned out, was not a well-omened setting for the minister and his family. In between the two children's deaths came a considerable scandal which convulsed church circles as 'rumours besmirching the character and conduct of Mr Morrison' began to circulate. What had he done? The thing is wrapped in mystery and speculation as close-mouthed elders kept the story from ever reaching the wider public; but one (watered-down) version has the minister casting a lascivious glance at a lady's ankle as she stepped from a carriage. There were also stories concerning afternoon visits by Mr Morrison to farmers' wives, while the farmers were occupied elsewhere.

But if that's what all the fuss was about, you'd have to say the business engendered as absurd an outcome as our Rannafast caper. Morrison was summoned to appear before a Church Tribunal – a grave and disagreeable proceeding – and after much solemn deliberation, the Presbytery came out in support of him. But this verdict so incensed half Morrison's congregation – including, no doubt, the outraged farmers with untrustworthy wives – that they took themselves off in high dudgeon to perform their heavenly worship elsewhere. (I have a good deal of fellow-feeling for the beleaguered Mr Morrison, and not only because it's likely that it was in this very room – though with a view stretching all the way to Lough Neagh and not curtailed after sixty feet by a hedge blocking off the bungalow next door – in this very room that his defence to the Church Tribunal was prepared.) Following the large-scale defection, the humiliated cleric stuck it out for a time, doggedly going about his duties; but the hostility of his former parishioners must have had a dejecting effect. After the adversities of Antrim, the Hackney appointment probably came as a godsend.

In Ireland, nothing remains of the Revd Charles Morrison but the melancholy gravestone commemorating his sons and a few scattered references in church documents. Oh, and the house he built, of course, which now forms a part of the North's very rapidly dwindling heritage. 'Protestant or Catholic,' Frank O'Connor noted, 'we are as decent a race of people as you are likely to find, but without the black of your nail of any instinct for conserving things.' It was 1947 when this fact struck him, and things since then have not improved. All the town- and country-house murders, or deaths by neglect, make a painful panorama. Some buildings on the verge of extinction could still be revived if anyone cared: the eighteenth-century courthouse in Antrim town, the once grand, neo-classical Upper Crescent in Belfast ... The custodians of these and so many other treasures of architecture are useless, swamped by bureaucracy, without a vision, careless of the future. However you look at it, the future *depends* on the past, on continuities understood and assimilated, on the psychic wellbeing engendered by the simple presence of survivals from a different age. It would be well for Northern Ireland if its people could learn to cherish the past more, and remain stuck in it less.

If we had to enumerate the components of the force that plucked us out of elegant Blackheath, and deposited us on the outskirts of rural Antrim, we'd have to place conservation among them: it was Ashville that attracted us. Once found, it made its claims on our commitment irresistible. The project of renovation wasn't, and isn't, without plentiful anxieties. Arriving ahead of our removers, we sat on the stairs in an empty house (there was nothing else to sit on), with a tranquillised ginger cat, contemplating the fungus growing up the walls and the row of obsolete servants' bells. Since then, the pleasures of inhabiting a house with a history have won out over the drawbacks inseparable from coping with its enormous demands: the unreclaimable garden, the still unconverted outbuildings. But it took a while before we were settled here, in any practical sense. After a week or two of trying to find shops that sold anything we could eat, and coping with life amid piles and piles of packing cases, my husband, an artist, began a huge painting called 'Landing on the Moon'. It adequately reflected our state of mind at the time.

My parents came to visit, and my mother's verdict was: it would be a lovely house if only it was new. The amount of work to be done and the current chaos dismayed her. And how would we earn a living, so far away from our previous sources of income? … Virtually without my noticing it, my dear parents had grown old and anxiety-ridden; and although they deserved a more efficient and selfless daughter to keep an eye on them, I was the only daughter they had. To be within reach of them, though not so close that we'd be living on top of one another, was among our reasons for uprooting ourselves. Another was London itself. For some time, the feeling had been growing on us that a less frenetic and clustered way of life was something we ought to try to cultivate while we had the chance. And our main requirement, if we were going to turn our back on everything familiar and step into the unknown, was an old Ulster house, preferably a listed house; never mind its state of repair, its practicality or even its situation on the outskirts of a town rendered ugly and damaged by redevelopment. Well, that's Ashville: we've got it, with its precarious tranquillity, its hidden impairments – may they stay hidden – and its romantic aspect.

★

In fact, not only the house, but the whole surrounding countryside abounds in historical associations. The impact of these has been diminished, but not completely vanquished, by the transformations of the last forty-odd years. Once a sleepy little place with a population of 3,000, 'mild and virtuous looking', according to the social commentator Hugh Shearman, Antrim town has now been catapulted into the twenty-first century, with its terrible shopping precinct, its vast surround of housing estates – proliferating in all directions – and its new reputation for delinquencies of various kinds, many of them drug-related. Not that a dubious reputation is entirely new to it. Hugh Shearman, in his comments on the town, makes a little joke about its one-time supposed depravity, at least in the eyes of a raving cleric who rechristened inoffensive Antrim Sodom and Gomorrah, in a sermon denouncing its laxity in the matter of licensing hours. Shearman's joke, with its note of quaintness, underscores the whole quaint element attaching to bygone Antrim – exemplified, perhaps, in its famous Pogue's Entry, in which a boy destined for more than local celebrity was once squashed into a miniscule dwelling along with his parents and siblings. Alexander Irvine, whose account of nineteenth-century poverty and uprightness in a lowly setting (very lowly: how they all crammed into the tiny space I do not know), *My Lady of the Chimney Corner*, commends, among other virtues, the lunatic honesty of his mother, who made him take back to its owner a turnip he'd uprooted from a field.

The subject of mild jokes, a centre of egregious sermonising, possessor of a picture-book round tower and, in Pogue's Entry, a miniscule literary landmark, along with aloof local toffs in the persons of Lord O'Neill and the Viscounts Massareene: Antrim, in this view, begins to take on a tinge of Ulster unctuousness. These things connect it to a bland past, a kind of countrified idyll in which even the most fearsome of social and physical deprivations are somehow rendered a bit folksy and – well – chimney-cornerish. But it's not a true picture of course, or even a very potent figment to superimpose over historical actualities.

History discloses many more compelling images, from the burning of the town in 1649 during the Cromwellian wars to the day in June 1798 when pikes in the hands of United Irishmen could be seen moving along apparently of their own volition above the tops of hedges lining the roads into Antrim. It is likely that, as they marched, the bearers of these pikes had in mind the fate of local man William Orr, accused of administering the United Irish oath to a couple of soldiers of the Fifeshire Fencibles and hanged near Carrickfergus in 1797 after a farce of a trial. This, on top of all the grievances fostering rebellious activity in the region, would have strengthened their resolve. For some, though, ordinary countrymen untrained in military operations, it wasn't enough.

James Orr, accomplished dialect poet and himself a participant in the Rising, details in one poem the evasive antics of many would-be insurgents who lost their nerve when it came to the bit:

> Some lettin' on their burn to mak',
> The rear-guard, goadin', hasten'd;
> Some hunk'rin' at a lee dyke back,
> Boost houghel on, ere fasten'd
> > Their breeks, that day.

Trousers round the ankles is somewhat at odds with the heroic aspect of the Rising, though it introduces a welcome note of humanity. Others in Orr's satirical account, misliking the look of General Nugent's Redcoats when they appeared on the horizon, threw down their weapons and promptly fled, sometimes making it home to the surprise and pragmatic thankfulness of their wives:

> 'Guid God! is't you? fair fa' ye! –
> 'Twas wise, tho' fools may ca't no' brave,
> To rin or e'er they saw ye.' –

By all accounts, James Orr's own conduct at the time entitles him to take a less than commendatory view of the shambles he witnessed and later inscribed in sterling verse. There were those in the company who deserved the epithet 'truly brave' among the hordes of scarperers. The mustering point for all the local United Irishmen was Donegore Hill, which supplies a title for Orr's poem. A mysterious and alluring hill on the outskirts of

Antrim, Donegore goes on distilling a sense of the numinous, despite the motorway at its foot and a garden centre and a couple of inappropriate new buildings wrecking its integrity. Like Ashville House, it suggests itself as the setting for a ghostly occurrence – and Maurice Leitch, born and raised in Muckamore, a mile south of Antrim town, clearly had Donegore in mind when he wrote the resonant ghost story 'Green Roads', in which the suicide of a British soldier serving in Northern Ireland in the 1980s is presided over by a line of long dead pikemen, implements clasped in their charnel hands, 'a few scythes, but mainly pitchforks and long poles tipped with metal. Their clothes looked outlandish as well, old and worn out from the effect of long drudgery in the open.' The position occupied by this unearthly company, if indeed it was the top of Donegore, would have given them a view of the subtle and seductive south Antrim countryside with its fields and farms and woodland and gorse-filled meadows rolling away in the distance.

We've hardly cast off our qualms and disorientation, transplanted quasi-Londoners that we are, before we are up at Donegore admiring the lovely small stone church and the quiet burial ground located there, both redolent of a kind of aesthetic and social wellbeing to do with old Antrim (yes, I know I'm indulging in an excess of blitheness here, but the setting calls for it). And the next minute we stumble on a woefully neglected, important grave behind the church: cracked and lopsided tombstone, rusty railing, nearly indecipherable inscription: Sir Samuel Ferguson 1810–1886 ... It's a good many years, it turns out, since the poet John Hewitt and his wife Roberta used to come up here, bearing flowers and gardening implements, to tend the grave and pay homage to a fellow Belfastman of Antrim ancestry whose life was largely spent in Dublin, though his burial spot indicates the importance to him of his northern roots. Fellow poet too – and now I'm standing half-way up Donegore Hill in the summer twilight, in a Christian churchyard with pre-

Christian thoughts surging into my head and the motorway only a distant annoyance down below, I have to wonder if 'The Fairy Thorn' with its overpowering uncanniness, its eldritch felicities, had its origin in this strange place:

> For, from the air above and the grassy mound beneath,
> And from the mountain-ashes and the old white-thorn
>   between,
> A power of faint enchantment doth through their beings
>   breathe,
> And they sink down together on the green.

Ferguson wrote 'The Fairy Thorn', based on a local legend, before he was twenty-four, and the first thing to note about the poem is the way it is charged with erotic energies – a merit you can't claim for his later exercises in Victorian subfusc, such as 'Congal'. Four young girls, bent on merriment, thoughtlessly arrange an evening out on a piece of enchanted ground, the upshot of which is the fairy abduction of one and the slow decline of the other three …

Ferguson's perfect fairy poem, as many critics have pointed out, underpins the whole Celtic Twilight movement in the later part of the nineteenth century. It's an unexpected accolade to fall on the shoulders of a Belfast unionist and barrister who married an heiress (Mary Catherine Guinness) and practised law in Dublin. But paradoxical elements are a feature of Ferguson's life, at least in the eyes of those for whom his Belfast Protestantism chimes oddly with his enthusiasm for Gaelic culture. Not that, at the time, there was anything unusual about this. Born in High Street when it was still mainly a residential quarter, Ferguson would have been a boyhood neighbour of Robert MacAdam (two years his senior), and also a fellow Instonian (Charles Morrison was at Inst about the same time too); and we know from MacAdam's correspondence that the two remained friends at least until well into middle age. We also know that Ferguson attended Irish classes in Hill Street, Belfast, in the early 1830s – though his proficiency in the language never matched MacAdam's, however much he outstripped his old contemporary in social aggrandisement and poetic ability.

When he composed his epics he relied on prose translations of the sagas by other people.

A hundred years after Ferguson's birth, in 1910, his contribution to Irish literature was acknowledged in a celebration which took place by his graveside in Donegore. Among the organisers of this event was the flamboyant Belfast solicitor, antiquary, historian, after-dinner speaker and famous dispenser of hospitality at his home, Ardrigh, on the Antrim Road, Francis Joseph Bigger, who ceremoniously laid a wreath of bays on Ferguson's grave. Equally ceremonious was the commemorative address by Alfred Perceval Graves, the father of Robert Graves and future expunger of 'embarrassing matter' from some of Ferguson's works. The expurgatory impulse, which we've noted before, was still going strong in relation to Ireland, literature and translation from the Irish – all areas in which Ferguson was hugely distinguished.

Indeed, in some ways the same impulse is still going strong – or at least, there are those who would like to see it reinstated: old-style, rock-solid Catholic puritans, many of them survivors from the generation born before the 1930s (say). These hold fast to Catholic-Irish rules of propriety as they first imbibed them. They are either deaf and blind to (so-called) obscenity, or, if the thing is persisted in, put on a display of old-fashioned dudgeon. They can't help it. They belong to an era in which any degree of sexual frankness is simply accounted nasty and shocking.

A couple of years ago I went to a talk in Belfast, partly because the lecturer was someone I'd known slightly at school, though she was a few years ahead of me and had since gained something of a reputation as an academic in the South. The subject of the talk was masterpieces of modern Irish language fiction or something of that sort: a topic that interested me, or at least one about which I felt I ought to be more knowledgeable. I mean, I knew I was never actually going to sit down, dictionary at hand, to read Máirtín Ó Cadhain's *Cré na Cille* (Churchyard Clay), or, for that matter, the Irish version of Flann O'Brien's *An Béal Bocht* (*The Poor Mouth*), but that was no reason not to gain some extra insights into these and other similar works.

So I find a suitable spot and fix myself in it half-way down the lecture hall. It proves to be a first-rate paper. The speaker begins by quoting Breandán Ó hEithir on *Cré na Cille*: young Gaeltacht people like himself, Ó hEithir says (the date of his comments is 1949), fed up with *an teach beag in ascaill an ghleanna* (the little house in the corner of the glen), 'the sexless Nabla and the gormless Tadgh, could hardly believe our eyes when we read in the pages of this whirlwind of a book that the man with the dole form to fill, coming silently to the school after three o'clock saw An Máistir Mór having it off with his assistant in the classroom.'

This and other like observations cause a frisson of dissent, nothing more, to ripple through a section of the lecture room containing people who'd probably come to the talk expecting *an teach beag in ascaill an ghleanna*. What happens next is that the speaker, after delivering her paper with fluency and equanimity, appears to lose her head during the session of questions and comments which follows. My recollection of her suggests to me that she is actually a person who subscribes to a moderately puritan code – not, I think, out of any instinctive prudery, but rather from a kind of natural distaste for disorder. All the weirder, then, to find her coming out with wild allusions to all kinds of dangerous modern topics, unrestrained copulation, drugs, unnatural practices, fornicating bishops and all the rest of it. (Someone in the audience has raised the question of whether or not the Irish language is fashioned to cope with every facet of contemporary life.)

An elderly gentleman sitting behind me is propelled right out of the lecture hall in a puff of embarrassment and disgust. Having allowed a sufficient interval – no doubt he thinks – for decency to be resumed, he returns to his seat just in time to hear someone praise the vivid homoerotic outpourings of the Irish language poet Cathal Ó Searcaigh. Himself an Irish-speaker, '*Tuilleadh salachair*,' the outraged *Gaeilgeoir* growls at the woman next to him, in a tone of utter affront. *Tuilleadh salachair* – more filth: this might stand as a catchphrase for those who believe such nastiness is best stowed out of sight beneath the increasingly threadbare carpet of Irish decorum.

★

Tuilleadh salachair … this incident illustrates the overwrought condition a strict *Gaeilgeoir* can get himself into when obnoxious allusions are freely bruited about and previously sacrosanct matter, the literature of Ireland in the Irish language, proves susceptible to adulteration. (Never mind Merriman, Cathal Buidhe, a selection of those Rannafast songs mentioned earlier, and so on and so forth.) This attitude of mind (as I've indicated) is a hangover from the past, from an era when not only the-little-house-in-the-glen but novels like *Mo Dhá Róisín* (My Two Roses) – in which a pure Irish girl called Rose takes a vow of celibacy, to remain in force until Ireland should be free, leaving her boyfriend with no alternative but to go out and, incidentally, get himself killed in pursuit of that purpose (it's 1916) – when works like these were taken seriously. At fourteen or fifteen I read them myself without too much dissent, indeed with admiration for the noble standpoint and with only a small amount of perplexity over the incessant high-mindedness of life in the Donegal Gaeltacht.

Poems and novels enshrining Ireland's wrongs alternated with P.G. Wodehouse and Agatha Christie to bridge a gap in my reading pursuits between *The Girls of St Bride's* and *The Girls of Slender Means*. In much the same way, during her own adolescence in the 1920s, my mother had latched on to Irish Catholic writers such as Annie M.P. Smithson (*The Light of Other Days; The Walk of a Queen*) to help her effect the transition from *Anne of Green Gables* to Graham Greene.

Was nationalist reading only a stop-gap or a transitory resource, then? Not really; but there was a limit to what was available in this area. I was pleased at sixteen to come by chance on a work entitled *The Green Cravat*, a thrilling patriotic farrago in which Lord Edward Fitzgerald is remodelled on Scarlet Pimpernel lines. *The Black City*, set in Belfast, was another novel I carried home from the Falls Road Library, but it proved deficient in republican glamour … We were Irish first and foremost, readers of my mother's generation and my own, but it didn't stop us revelling in imported entertainment by the cartload. As Seamus Heaney acknowledges in one of his essays, indigenous Kitty the Hare never stood a chance against Rockfist Rogan in the *Champion*, or even Korky the Cat. Kitty the Hare … what else was there? Patricia Lynch, I think, had something to offer the discerning child reader – but perhaps not *Brogeen*. I never really took to retellings of folk or fairy tales, Irish or otherwise; and – leaving Ireland far behind – exotic adventure stories by Rider Haggard or Baroness Orczy left me cold.

It was this sort of thing Elizabeth Bowen had in mind when she recalled its soul-stirring power with gratitude, but also with full awareness of its suitability for readers of unadvanced years only. It fell apart once an adult knowingness began to kick in – or if it didn't, it suggested an unfortunate adherence to an infantile mode. Well, perhaps. Some of us, though, not ill-equipped for ratiocination, continue to gain a modicum of sustenance from our childhood books, those that remain re-readable, even if the feast they once constituted is immensely watered down.

Other things are watered down too: domestic security, anticipation of some exciting social occasion, the sense of limitless possibilities for the future. But never mind: the passing of time brings with it the pleasures of retrospection. I've never been prone to sleepless nights, but I understand perfectly the delight in 'sweet insomnia' expressed by Mrs Hawkins in Muriel Spark's novel *A Far Cry From Kensington*; Mrs Hawkins who lies awake revisiting the past, letting her thoughts of the night mesh with earlier thoughts of the night, until a state of productive reverie is attained.

For me, at present, it's a far cry from the Donegal Gaeltacht and the tangle of emotions surrounding it, the place itself and what happened there, the unwarranted outcome. Why did we act as we did? Sixteen years old, that's the reason – a pretty obvious reason for a pretty routine carry-on, to which a proper adult response might have been a shrug, or, at most, a sardonic reprimand. It was nothing to treat punitively or get into a tizz about. But there, the time and the place decreed differently. 'I am now,' William Carleton wrote, 'painting the state of education and society in the north when I was a boy' – and I suppose some similar objective was lurking at the back of my head when I succumbed to the impulse to get going on this fragment of autobiography. Perhaps it had better be called deflected autobiography, since it was never meant to run on straight lines or tell an unvarnished tale.

I also started off with some notion that I would write a book about Ulster puritanism, Catholic puritanism in particular, and its insidious effects – but then, I found my attitude to the puritan ethic was less straightforward than I'd supposed. As a means of fending off anarchy it is not to be deplored. Of course, as a result of my own experience, and for common-sense reasons, I am glad that sex is no longer regarded as a sin; but still, in this area no less than others, it's desirable to have some kind of social force acting as a curb on profligacy. Otherwise, you just get hedonism gone haywire. It's axiomatic that everyone in their right mind would want to see an end to all the old abominations, deprivation and discrimination and social ostracism, cruelty and sectarianism and oppression. But we still need guidelines to keep things functioning equitably. Identifying an abuse and then going to the other extreme isn't always well advised. To cite an infinitesimal example: achieving a good examination result no longer means very much since no one fails. And, a more urgent concern, at no time in history has the asininity of the law been more apparent than it is at the moment, when it bends over backwards to protect and even reward the criminal, while often showing no such regard for the victims of crime.

Education and society in the north. Well, in the 1950s, I was better off than William Carleton 170 years earlier, Carleton who got all the schooling he ever received in a barn, albeit one of the largest barns in the parish of Aughentain, or in a sod house scooped out of a bank in the roadside. When he set out for Dublin to make his way in the world, like the youngest son in a rollicking folk tale, Carleton had two shillings and ninepence in his pocket, a bundle on his back and a new pair of shoes on his feet. The shoes were important, for he had to walk the whole way. His journey was punctuated by the sight of hanged Ribbonmen dangling from wayside gibbets. 'Merciful God!' he wrote. 'In what a frightful condition was the country at that time … It was then, indeed, the seat of Orange ascendancy and irresponsible power … There was then no law *against* an

Orangeman, and no law *for* a Papist. I am now writing not only that which is well known to be historical truth, but that which I have witnessed with my own eyes.'

We have all, with our own eyes, seen comparable sights in the North, as new outlets arrive for barbarity and nightmare. Each generation reinvents its own version of Orange and Green, Catholic and Protestant, Ribbonmen and Yeomen, Cowboys and Indians. Here in County Antrim they're still at it, waving flags and shouting slogans to provoke their counterparts across the way. Of course, if it wasn't the Union Jack and the Tricolour it would be something else; but the way gang warfare happens here takes it out of the sphere of transitory juvenile hostilities and into deep-rooted dissension.

One of our moving-in presents, when we came to Ashville, was a large and elaborate family tree prepared for me by an old friend who is an expert in genealogy. (It was a present for me, rather than Jeff, since my Irish ancestry was more amenable to investigation by the genealogist than his Welsh ancestry.) The chart is in two sections, meticulously mapped out and not altogether to be taken seriously, since the top half traces my ancestry via such figures as Robert the Bruce, Jehosaphat, Abraham, Noah and so forth, right back to Adam and God. The bottom half, on the other hand, is rather more particularised and historically accurate, although it moves horizontally as well as vertically, to accommodate a lot of notables such as Queen Elizabeth I, Mary Queen of Scots and all the rest of them, Sir Arthur Chichester, John Knox, the Bonnie Earl of Murray, Parnell, the Sitwells and Sir Basil Brooke.

Well! How have I acquired such exotic offshoots on my very plain family tree? It came about because my friend had asked for a copy of a straightforward chart I'd mentioned as having come into my possession, in case he might spot a name among my antecedents that would set him off. Sure enough, he did. Around 1670 an ancestor named John Tipping had married Frances

214

Blacker of Seagoe near Portadown in County Armagh; and in the hands of an adept genealogist, the Blacker connection burgeoned outwards into all kinds of ornamental areas.

Frances Blacker, my seven-times-great-grandmother, her husband and other relations died in 1689; fantasy or not, the most persuasive explanation has them heading for Derry, among the thirty thousand panicking Protestants converging on the city from all over Ulster in search of sanctuary – and not making it, whether through illness, exhaustion or foul play. However, at least one of the Blacker/Tipping sons survived; his son Henry went on to marry a Catholic named Esther O'Neill, and thereafter the plunge down the social scale was swift and severe. While the Blackers of Carrickblacker were maintaining their wealth and prominence, with a progeny conspicuous among churchmen and military men, and had a hand in the founding of the Orange Order (this is the Catholic side of my family I'm delving into) – while this was happening, their relatives by marriage, the Tippings, were ekeing out a living as small-scale farmers and linen-weavers.

When famine struck the North in the late 1840s, and the Revd Charles Morrison was mourning his infant son and trying to appease the Presbyterians of Antrim, my great-grandfather Matthew Tipping – who would then have been a youth of fourteen or fifteen – was growing up in a townland called Crossmacahilly, in a house his family had occupied since the 1790s, when the whole area consisted of bogland. A long, low farmhouse with a section at one end given over to hand-loom weaving, it held not only Matthew, his parents and seven brothers and sisters, but also his uncle John and his four children. (John died of famine fever in Lurgan Union workhouse in 1848.) Great-grandfather Matthew seems to have been quite a boy. Before he was twenty, he had impregnated a local fifteen-year-old named Eliza O'Hara; but no marriage took place until the couple's daughter Helena was over a year old. It's a wonder they bothered to marry at all. Given the social and economic conditions prevailing at the time, it's unlikely that an illegitimate birth or two would have caused a stir in the neighbourhood of Legahory and Crossmacahilly; a more urgent concern was getting the rye-grass, turnip and parsnip seeds needed to replace the rotting seed potatoes, as potato blight persisted. Semi-starvation and household congestion were the order of the day.

Once married, Matthew brings his wife and daughter to live in the two-roomed farmhouse, which he shares with an older brother and a cousin (his father having died in 1853), and goes on procreating until the place becomes as densely populated as one of Daniel O'Connell's monster meetings. In the end, it makes sense for Matthew, Eliza and their brood to leave the meagre smallholding, which they do in the late 1860s, moving on to a huxter life in John Street, Lurgan.

It took another couple of generations to get their descendants as far as the city of Belfast, but the movement from country to town was typical of migratory patterns established during the nineteenth century, once the Industrial Revolution, with its dire implications for hand-loom weaving, had begun to bite. Life for the Tippings goes on, in the new surroundings. When the luckless Eliza dies in childbirth – what else?– at the age of forty, Matthew doesn't waste a minute before rushing into wedlock once again. His eye has lighted on a widow with three children, Ellen Dowds (née Jordan) – and she and he will produce two further daughters to add to the melee. The youngest of these, born in 1881, is my grandmother Sarah Tipping.

To raise the domestic snarl-up to monumental proportions, Ellen's daughter by her first marriage, Mary Ann Dowds, in 1886 marries Matthew and Eliza's son Henry Tipping – a shotgun wedding, for which, no doubt, contiguity is to blame. It's Matthew and Eliza all over again – but a different era, in which town life with its lace-curtain gossip-mongers and its priestly pressures bolsters up respectability. Respectability is the new social aspiration – and you've only to look at the sole surviving image of Ellen Jordan, cloaked and bonneted in full Victorian glory, eyes sparkling with intelligence and will-power, to understand that she at least will see to it that her daughter's reputation is not destroyed, whatever the ensuing complications on the domestic front.

As for Matthew – he remains a wicked old man who endangers the family's precious, and precarious, respectability by getting himself arrested and brought to court on a charge of selling intoxicating liquor without a licence to do so. On a morning of July in 1889, after a tip-off from a begrudger, police had raided Matthew's John Street home and taken away a half-barrel of ale from a parlour-shop premises supposed to deal only in vegetables and buttermilk. The indignant shopkeeper – 'a respectable looking man' according to a subsequent newspaper report – claimed the ale was for his own consumption, since a weakness of the digestive system made him unable to stomach milk or tea. His protest went down well with the magistrates, who dismissed the case. It was a victory for proletarian principle. Counsel for the defence, a Mr Menary, was cheered in the courtroom when he wondered aloud why a rich man's cellar was safe from police intrusion, while 'a poor man couldn't keep a half-barrel of ale without having to explain his conduct in a criminal prosecution'. The barrel of ale was returned to its owner. His wife, though, was immensely put out to hear him described as 'a poor man' for all the Lurgan world to sneer at.

Matthew lived on until 1910, when he suddenly dropped dead in the street on his way to the workhouse infirmary for medical advice. His wife Ellen outlived him by seventeen years, becoming an autocratic old lady who, in her final bedridden state, imposed on her irreverent grandchildren the duty of carrying her downstairs and depositing her in the front parlour where she presided over the affairs of the day. 'Go canny wi' your granny,' the merry grandchildren would urge one another while transporting their burden.

All I know about these old Victorian people, my great-grandparents, comes from hearsay; but I envisage them as a notable pair, he incorrigible, she indomitable. Most relatives who knew them, or knew about them, were apt to regard the two indulgently, some holding Ellen and her daughter Mary Ann Dowds to be a civilising influence on the earthy Crossmacahilly Tippings. But my grandmother disliked her mother, for reasons unfathomable to me; and she never, in all the time I knew her, made any reference at all to her father, Matthew. Clearly, there are interstices in my family history, no less than anyone's, which would bear investigation.

A pioneer of the Tipping trail is my cousin Harry Tipping, whose researches I've plundered for the preceding paragraphs. (He's a distant cousin, but not as distant as it might be, since we are doubly related. His grandparents were Henry Tipping and Mary Ann Dowds: work it out for yourself.) This is the only strand in my background I can trace back as far as the Plantation era; but it confirms my belief that we're all, in the North, so religiously and culturally intertwined that it's just pot luck whether you come out Catholic or Protestant …

My cousin Harry is a retired schoolmaster and bibliophile, whose scholar's library of Irish books and specialist dealers' catalogues testifies to a collecting gene which must have originated somewhere along the Tipping line, but seems to have come out, in the twentieth century, only in him and me. It was in his company that I recently, and for the first time, visited the remains of the Crossmacahilly farmhouse, now used to store cattle-feed. To approach it, you take a turning off the Lurgan/Craigavon road, and park by a gate at the end of an unfrequented lane.

It is unfrequented for a reason. You climb the gate and lower yourself into a morass. I'd been warned to wear wellingtons, and I can see why. Mud is not the word. Perpetual rainfall and copious cow dung descending on the residue of the old bog have turned the whole area into a squelching mass. It provides a new insight into the expression 'clabber to the knee'. You need a strong incentive to subject yourself to its mucky viscosity, which calls to mind (among other things) the Dormouse's treacle-well. And there it is, a hundred yards away at the end of the lane: the old Tipping residence, last inhabited in 1941, now covered by a corrugated iron roof (to keep the bales of cattle-fodder dry), empty door and window frames, walls of decomposing plaster. We regard it intently. It's a heady experience, coming face-to-face with your ancestral home, even if it's nothing but a shack in a swamp.

I doubt if the farmhouse was ever picturesque, but it would once have been clean and more or less orderly: old Ann Tipping, Matthew's mother, would have seen to that. It is partly the rundown surroundings, the November gloom with full complement of clabber, that makes it so wretched. Once, it would have been cosily thatched, with neat patches of grass – perhaps even a vegetable garden – around it. It probably contained a dresser full of spongeware (crockery for the poor) and a settle bed or two. Its floor might have been stone. It included a stone outbuilding which might even have accommodated the overflow from the house. (All that ancestral fecundity in a small space perhaps was bound, eventually, to breed its opposite; and true enough, one branch of the family line will peter out with me. Never mind, the same fecundity has ensured there are plenty of others to carry on till the crack of doom.) There would have been neighbouring houses. There are trees all around, wild flowers no doubt at appropriate seasons, and fields to graze cattle. The current cattle eye us distrustfully, with much swishing of tails. I am not afraid of cows, I *like* cows, but these are very large and not fenced off. It's their mud we're up to the oxters in. The ancestral pull is getting undermined by accumulating discomforts of the spot.

And yet. There is something here that gets under one's skin and into one's mental landscape, a hint of another world and time, both endlessly alien and utterly ordinary, suffused with imaginary memories. This is especially true, of course, of a place that holds powerful associations, as the Crossmacahilly clachan does for us, your actual descendants of the Tipping household; but you get a charge of historical apprehension from any weed-encrusted remnants in a field, or bits of stone walls returning to rag and bone.

It would be patronising to imagine this household, and the thousands like it, as being deficient in intellectual or aesthetic stimulus: one simply doesn't know. Of course, in the harsh past, mere subsistence would have taken precedence over everything else, but it's tempting to hope enough energy was left over for non-workaday pursuits. We do know that a fierce republican ideology took root within the Crossmacahilly clan, coming to a head in early-twentieth-century Lurgan among the town-bred Tippings. The sons of Henry and Mary Ann Dowds were especially prominent in rebel circles. Night raids, arrest and internment grew as familiar to them as scallion champ. 'No doubt the Tippings are a bad lot,' reads a 1923 memo from the Lurgan office of the Royal Ulster Constabulary.

My solitary brush with the RUC occurred when I was seventeen. It's the Easter holidays, during my Ballynahinch year. With a couple of seditiously minded friends, I have come to Milltown Cemetery for the annual republican ceremony in honour of Easter Week. Well, one of these not entirely law-abiding girls is a friend – Maire, my Rannafast companion; the other is a friend of hers, or at least a fellow dissident. Her name is Lizzie O'Rawe. The two are up to something; I've received hints, all the way up the Falls Road in the wake of the Easter parade, that more is on the cards this afternoon than a jolly Sunday outing. Eventually they decide to come clean. They're on an assignment for the 'Army' (the Irish Republican Army). Am I willing to help? Well! Here are my republican protestations being put to the test. I can do nothing but nod solemnly, stifling any unworthy qualms which threaten my equanimity. I do not have the temperament of a conspirator!

Still, there's nothing much to this afternoon's exploit. Lizzie has a camera – but so have many people, who've stood by the roadside snapping the marchers as they pass along bearing flags and banners emblazoned with patriotic devices. The old guard of the IRA, upright men in their sixties and seventies draped in tricoloured sashes, are at the forefront of the procession, and after them come troops of Irish dancers wearing embroidered kilts of purple or green, topped by saffron cloaks held in place with Tara brooches. It is all very showy and animated. But the carnival atmosphere has a steely undertone. The purpose of the occasion is to uphold the concept of a united Ireland, and to this end rousing speeches are delivered from a platform set up in the middle of the republican plot. While preparations for the speeches are going on, Lizzie mingles with the crowd, pointing her camera at the faces of policemen and B-Specials monitoring the event. The resulting photographs, passed into the hands of the right people, will be used for identification purposes. The role of Maire and myself is simply to act as camouflage, to help create an impression of innocent skylarking.

Once it's reached the cemetery, the parade disperses, to reassemble in an approximate circle around the republican plot. While microphones are being positioned the orators consult pieces of paper and smoke cigarette after cigarette to calm their nerves. People stand about in groups admiring the bravado of the occasion. Unruly children swarm all over the gravestones and shin up Celtic crosses while their elders' backs are turned. The admonition 'Don't you do that again' is heard on all sides, accompanied by the noise of slapping and resultant wails.

Lizzie is still snapping away, focusing on any RUC constable she spots keeping an eye on things. She claims a couple of plain-clothes-men are on the film too. She and Maire exchange jubilant glances. Lizzie is a rough-looking girl with coarse black hair and turned-up nose. Severely cross-eyed, she wears dark-rimmed glasses which do little to moderate this defect. Her manner is very loud and boisterous. In a moment of censoriousness, it strikes me that nothing but the republican movement stands between Lizzie and juvenile delinquency.

Milltown Cemetery is like Piccadilly Circus this afternoon: sooner or later you're bound to meet someone you know. It isn't long before we bump into a group of Cluan Ard regulars, a bit older than us, including one, tall and curly-haired, on whom I've been casting a mildly infatuated eye. His name is Fergus Hegarty, he is sensible and kindly and takes a schoolmasterly interest in us. 'Taking photos, are you,' he beams – fortunately making this unwelcome observation in Irish.

Nevertheless, it elicits no reply. Three conspicuously cagey faces are turned towards him.

The film is now used up, and Lizzie sits on the edge of a grave to unload it. She slips the exposed roll into the pocket of her off-white duffle coat. At this point the speeches begin. 'The proclamation of the Irish Republic in 1916 and its establishment in 1919 was a clear and definite expression of the will of the vast majority of the Irish people for an ending of British interference in the affairs of the Irish nation.'

This particular orator, blunt and indignant, has the right approach for getting everyone stirred up. 'In 1922, Dáil Éireann, the established government of the Irish Republic, was overthrown, and partition of the national territory was imposed by Britain on the Irish people. Thus Britain remained in occupation of part of the Irish nation.'

The voice booms on. 'The professional politicians realised they had failed in their perverting activities when the young men and women of the occupied area – the six north-eastern counties – revolted once again against British tyranny; they banded themselves together and on December 12th, 1956, they challenged the right of the British Empire to hold any part of the territory of Ireland. On that eventful day they reasserted in arms the right of the Irish people to the ownership of *all* Ireland ...'

You can feel the righteous outrage emanating from the listeners, apart from those children who are really more interested in extracting the fullest entertainment from whacking gravestones with sticks. The rest of the audience appreciates these reminders of England's iniquity, and the worse behaviour of her unionist hangers-on. These people gathered in the cemetery believe they've retained their national identity in the face of fearful odds. To prove it, they have their party songs, their heroes, their tales of atrocities going back to the time of Cromwell, their memories of barricaded streets on the Falls Road, their religious emblems, the disgust aroused in them by Protestant bigotry, their sense of being done out of something as far as material welfare is concerned. It doesn't make for an equable way of going on.

I'm craning my neck trying to see where Fergus Hegarty has gone, when Maire gets to her feet and starts brushing gravel off the back of her skirt. 'Come on, it's time to go.' We're half-way towards the exit opposite the Falls Park when Lizzie suddenly nudges Maire with an importunate elbow. Speaking in a voice hoarse with intensity, she urges her not to look round. 'We're being followed.'

It occurs to me that the excitement of the occasion has gone to Lizzie's head. Why on earth should we be singled out for attention among all the amateur photographers milling about the place? It isn't reasonable. But Maire takes the warning seriously. 'Don't do anything drastic,' she whispers. 'Just walk naturally towards the gate. Have you got the film?'

'Pass it to me,' I catch myself saying, entering into the spirit of the thing. I am wearing a lime-green blouse elasticated round the top. 'I'll just shove it down my front. They're not likely to look there.' A brief fit of giggles overtakes the three of us. It passes off leaving us more apprehensive than before.

'Oh Jesus, Mary and Joseph,' Lizzie moans. 'We're never going to get out of this in one piece.'

Maire shrugs. 'Don't panic.'

By now it's dawned on me that Lizzie's alarm is perhaps not wholly without foundation. I begin to wish I hadn't been quite so precipitate in the matter of the film. Now the vital object is landed on me! Maire is saying we should make a run for it once we reach the main road. I'm not convinced this is a good idea, having had it drummed into me from an early age that every member of the Royal Ulster Constabulary is issued with a gun. But Maire, having a better grasp of what is expedient for the civic authorities and what isn't, understands that no policeman would ever fire in such a situation. If we'd made it to the gate, indeed, we might have had a chance of escaping with our trophy. But we're not allowed to get that far. Two or three policemen close in around us, cutting us off from the nearest republican supporters who stand there gaping. Several conversations break off in mid-sentence.

My shoulder is gripped by a uniformed policeman who instructs me to hand over at once the article I'm carrying for an unlawful purpose. I demand to know what he means – the others having conveyed to me, by scowling and snorting, that it's best to brazen it out. It doesn't do any good, of course. The constable patiently explains that it's in our own interests to do as he asks without further fooling around. Otherwise we may find ourselves at the near-by barracks facing a serious charge. At this, Lizzie makes a grunting noise to show she isn't going to be intimidated. Maire offers the opinion that a mistake has been made. On the face of one policeman I catch an indulgent expression which indicates he doesn't consider us a serious threat to the British Empire.

We're advised not to behave like silly girls. When this produces no effect, we find ourselves being marched across the road to the police station at the junction of the Glen and Andersonstown roads. It's such an unusual predicament that I hardly know how to act. I do my best to assume a dignified and impassive look, as befits a potential martyr for old Ireland. At least, I hope this is how I appear to Fergus Hegarty, whom I've sighted once again standing just inside the cemetery gate, regarding the scene with astonishment.

At this stage in my life, I don't want to lose face as an intrepid republican; but far less would I want word of this exploit to reach the ears of my family, or my school. (Though nearly all my doings are relayed to my mother, this is one incident I will keep to myself, if I'm allowed to.) Politics or not, it can only cause a headache for everyone concerned, if it should come out that I'm in trouble with the police. I wonder what kind of a ticklish situation – this time – I've got myself into. I'm regretting that imprudent impulse to take possession of the infernal film.

We're admitted into the police barracks through a heavy door which clangs alarmingly behind us. It isn't at all a suitable outcome for a gallant enterprise. You wouldn't catch Roddy McCorley or Fergal O'Hanlon making a hash of things like this. It's clear the constables regard us as wrongheaded nuisances, and not altogether unjustly. A mixture of chagrin and apprehension makes me retreat into silence, while the other two continue to act like people in the course of undergoing an outrage.

Our names and addresses are extracted from us and recorded in a book. Lizzie's name prompts a facetious enquiry as to whether she is so called in honour of the queen. She reacts predictably with a snarl: 'Like bloody hell.' Her voice is huskier than ever with defiance. The policemen's good humour begins to wear off. 'Just give us the bloody film like good girls, will you, and take yourselves off to your homes. You've committed an offence but we'll overlook that if you do the right thing now.'

'What film?'

'We haven't got it.'

'Come on, come on.'

'Have you got it, Pat?'

'No, I thought you had it.'

'I haven't got it.'

'You must have dropped it.'

'What do they want it for anyway? There's no law against taking photographs that I know of.'

'Call this a free country!' Maire exclaims.

I don't know where all this is getting us. A policewoman is sent for, since the next resort is to have us searched. After putting the police to all this trouble, no doubt the three of us will be charged and remanded in custody. A moment occurs when the policemen guarding us turn their backs to confer over some document laid on the counter. I seize the opportunity to extract the roll of film from my blouse and pass it to Maire with a frenzied surreptitiousness. Maire can do nothing but take it.

'I thought you'd have a better chance of saving it,' I explain later. We've been admonished, warned to behave ourselves in future, and sent on our way without further ado. The truth is – though all of us are implicated – I do not want the lion's share of the blame to fall on me. I'm trying to undo the effect of my foolhardy gesture. Fortunately my explanation makes sense to the other two.

'I tried to,' Maire says. 'I thought I could hide it underneath the seat of my chair, and then maybe get it back once they'd searched us and found nothing incriminating. But that great bully saw what I was doing and made a grab.'

'Orange bastard,' Lizzie mutters.

Maire advises me to keep a look-out for this policeman, whose name is McGinty. Now that I've got a criminal record, they may well decide to put a tail on me. She confides that she has been kept under constant surveillance since the occasion, a few months back, when she refused point-blank to sign a document repudiating unlawful behaviour undertaken for political ends. 'Of course they had to let me go. They couldn't do a thing. But they've kept a close watch on me ever since. I don't know what they expect me to do – blow up the City Hall, perhaps.'

'It wouldn't be much of a loss if you did,' I respond automatically; the fashionable attitude of the day is to cast aspersions on that remarkable building. 'I'm sorry we lost the film.'

'Never mind, perhaps we can try again.'

Some months after this event, Maire and Lizzie O'Rawe are peripherally involved in an arms raid which goes wrong. The principal raiders are caught and sentenced to a long term of imprisonment. This incident marks the end of a revolutionary phase in Maire's life. Henceforth her nationalist energies, like mine, will be concentrated on the language issue. As for Lizzie O'Rawe – she is so unnerved by the arms disaster (Maire tells me) that she has gone away to be a nun.

As far as I know, whatever revolutionary leanings I possessed (shaky and all as they were) came via my Tipping grandmother: the Tippings are exceedingly knowledgeable about evictions and coffin ships, ancient wrongs and rebel feats, a whole heritage of injustice and subversion. Repudiators to a man of *English* claims to cultural supremacy, they stand for Irish Ireland at its most assertive. I am therefore mystified when a Lurgan relative alludes to my half-great-uncle Henry's fondness for *Little Lord Fauntleroy*, a work (it appears) which he would often recite in its entirety within the family circle. 'Recite' is the word – but surely he couldn't have had the whole book by heart? Did she mean he would read this story to the children in the family? If indeed he'd learned the whole thing, is this the source of both my parrot memory and my addiction to children's books? None of this seems very plausible. Great-uncle Henry was over thirty by the time Mrs Hodgson Burnett's stirring tale of a velvet-clad-heir-to-a-fortune came out in book form, and one would not want to overestimate its impact on Fenian rebels in the back end of Lurgan. Neither, one would think, would Uncle Henry's rough Crossmacahilly boyhood have predisposed him to applaud bland juvenile literature, or to use it to divert younger members of the household. Other reports of Uncle Henry make him seem a bit testy and uncouth.

This mystery, if no other, is easily solved by an act of memory. I am back in the Donegall Road, *c.* 1950, listening to my grandmother recall how her much older half-brother Henry had frightened the life out of her with his rendering of the patriotic ballad 'Fontenoy': 'At Fontenoy, at Fontenoy, like eagles in the sun, / With bloody plumes the Irish stand. The field is fought – and won!', which he declaimed with such vehemence that she hid under a table until he had regained his everyday demeanour. So the misattribution leads gradually backwards in time to the comforting ambience of a well-remembered 1950s kitchen-cum-living-room, complete with coal fire and worn art-deco hearth rug, and then back further again to a more distant scene – imagined this time – involving a scared toddler in a back room of a small row house in 1880s Lurgan, scurrying under a table.

I don't have many images of my grandmother as a child – and only one, the Minnie Cochrane one, of her as a young girl. This is probably because she died before I'd have found it worthwhile to cross-question her: but I do remember 'Fontenoy' and a couple of other incidents, all involving fear and distress. One bad experience, which she sometimes recalled, had herself and her sister Ellen being menaced by an angry goose, a scene that takes shape in my mind with the two small girls, either barefoot or wearing black laced ankle boots and late-Victorian pinafores, immobilised in a back lane straggling off into the country, uncertain whether to run or to face it out. On another occasion, young Sarah was locked, for some reason, in – I think – a cupboard under the stairs (this may have taken place at school), an experience associated in her mind for ever after with Jane Eyre in the Red Room.

If you can't write fiction, as I can't, though I've spent my whole life besotted with fiction – well, maybe it's possible to make some kind of a story out of shreds and shards of the past, your own past and the pasts of others, real or in books. The central story I've tried to tell concerns the Rannafast affair. (I couldn't have written about it while my mother was alive; it would have caused her distress to have the agitating business raked up again, even after all this time.) But that story has led to all manner of surrounding stories, reminiscences, bookish reflections, social comment and so on, in the normal way of one thing leading to another. Early on, I took a look at Robert MacAdam, Belfast Presbyterian and outstanding advocate of Irish, because he was one of those who changed the way the language was perceived in the nineteenth century. He helped to create a climate in which the Gaelic League could come into being and flourish; the Gaelic League started the Irish summer school, and so on, and so on. As for me and my minor *mí-ádh*: enough good fortune has occurred in my life to tone down the bad bits, in retrospect anyway.

The gifted Armagh author John O'Connor, in his single novel *Come Day – Go Day* (1948) employs a rich local vernacular full of eccentric flourishes to gain an effect of quotidian exuberance. 'If I wouldn't be better off handcuffed to a ghost it's a quare thing to me' (the things I have to put up with); 'Don't get your be'rd [beard] in a blaze' (Calm down); 'Ah for God's sake give our heads peace' (Leave off). These and other striking catchphrases were current in our house in Belfast as late as the 1950s, whether articulated wholeheartedly (by my grandmother) or self-mockingly (by my mother). 'Dear God this holy day and hour' was a frequent exclamation denoting full-blown dismay, one no doubt springing to the lips of bygone Tipping females as their menfolk exited the house in police custody yet again. A lesser cause of consternation, the arrival home of a couple of children soaked to the skin by a tremendous downpour, might result in the following avowal: 'My head's astray. These ones are only after coming in on the top of me like drownded rats.'

Like drownded rats. As everyone is aware, a cultural and merchandising takeover on a global scale is ironing out all such quirks of speech, like the levelling of drumlins in a landscape. No one asks a child if she's 'progling' (rummaging aimlessly in a drawer – I think that word must have been peculiar to our family, like Paul Muldoon's 'quoof' for 'hot water bottle'; I've never come across it anywhere else). Phrases such as 'They're coming like the half of Newry' (at full tilt) have gone with the corner shop dispensing vegetables and buttermilk.

I've got to get my tone right here: I wouldn't want to be accused of profitless nostalgia, or indifference to shocking one-time privations. Other things have gone, like the danger of children being got hold of by nuns, or having no redress when caught in a fix. But progress shouldn't entail so many dead – or deadly – ends, so much destruction. Of course, like almost everyone over the age of forty-five (say), I'm susceptible to the backward look, to anything that unlocks a door into a more vivid domain. I want to preserve in some form the spirit of the past, the distant past and the more recent past, even though I'm aware that one is essentially as elusive as Sir Percy Blakeney, and the other is filtered through goodness knows what degree of pig-headedness and fixation.

I want to reinstate 'all the dead dears', as enumerated in the Plath poem, 'mother, grandmother, great-grandmother … ', right down to those unknown 1950s schoolgirls in their blazers and pastel-coloured dresses, marching straight ahead along the road beside St Brigid's College in Rannafast, savouring the pungent odours of turf smoke and sea wrack, and envisaging an unclouded future.

ACKNOWLEDGEMENTS

I should like to record my gratitude to the Harold Higham Wingate Foundation whose award of a Wingate Scholarship enabled me to write this book. I am also grateful to the Arts Council of Northern Ireland for financial assistance.

As far as family history is concerned, I was lucky enough to have cousins on both sides whose researches I found invaluable. In this area Harry Tipping and George Hinds provided the greatest help. I should also like to thank Craig Hutchinson.

Among those who read the manuscript and made valuable comments or suggestions are Gerry Keenan, Douglas Carson, Mary Denvir and Brice Dickson. I owe thanks also to Chris Agee who published a lengthy extract from the book in the magazine *Irish Pages*. I am grateful to Emma McDowell, and to Monika McCurdy who translated the poem on pages 64–5. I have benefited greatly from the enthusiasm for the project of the wonderful Blackstaff team, in particular Patsy Horton, Helen Wright, Janice Smith, and Cormac Austin; and from Anne Tannahill's knowledge and expertise. Thanks also to Wendy Dunbar who designed the cover. My greatest debts, however, are to my mother Nora Craig, for reasons which will be clear to every reader of *Asking For Trouble*; and, less obviously perhaps but no less crucially, to my husband Jeffrey Morgan.

PATRICIA CRAIG, Antrim, 2007